JÜRGEN KLOPP

80 Attacking Combinations, Finishing, Positional Patterns of Play, Transition & SSGs Direct from Klopp's Training Sessions

PUBLISHED BY

JÜRGEN KLOPP

80 Attacking Combinations, Finishing, Positional Patterns of Play, Transition & SSGs Direct from Klopp's Training Sessions

First Published April 2023 by SoccerTutor.com
info@soccertutor.com | www.SoccerTutor.com

UK: 0208 1234 007 | **US:** (305) 767 4443 | **ROTW:** +44 208 1234 007 **ISBN:** 978-1-910491-61-4

Copyright: SoccerTutor.com Limited © 2023. All Rights Reserved.

All rights reserved. No part of this publication may be reproduced, stored in a retrieval system, or transmitted in any form or by any means, electronic, mechanical, photocopy, recording or otherwise, without prior written permission of the copyright owner. Nor can it be circulated in any form of binding or cover other than that in which it is published and without similar condition including this condition being imposed on a subsequent purchaser.

Edited by
Alex Fitzgerald - SoccerTutor.com

Diagrams
Diagram designs by SoccerTutor.com. All the diagrams in this book have been created using SoccerTutor.com Tactics Manager Software available from www.SoccerTutor.com

Cover Design by
Alex Macrides, Think Out Of The Box Ltd.
Email: design@thinkootb.com Tel: +44 (0) 208 144 3550

Note: While every effort has been made to ensure the technical accuracy of the content of this book, neither the author nor publishers can accept any responsibility for any injury or loss sustained as a result of the use of this material.

CONTENTS

Jürgen Klopp's Achievements 8
Klopp's Trophies and Records at Liverpool 9
Jürgen Klopp's Philosophy: Best Quotes 11
Diagram Key 12
Practice Format 12

Attacking Positional Patterns of Play 13

Liverpool's 4-3-3 Formation 16
1. Central Midfield Combinations, Switch of Play to Winger, Cross & Finish 17
2. Double Switch of Play with Lay-offs and Full Back's Overlap Run 18
3. Triple Switch of Play Combinations and Movements + Play into Forward to Shoot 19
4. Switching Point of Attack in Behind to Opposite Winger with Lofted Pass into the Box 20
5. Switch of Play + Quick Combinations with the Defensive Midfielder Moving Forward to Join the Attack 21
6. Switching Play for Advanced Run of the Full Back into the Box 22
7. Winger's Movement Inside to Create Space for Midfielder's Through Pass to Full Back on Overlap 23
8. Playing THROUGH a High Defensive Line and Advanced Runs to Finish the Attack (vs. 4 Defenders) 24
9. Playing OVER a High Defensive Line and Advanced Runs to Finish the Attack (vs. 4 Defenders) 25
10. Maintaining Possession + Quick Reactions to Launch Attack and Score (Reduced Width) 26
11. Maintaining Possession + Quick Reactions to Launch Attack and Score (Full Width) 27

Attacking Positional Patterns of Play + Counter-pressing 28

1. Moving the Ball Quickly to the Winger for a Cut Back and Finish + Counter-pressing 30
2. Combination Play on One Side of the Pitch and Switch of Play Over the Top (in Behind) + Counter-pressing 31
3. Attacking Pattern of Play, Counter-pressing, and Fast Break Attack in a 2-Ball Practice 32

Positional Patterns of Play with 2nd/3rd Ball Attacks 33

1. Play Through Midfield, then Wide for the Winger to Cross + 2nd Ball Attack .34
2. Through Pass for Left Winger's Cut Back + 2nd Ball Attack on Right Side 35
3. Possession in Midfield with Lay-offs, Play into Forward, and Lofted Pass in Behind to Winger + 2nd Ball Attack 36
4. Short Fast Combination Play Around the Box + Finishing Inside and Outside the Box 37
5. Pass and Move in Centre + Fast Attacks with 2nd/3rd Balls 41

Attacking Combinations and Finishing 43

1. Pass Under Pressure, Curved Run into Box + Finish 45
2. Short Passing Under Pressure, Movement + Finish 46
3. One-two, Lateral Third Man Run for Through Pass + Finish 47
4. Double One-two and Through Pass for Lateral Third Man Run + Finish 48
5. One-two, Open Up to Receive and Finish + 2nd Ball Finish 49
6. Diagonal Lofted Pass in Behind with Fast Supporting Runs into the Box 50
7. 3-Player Combination + Cross for Timed Runs into the Box 51
8. Switch Play Wide, Give & Go, and Cross for Timed Runs/Box Finishing 52
9. 4-Ball Long Range Finishing Drill with Support Play 53
10. Quick Combination Play to Set the Ball Back to Finish from Different Positions 54
11. Moving to Receive and Finish from Different Angles + Finishing in a 1v1 Duel (Multiple Balls) 55

12. Simultaneous 3-Player End to End Mixed Combination Play with Long Range Finishing... 56

13. Simultaneous 3-Player Combination Play with Overlap Third Man Run + Cross and Finish... 57

14. Fast Break Attack from Centre Circle with Deep Forward Runs............. 58

15. One-two Set to Shoot + Sprint to Receive for 1v1 vs Goalkeeper Circuit..... 59

16. Attacking Runs and Finishing in Pairs with Double Switch of Play and Wide Crossing Zones... 60

17. 4-Player Attacking Wave Break Always with Multiple 1-Touch Overlaps + 2nd Ball Fast Break Attack.. 61

18. Various End to End Attacking Combinations and Finishing in Groups of 3... 62

19. Possession Play in Zones + Fast Break Attack Combinations and Finishing.. 63

Multi-Ball Attacking Combinations and Finishing 64

Klopp's Multi-Ball Finishing Drills.................................. 65

1. 3-Balls: Two Player Central Finishing, Cut Back & Finish + 3v2 Attack......... 66

2. Through Passes to the Wingers for Runs into the Box in a 3-Ball Finishing Drill.. 67

3. Crossing and Finishing + Receive and Shoot in a 4-Ball Finishing Drill........ 68

4. Different Finishes + Quick Passes and Switch of Play for Cross in a 4-Ball Finishing Drill.. 70

5. Positional One-touch Combination Play in and Around the Box in a 4-Ball Finishing Drill.. 72

6. Centre Forward & Wingers Combine in and Around the Box in a 5-Ball Finishing Drill.. 74

7. 3 Forwards Continuous Finishing from Various Types of Assists (7-Balls)..... 76

8. Technical 8-Ball Finishing Variations from Central Positions 78

9. Positional Attacking Combinations Around the Box in an 8-Ball Finishing Drill.. 80

10. One-twos, Turn & Shoot, Give & Go, & Crossing in a 4-Ball Finishing Drill ... 83

11. Dynamic Wing Play, Dribbling, and 1v1s in a 5-Ball Finishing Drill............ 85

12. Shoot, Lofted Pass Finish, Combination + Fast Counter Attack in a 4-Ball Finishing Drill 88

13. Feint, Move & Shoot, Lofted Pass, and Give & Go Finishing + 3v2 Attack. . . . 90

14. Turn & Shoot, Lofted Pass, and Give & Go Finishing + 3v2 Attack. 92

15. Pass, Receive, Shoot, Give & Go Finishing + 6v4 Attack in a 5-Ball Finishing Drill 94

16. 4-Ball Finishing + Quick Transition to 7v4 Attack. 96

Small to Large Sided Games 98

1. Receiving from a Throw-in and Breaking Out of Pressure in a 3v2 Game 100

2. Receiving from a Throw-in and Breaking Out of Pressure in a 5v4 Game. 101

3. High Tempo 4v4 (+GKs) "Shoot On Sight" Small Sided Game 102

4. Shooting at Every Opportunity in a "Winner Stays On" 3v3 (+GKs) SSG 103

5. Direct Play, Shooting Early and from Deep in a 4v4 (+GKs) SSG 104

6. Support Play and Finishing in a 4v4 (+4) + GKs SSG with Outside End Players 105

7. Attacking Using the Full Width in a 5v5 (+GKs) SSG with Side Zones 106

8. Playing in Behind + Attacking Against a Low Block in a SSG with Changing Conditions. 107

9. Play Out and Score Quickly in a 5v5v5 (+GKs) 3-Goal Game 109

10. Playing Through Pressure and Collective Defending in a 5v5 (+1) +GKs SSG 110

11. 5v5 (+GKs) Small Sided Game with Possession Play Conditions 111

12. Attacking and Defending Corner Kicks + Counter Attacks in an 8v8 (+GKs) Game. 112

13. Attacking and Defending Free Kicks + Counter Attacks in an 8v8 (+GKs) Game. 113

14. Possession Play in a Conditioned 10v10 (+GKs) 4-Sided/4-Goal Game. 114

Transition Games 115

1. Supporting Runs to Score Quickly in a Dynamic 2v1 Attack / 3v2 Transition Game. 117

2. Receive and Finish, 3v2 Transition + 4v6 Transition Game 118

3. Receiving from Different Angles and Finishing + 3v3 Transition 120

4. 5-Ball Finishing Drill with Give & Go + 4v4 (+4) Transition to Defend 122

5. 3-Ball Finishing + 4v4 Transition + 5v4 Transition Game. 124

6. Crossing & Finishing with Side Zones + 5v4/5v8 Transition Game 126

7. Wingers/Centre Forward Finishing in and Around the Box + 9v7 (+GKs) Transition. 128

8. 3-Team 5v5v5 (+GKs) 2-Zone Counter Attack Transition Game 130

9. 3-Team 6v6v6 (+GKs) 4-Zone Counter Attack Transition Game with Time Limit to Score. 131

10. 3-Team 6v6v6 (+GKs) 4-Zone Counter Attack Transition Game with Offside Rule 132

11. 3-Team 6v6v6 (+3) + GKs Counter Attack Transition Game with Side Zones. 133

12. 8v8 (+3) + GKs "5-Second Rule" Fast Counter Attack Transition Game 134

JÜRGEN KLOPP'S ACHIEVEMENTS

COACHING ROLES

- **Liverpool F.C.** (2015 - Present)
- **Borussia Dortmund** (2008 - 2015)
- **Mainz 05** (2001 - 2008)

HONOURS (Europe / World)

- **UEFA Champions League** (2019)
- **UEFA Champions League Runner-up** (2013 & 2018)
- **UEFA Europa League Runner-up** (2016)
- **FIFA Club World Cup** (2019)
- **UEFA Super Cup** (2019)

HONOURS (Domestic Leagues)

- **English Premier League** (2020)
- **German Bundesliga x 2** (2011 & 2012)

HONOURS (Domestic Cups)

- **English FA Cup** (2022)
- **EFL Cup** (2022)
- **German DFB-Pokal** (2012)
- **German DFL-Supercup** (2013 & 2014)

INDIVIDUAL AWARDS

- **The Best FIFA Men's Coach** (2019 & 2020)
- **Onze d'Or Coach of the Year** (2019)
- **IFFHS World's Best Club Coach** (2019)
- **World Soccer Awards World Manager of the Year** (2019)
- **Premier League Manager of the Season** (2020)
- **LMA Manager of the Year** (2020)
- **BBC Sports Personality of the Year Coach Award** (2019)
- **German Football Manager of the Year** (2011, 2012 & 2019)

KLOPP'S TROPHIES AND RECORDS AT LIVERPOOL

2018-2019

UEFA Champions League

2019-2020

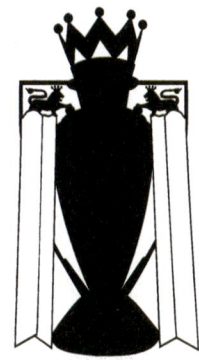

Premier League

+

UEFA Super Cup

+

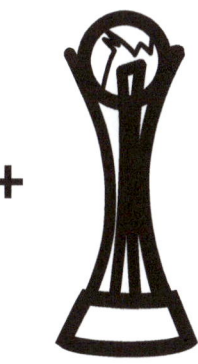

FIFA Club World Cup

In the 2018-2019 season, Jürgen Klopp's Liverpool team won the **UEFA Champions League** and also came close to winning the Premier League, finishing with a record breaking runner-up total of 97 points (losing only 1 game), just 1 point short of champions Manchester City. To win the UEFA Champions League, Liverpool beat **Bayern Munich**, **Porto**, **FC Barcelona**, and **Tottenham** with high intensity, attacking and exciting football.

In the 2019-2020 season, Jürgen Klopp's Liverpool team won the **UEFA Super Cup**, the **FIFA World Club Cup**, and the **Premier League** title with 7 games still to be played and another incredible points total of 99. Across these 2 Premier League seasons (2018/2019 & 2019/2020), Klopp's Liverpool had a record of 62 wins, 10 draws and only 4 losses (of which 2 losses were after they were already crowned Premier League Champions in 2020).

Jürgen Klopp's Liverpool have also achieved the following league records:

- Joint-record for **most Premier League wins in a season (32)** - 2019/2020.
- February 2019 to July 2020, Liverpool **won 24 consecutive Premier League home matches**.
- Joint-record for **most Premier League home wins in a season (18)** - 2019/2020.
- Joint-record for **fewest Premier League home defeats in a season (0)** - 2018/2019 and 2019/2020.
- October 2019 to February 2020, Liverpool **won 18 consecutive league matches**, a joint-record in English top-flight history.
- Liverpool remained **undefeated in 68 consecutive league games at home** (April 2017 - January 2021) - the third longest run in English top-flight history.

* Trophy images from PIXSECTOR.com

2021-2022

FA Cup   EFL Cup

In the 2021-2022 season, Jürgen Klopp's Liverpool team won the **FA Cup** and **EFL Cup** double, beating a strong Chelsea team in both finals.

They also came close to winning the Premier League again, finishing with another incredible total of 92 points after losing only 2 games, just 1 point short of champions Manchester City.

* Trophy images from **PIXSECTOR.com**

JÜRGEN KLOPP'S PHILOSOPHY:
BEST QUOTES

"Attack the opponent with, but especially without the ball - a chasing attitude over 95 minutes."

"Our way of playing is the central element in our training sessions."

"We have a team of 11 at a time, each of whom is an attacking forward and each of whom is a defender."

"We want to attack the opponent non-stop - when we have the ball, when we lose it and when the opposition have it."

"Fighting football, not serenity football - that is what I like."

"With a few new movements, with a few new passing options, you can change the whole game."

"He [Arsene Wenger] likes having the ball, playing football, passes. It's like an orchestra. But it's a silent song. I like heavy metal."

"Coaches will say that it's not important for their team to run more, and they prefer to make games the right way. I want to make games only the right way and run 10km more."

DIAGRAM KEY

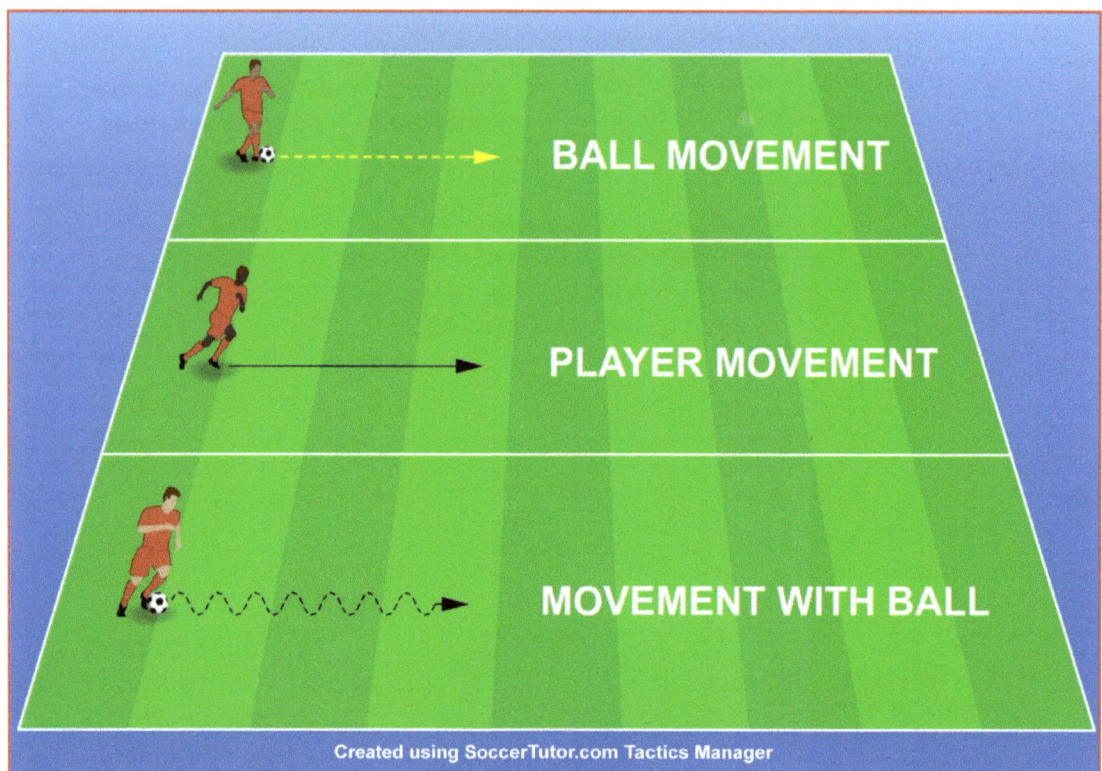

PRACTICE FORMAT

- The practices in this book are direct from Jürgen Klopp's training sessions at Liverpool F.C. between 2016 and 2022.
- Each practice includes the practice topic/name and clear diagrams with a detailed description.

Attacking Positional Patterns of Play

Direct from Jürgen Klopp's Training Sessions

"With a few new movements, with a few new passing options, you can change the whole game."

"Our way of playing is a central element in our training sessions. But I also look to details of opponents which can give us an advantage, like spaces they might leave open or other weaknesses which we can exploit. I always try to interweave those elements in our sessions without the players noticing it."

Pep Ljinders
Liverpool Assistant Manager

Jürgen Klopp Practices: Attacking Positional Patterns of Play

LIVERPOOL'S 4-3-3 FORMATION

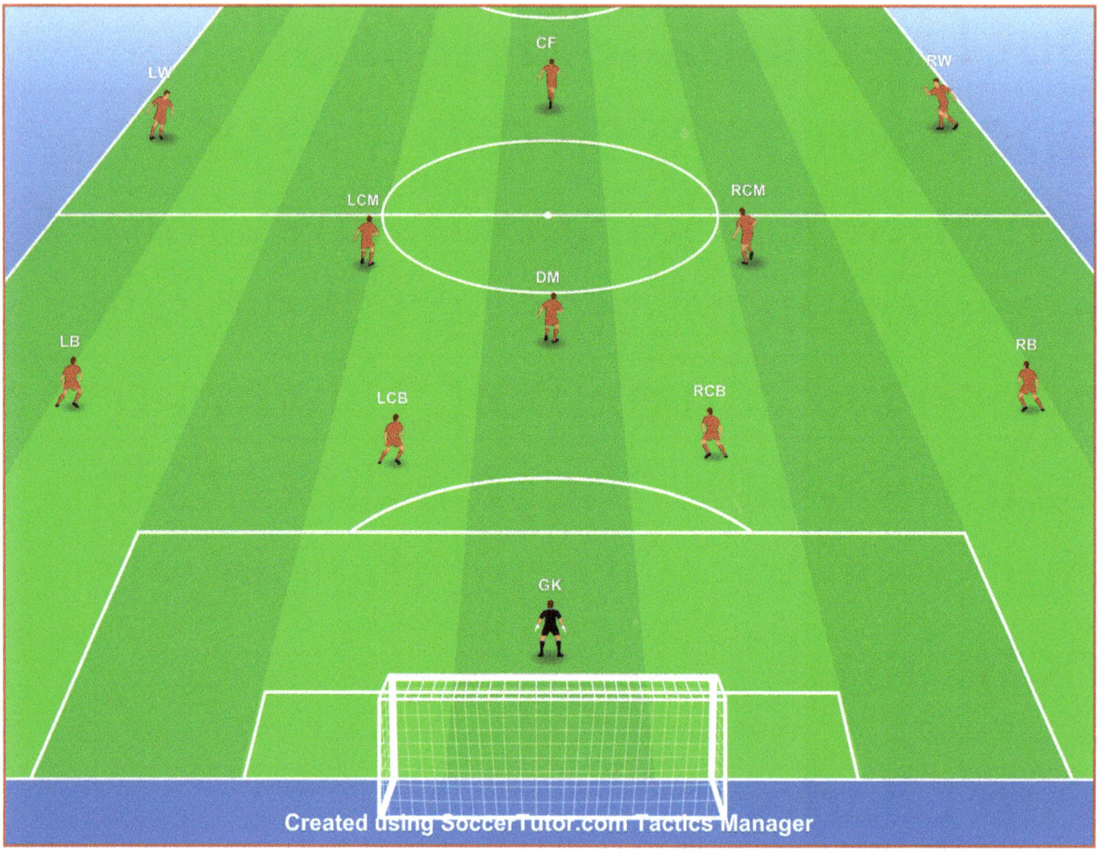

- **GK:** Goalkeeper
- **LCB:** Left Centre Back
- **RCB:** Right Centre Back
- **LB:** Left Back
- **RB:** Right Back
- **DM:** Defensive Midfielder
- **LCM:** Left Central Midfielder
- **RCM:** Right Central Midfielder
- **LW:** Left Winger
- **RW:** Right Winger
- **CF:** Centre Forward

Jürgen Klopp Practices: Attacking Positional Patterns of Play

1. Central Midfield Combinations, Switch of Play to Winger, Cross & Finish

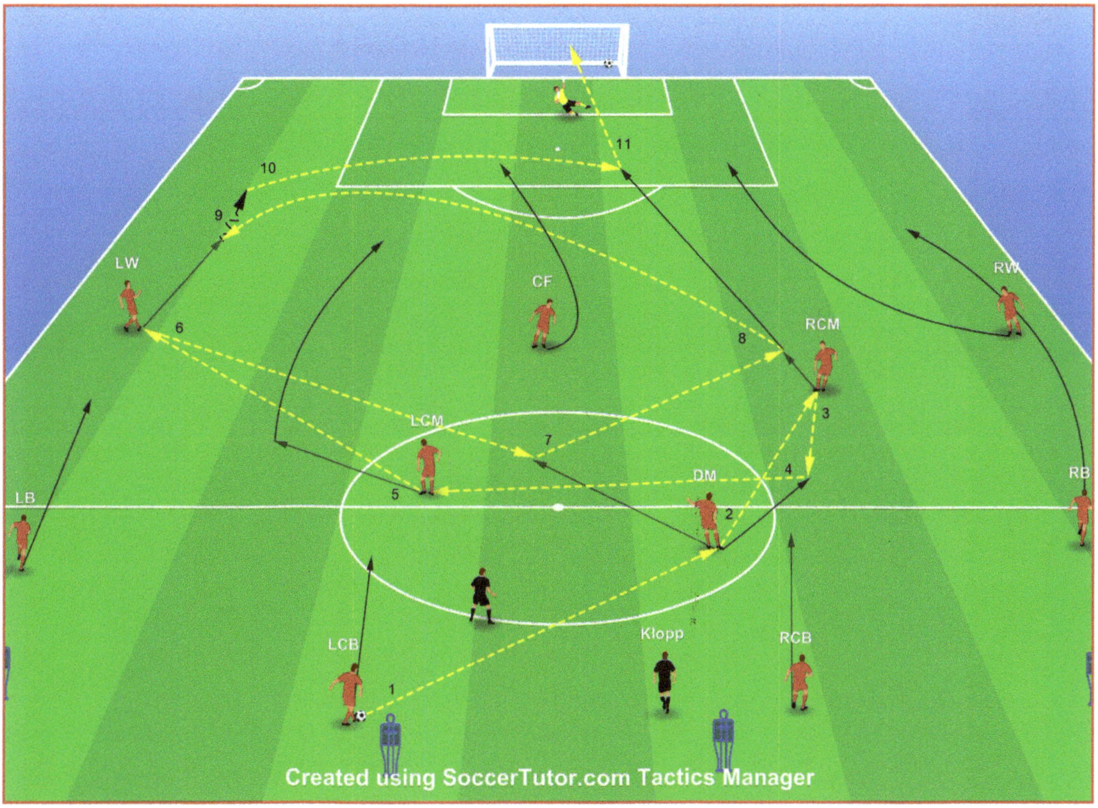

Practice Description

1. The left centre back (**LCB**) passes to the defensive midfielder (**DM**).

2-3. The **DM** plays a one-two with the right central midfielder (**RCM**).

4. The **DM** passes across to the left central midfielder (**LCM**).

5. The **LCM** passes out wide to the advanced left winger (**LW**).

6. The **LW** hits a firm ground pass all the way back to the centre of the pitch.

7. The **DM** moves inside and forward to receive and passes to the **RCM**.

8. The **RCM** plays an aerial pass for the forward run of the **LW** to switch the play.

9-10. The **LW** moves forward with the ball and delivers a cross into the box.

11. Many of the players have made forward runs towards or into the box. In this example, the **RCM** meets the cross near the edge of the box and scores.

Source: Jürgen Klopp's Liverpool pre-season training session at Stanford University, California - 23rd July 2016

Jürgen Klopp Practices: Attacking Positional Patterns of Play

2. Double Switch of Play with Lay-offs and Full Back's Overlap Run

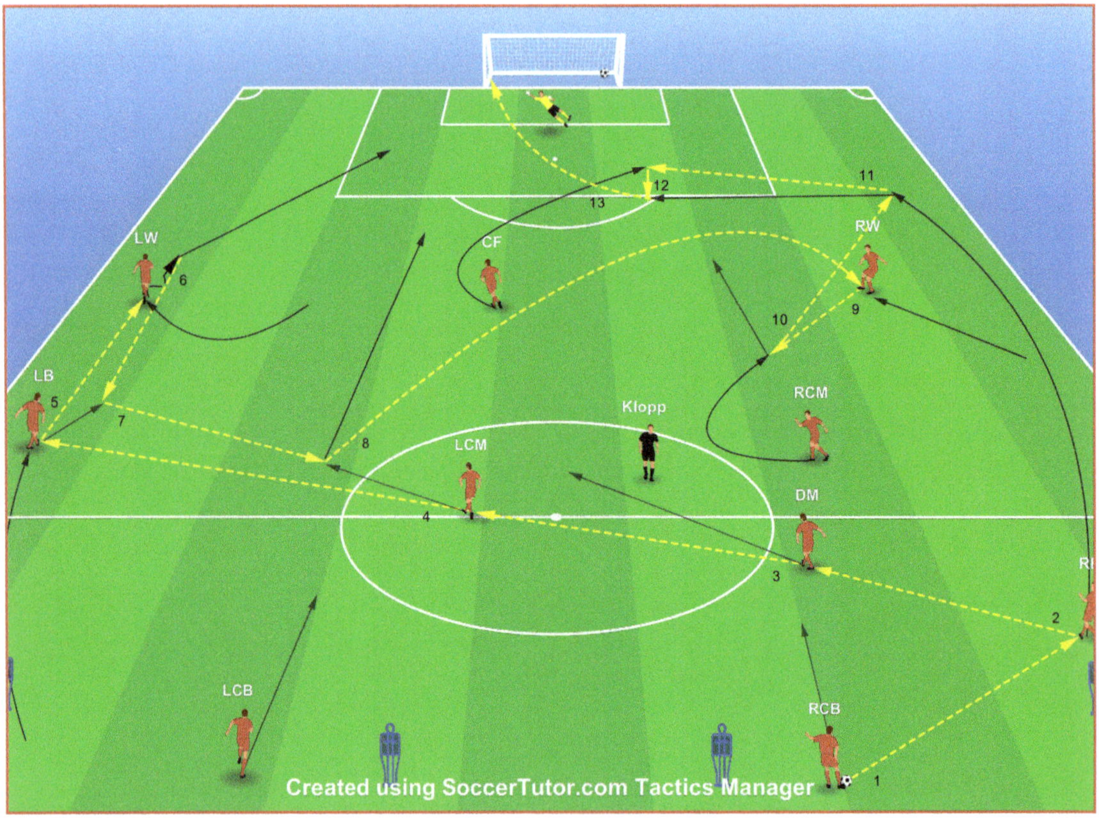

Practice Description

1. The right centre back (**RCB**) passes to the right back (**RB**).

2-3. The **RB** passes to the defensive midfielder (**DM**), who moves the ball onto the left central midfielder (**LCM**).

4. The **LCM** passes out wide to the oncoming left back (**LB**), which completes a switch of play.

5. The **LB** passes forward to the left winger (**LW**), who makes a curved run out wide.

6. The **LW** takes a touch forward and then plays the ball back to the **LB**.

7-8. The **LB** passes inside to the **LCM**, who opens up and switches play to the right winger (**RW**) with an aerial pass. The **RW** moves inside off the flank to receive.

9-10. The **RW** lays the ball back to the **RCM**, who then passes for the deep overlapping run of the right back (**RB**).

11-13. The **RB** passes to the centre forward (**CF**) in the box, who sets the ball back for the **RB** to shoot and score.

Source: Jürgen Klopp's Liverpool pre-season training session at Stanford University, California - 23rd July 2016

Jürgen Klopp Practices: Attacking Positional Patterns of Play

3. Triple Switch of Play Combinations and Movements + Play into Forward to Shoot

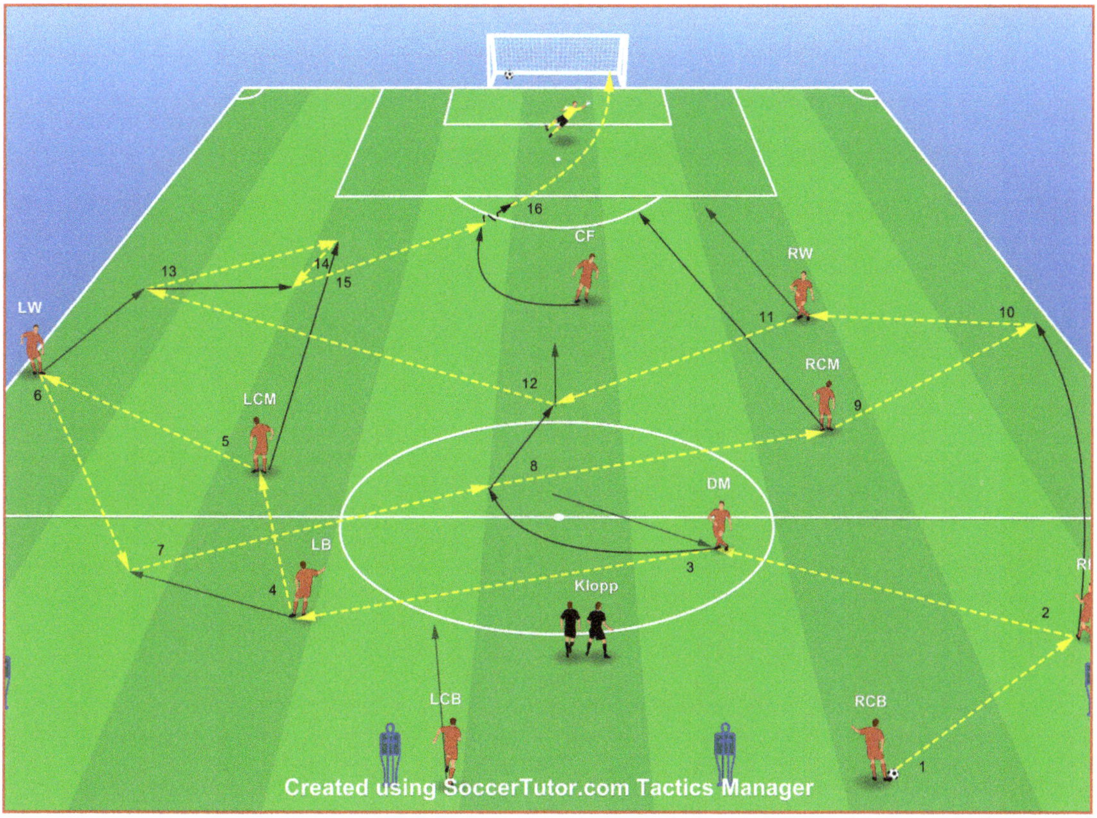

Practice Description

1-2. The right centre back (**RCB**) passes to the right back (**RB**), who passes to the defensive midfielder (**DM**).

3-4. The **DM** passes across to the inverted left back (**LB**), who passes forward to the left central midfielder (**LCM**).

5-6. The **LCM** passes out wide to the left winger (**LW**), who plays it back to the **LB**.

7. The **LB** passes inside for the curved movement of the **DM** to receive again.

8-9. The **DM** passes to the right central midfielder (**RCM**), who passes for the advanced run of the right back (**RB**).

10-11. The **RB** passes inside to the right winger (**RW**), who plays back into the centre for the **DM** to receive again.

12. The **DM** now passes towards the **LW** on the opposite side.

13-16. The **LW** passes for the advanced run of the **LCM**, who lays the ball back to the **LW**. **LW** passes to the **CF**, who opens up and shoots from the edge of the box.

Source: Jürgen Klopp's Liverpool pre-season training session at Stanford University, California - 23rd July 2016

Jürgen Klopp Practices: Attacking Positional Patterns of Play

4. Switching Point of Attack in Behind to Opposite Winger with Lofted Pass into the Box

Practice Description

1. The left centre back (**LCB**) starts with a pass to the defensive midfielder (**DM**).
2. The **DM** passes forward to the centre forward (**CF**), who drops towards the left side to receive.
3. The **CF** passes back to the left back (**LB**).
4. The **LB** passes inside to the left central midfielder (**LCM**).
5. 4 players make forward runs - *LW, CF, RCM,* and *RW*. The **LCM** plays a lofted pass into the box for the run of the right winger (**RW**) on the opposite side.
6. The **RW** receives in the box and scores past the GK.

Source: Jürgen Klopp's Liverpool training session at AXA Training Centre, Liverpool - 7th July 2022

Jürgen Klopp Practices: Attacking Positional Patterns of Play

5. Switch of Play + Quick Combinations with the Defensive Midfielder Moving Forward to Join the Attack

Practice Description

1. The left centre back (**LCB**) starts with a pass to the left back (**LB**).

2. The **LB** passes inside to the left central midfielder (**LCM**).

3. The **LCM** switches play towards the opposite right winger (**RW**) high up on the flank.

4. The **RW** lays the ball back for the oncoming right back (**RB**).

5-6. The **RB** dribbles inside and then passes back/inside, timed well for the forward run of the defensive midfielder (**DM**).

7-8. The **DM** plays a one-two combination with the centre forward (**CF**), so receives the ball back.

9. The **DM** plays a through pass into the box, timed for the third man run of the right winger (**RW**).

10. The **RW** takes a touch inside and scores past the GK into the far corner.

Source: Jürgen Klopp's Liverpool training session at AXA Training Centre, Liverpool - 7th July 2022

Jürgen Klopp Practices: Attacking Positional Patterns of Play

6. Switching Play for Advanced Run of the Full Back into the Box

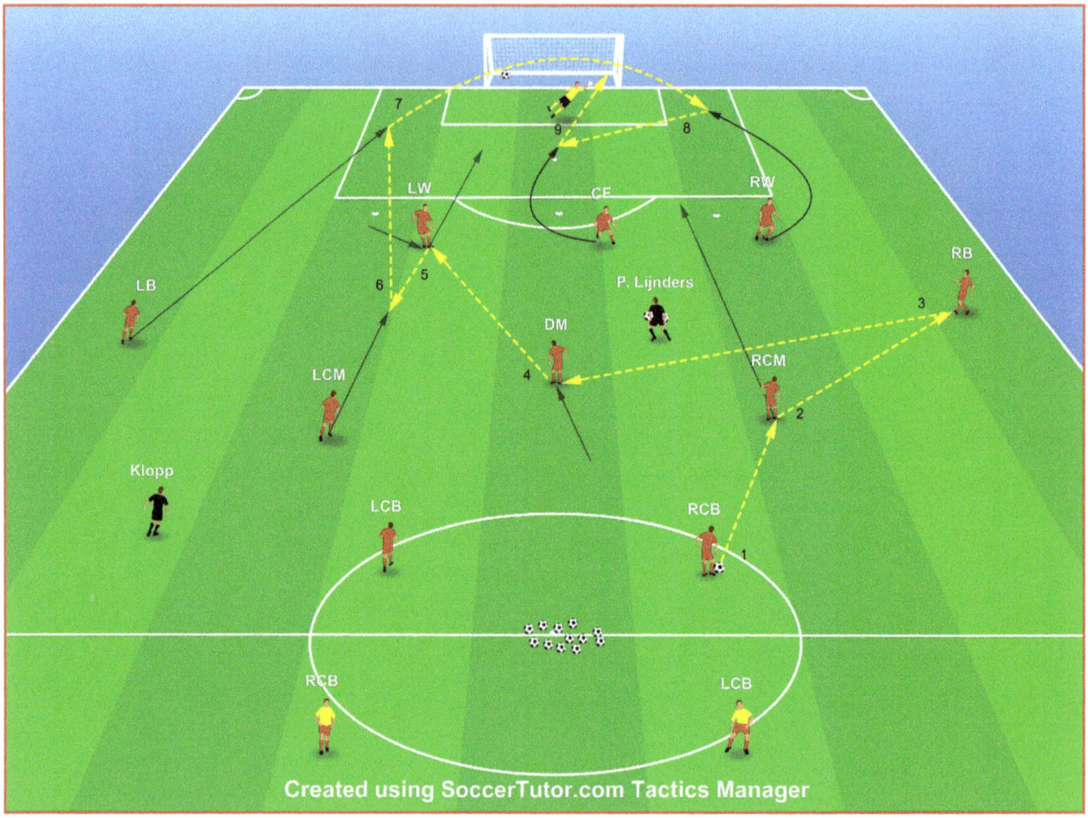

Practice Description

There are 3 white cones near the edge of the penalty area, which are the starting positions for the 3 attacking players.

1. The right centre back (**RCB**) passes to the right central midfielder (**RCM**).
2. The **RCM** passes out wide to the advanced right back (**RB**).
3. The **RB** passes inside to the defensive midfielder (**DM**), who has moved forward to receive.
4. The **DM** passes to the left winger (**LW**), who checks off the cone to receive.
5. The **LW** lays the ball off for the oncoming run of the left central midfielder (**LCM**).
6. The **LCM** plays a through pass into the box, timed well for the run of the left back (**LB**).
7-9. All 3 attacking players (*LW, CF & RW*) make movements into the box. The **LB** crosses to the other side where the **RW** cuts the ball back for the **CF** to score.

Source: Jürgen Klopp's Liverpool training session at AXA Training Centre, Liverpool - 7th July 2022

Jürgen Klopp Practices: Attacking Positional Patterns of Play

7. Winger's Movement Inside to Create Space for Midfielder's Through Pass to Full Back on Overlap

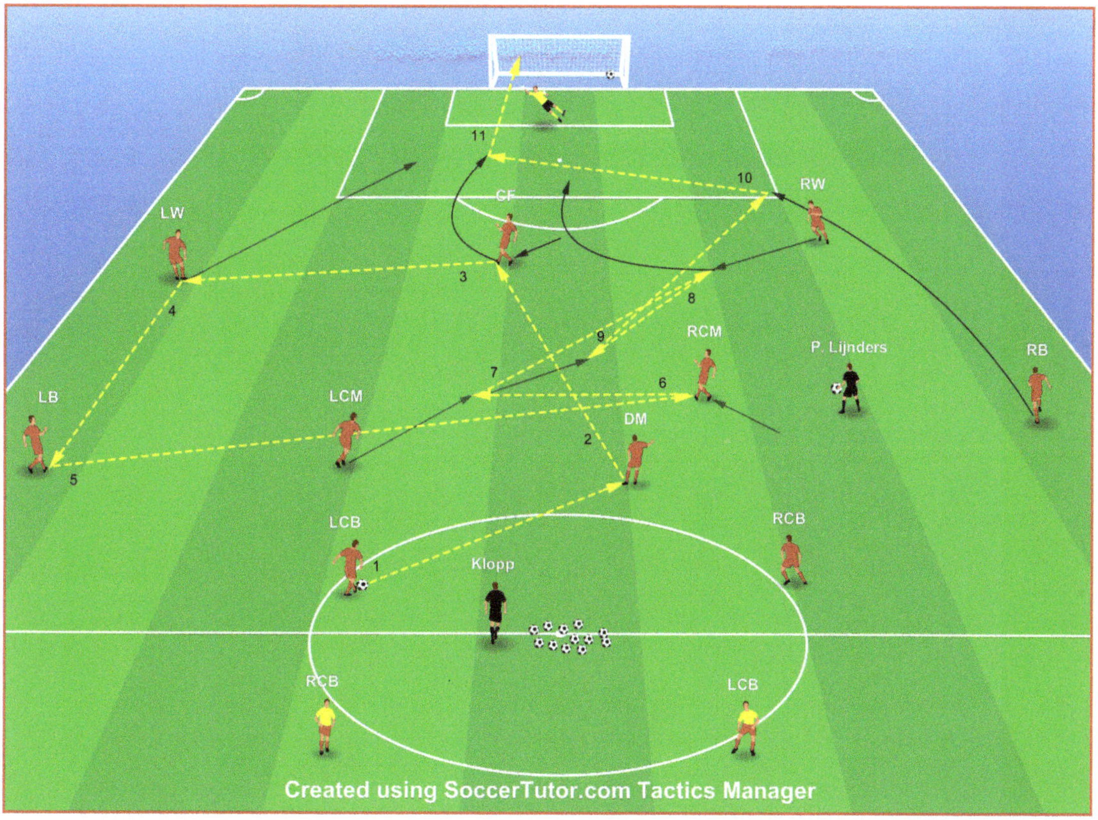

Practice Description

1. The left centre back (**LCB**) starts with a pass to the defensive midfielder (**DM**).

2-3. The **DM** passes forward to the centre forward (**CF**), who drops towards the left side and passes to the left winger (**LW**).

4. The **LW** passes back to the left back (**LB**).

5. The **LB** plays a firm pass across the pitch to the right central midfielder (**RCM**), who moves forward and inside to receive.

6. The **RCM** plays inside for the left central midfielder (**LCM**) to run onto the ball.

7-8. The **LCM** plays a diagonal pass to the right winger (**RW**), who drops back and inside, then lays the ball back to the **LCM**.

9-10. The **LCM** plays a pass in behind for the overlap run of the right back (**RB**), who then plays the ball into the box.

10-11. There are 3 players (*LW, CF & RW*) who make runs into the box and the **CF** scores at the back post in this example.

Source: Jürgen Klopp's Liverpool training session at AXA Training Centre, Liverpool - 7th July 2022

Jürgen Klopp Practices: Attacking Positional Patterns of Play

8. Playing THROUGH a High Defensive Line and Advanced Runs to Finish the Attack (vs. 4 Defenders)

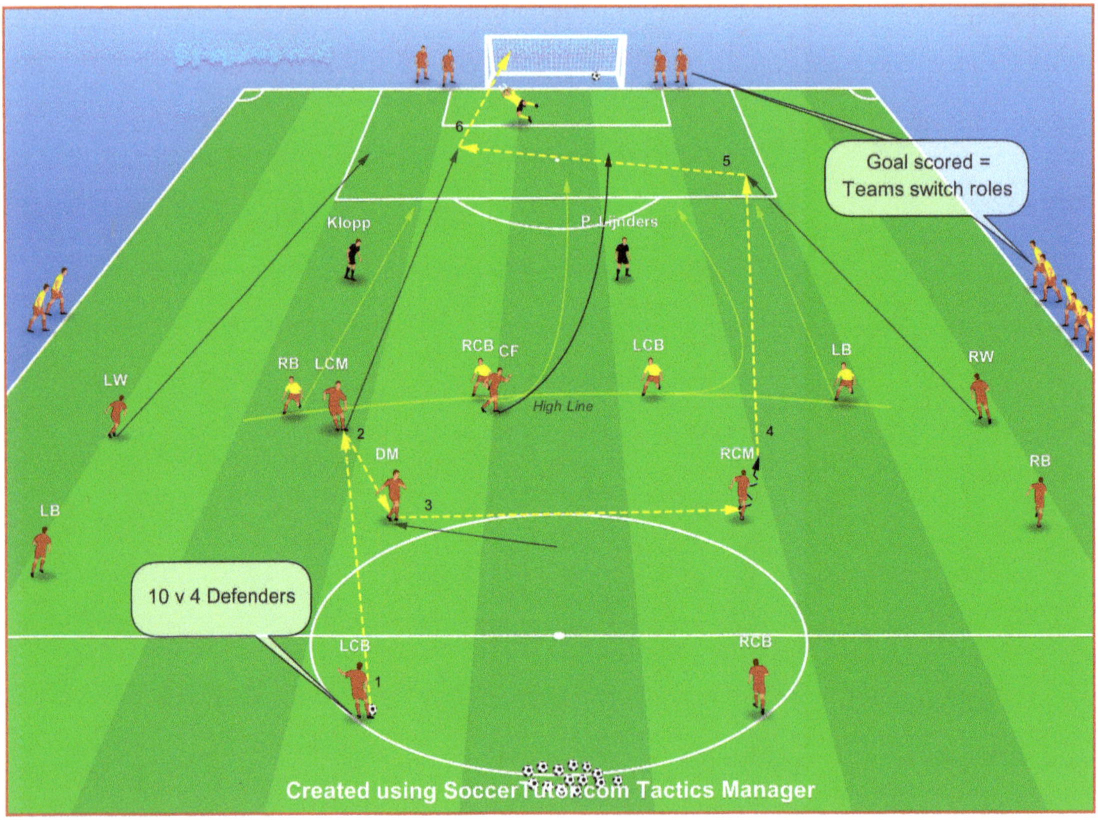

Practice Description

The Liverpool players play 10v4 and the attacking team try to score quickly using combinations and through passes.

The 4 yellow defenders start with a high line but when the ball is played in behind, they track the runners and defend their goal. When a goal is scored, the 2 teams switch roles.

1. The centre back (**LCB**) starts with a pass to the central midfielder (**LCM**).

2. The **LCM** lays the ball back to the defensive midfielder (**DM**).

3-4. The **DM** passes across to the right central midfielder (**RCM**), who moves forward with the ball and plays a through pass in between the yellow *LCB* and *LB*.

5. The right winger (**RW**) has made an advanced run to receive the through pass, and then passes across the box.

6. Many players have made runs into the box - the **LCM** scores at the back post.

Source: Jürgen Klopp's Liverpool training session at AXA Training Centre, Liverpool - 7th July 2022

Jürgen Klopp Practices: Attacking Positional Patterns of Play

9. Playing OVER a High Defensive Line and Advanced Runs to Finish the Attack (vs. 4 Defenders)

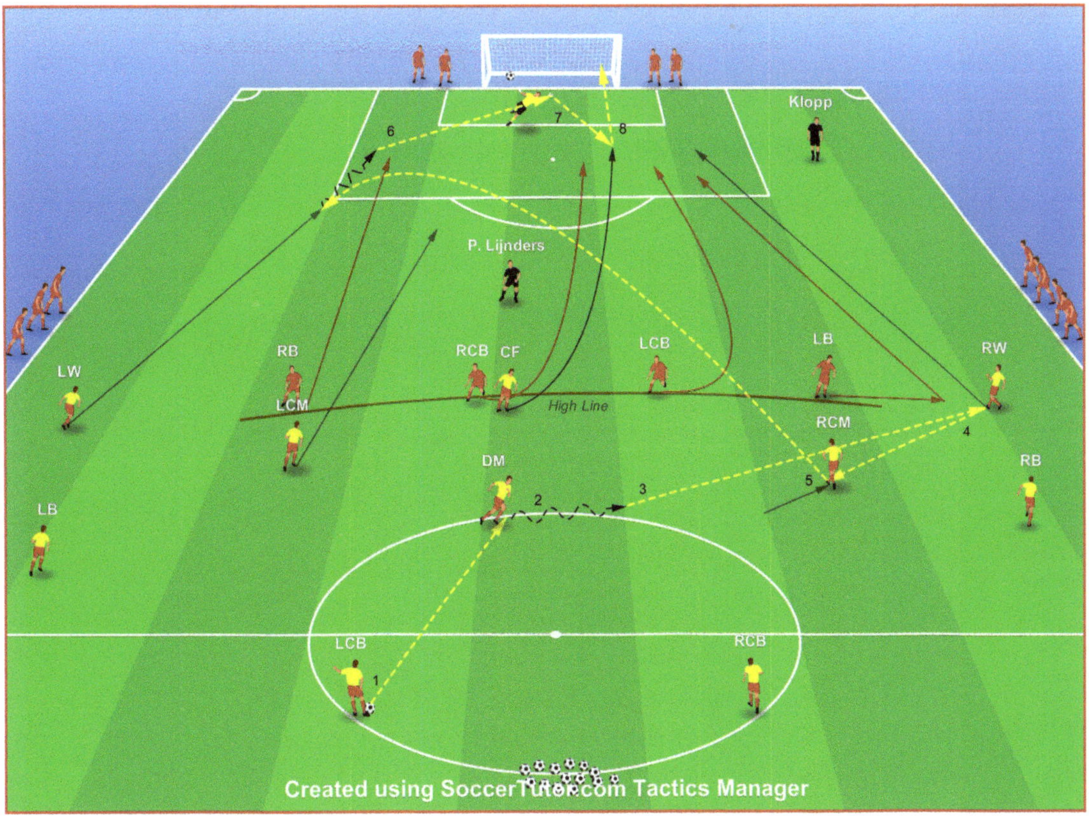

Practice Description

This is a variation of the previous practice which displays a different pattern of play.

1. The centre back (**LCB**) starts with a pass to the defensive midfielder (**DM**).

2-3. The **DM** opens up, moves sideways with the ball, and passes out wide to the right winger (**RW**).

4-5. The **RW** lays the ball off to the right central midfielder (**RCM**), who plays a long aerial pass to switch the play.

5. The switch of play is directed to the left winger (**LW**), who has made a well timed run to receive in an advanced position.

6-8. In this specific example, the **LW** carries the ball into the box and shoots. The ball is parried and the oncoming centre forward (**CF**) is able to score on the rebound. Many other players also made runs into the box to support the attack.

Source: Jürgen Klopp's Liverpool training session at AXA Training Centre, Liverpool - 7th July 2022

Jürgen Klopp Practices: Attacking Positional Patterns of Play

10. Maintaining Possession + Quick Reactions to Launch Attack and Score (Reduced Width)

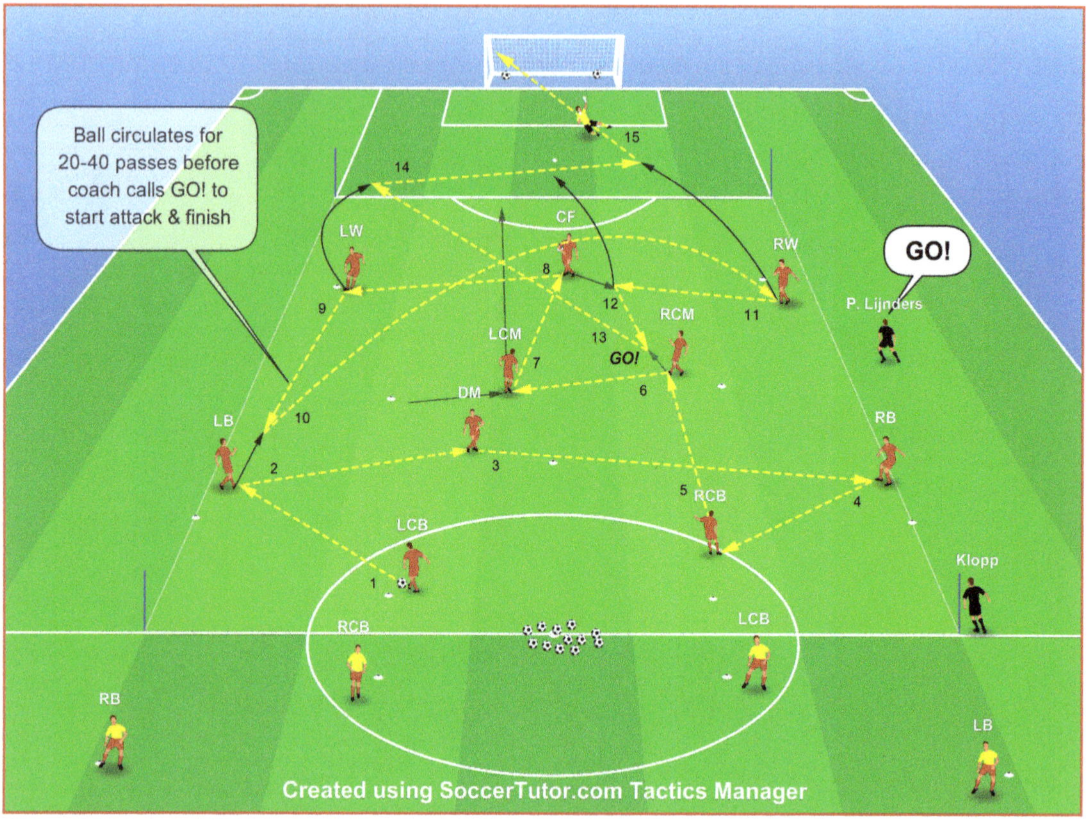

Practice Description

The players start the practice from one of the centre backs (LCB in diagram) and pass freely within their positional 4-3-3 roles with good combinations.

After 20-40 passes, the Coach calls out "GO!" - The players launch a fast attack to try and score. Here is the pattern observed:

1-12. The players pass the ball between each other at match speed with position specific combination play.

13. The Coach calls out **"GO!"** - The players must react quickly to attack and score. This starts with the right central midfielder's (**RCM**) diagonal through pass to the left winger (**LW**) inside the box.

14-15. The attacking players make runs into the box to support the attack. In this example, the **LW** passes the ball across the box for the right winger (**RW**) to score.

Source: Jürgen Klopp's Liverpool training session at AXA Training Centre, Liverpool - 17th August 2021

Jürgen Klopp Practices: Attacking Positional Patterns of Play

11. Maintaining Possession + Quick Reactions to Launch Attack and Score (Full Width)

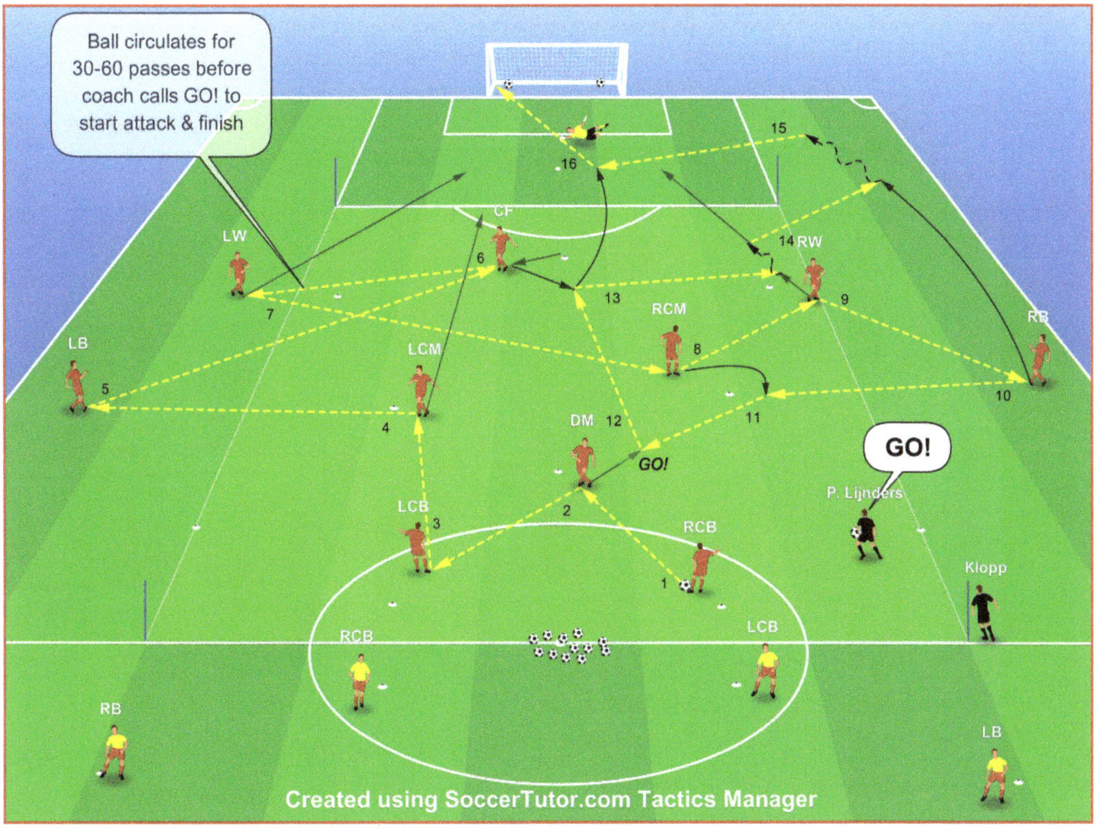

Practice Description

This is a progression of the previous practice with the players now able to occupy the wide spaces using the full width of the pitch.

1-11. The players pass the ball between each other at match speed with position specific combination play.

12. The Coach calls out **"GO!"** - The players must react quickly to attack and score. This starts with the defensive midfielder's (**DM**) pass to the centre forward (**CF**), who drops to receive.

13. The **CF** passes across to the right winger (**RW**).

14. The **RW** takes a touch forward and passes out wide to the right back (**RB**), who makes an advanced overlapping run on the outside.

15-16. The attacking players make runs into the box and the **RB** cuts the ball back for the centre forward (**CF**) to score.

Source: Jürgen Klopp's Liverpool training session at AXA Training Centre, Liverpool - 17th August 2021

Attacking Positional Patterns of Play + Counter-pressing

Direct from Jürgen Klopp's Training Sessions

"The best moment to win the ball is immediately after your team just lost it."

Jürgen Klopp Practices: Attacking Positional Patterns of Play + Counter-pressing

1. Moving the Ball Quickly to the Winger for a Cut Back and Finish + Counter-pressing

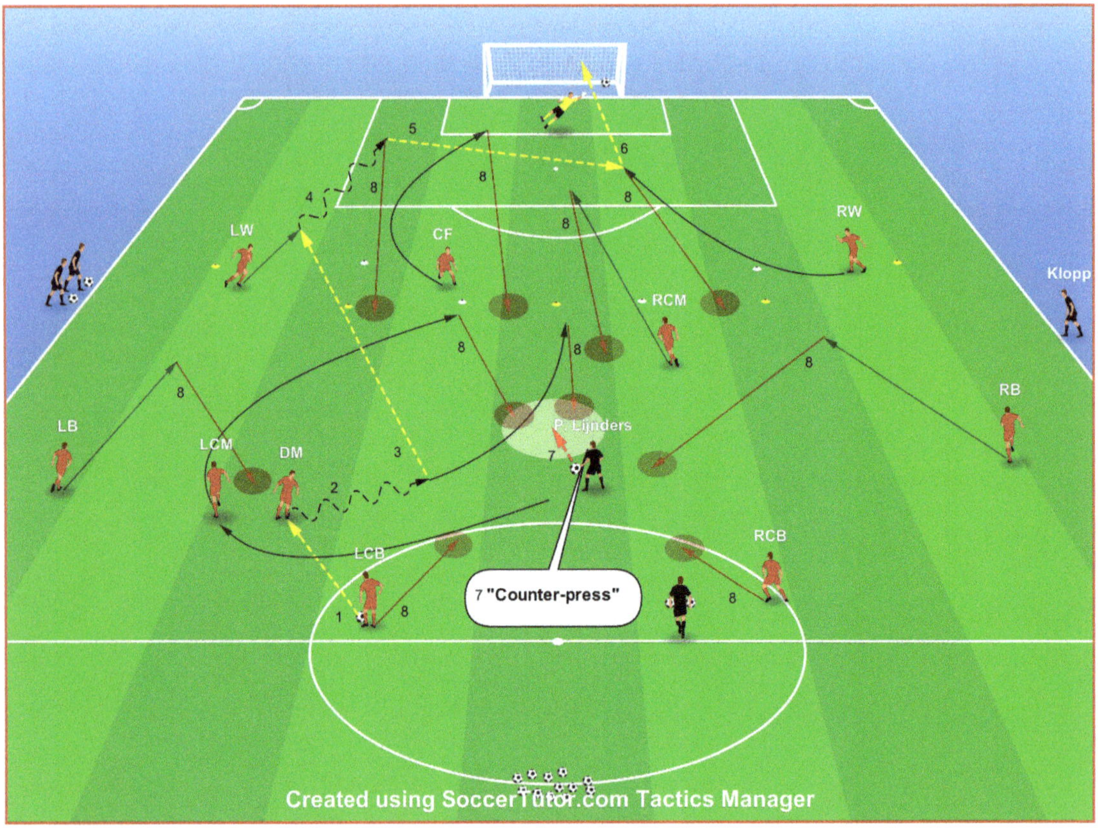

Practice Description

The players perform a set pattern of play and once the attack is complete, they react to the Coach's call and where the ball is to counter-press in relation to the position of the ball.

1-3. The left centre back (**LCB**) passes to the defensive midfielder (**DM**), who carries the ball inside and then plays a firm diagonal pass to the advanced left winger (**LW**).

4-6. The **LW** drives with the ball into the box and cuts the ball back for the opposite right winger (**RW**) to score. The **CF** and **RCM** also made runs into the box to support the attack.

Counter-press (7-8). After the attack is complete, the Coach calls out **"Counter-press"**, and all 10 players make counter-pressing movements in relation to the position of the new ball. These movements are shown by the red arrows.

Source: Jürgen Klopp's Liverpool training session at AXA Training Centre, Liverpool - 17th August 2021

Jürgen Klopp Practices: Attacking Positional Patterns of Play + Counter-pressing

2. Combination Play on One Side of the Pitch and Switch of Play Over the Top (in Behind) + Counter-pressing

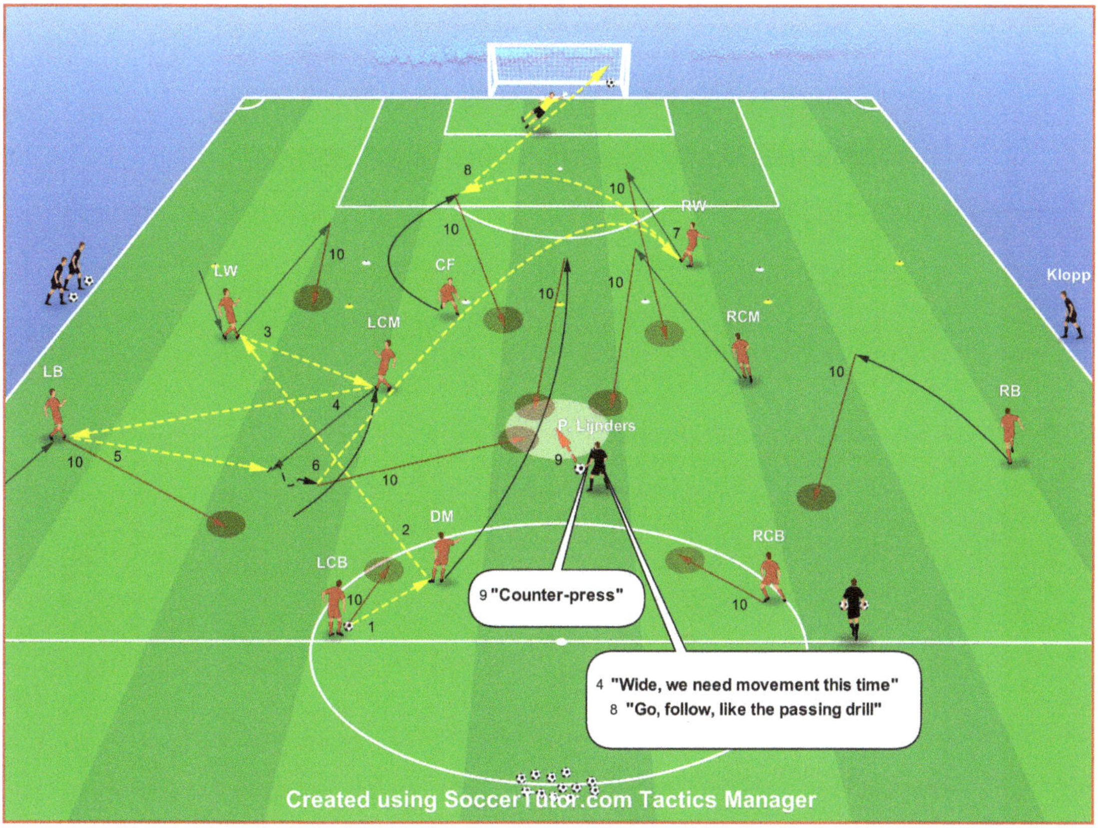

Practice Description

This is a variation of the previous practice with a different pattern of play displayed:

1-2. The left centre back (**LCB**) passes to the defensive midfielder (**DM**), who plays a firm diagonal pass to the left winger (**LW**), who has dropped back to receive this time.

3-4. The **LW** passes to the left central midfielder (**LCM**), who passes wide to the left back (**LB**).

5-6. The **LB** passes to the **LCM**, who drops back to receive, opens up, and hits a long aerial pass to switch the play to the right winger (**RW**).

7-8. The **RW** plays a chipped pass into the box for the centre forward (**CF**) to score.

Counter-press (9-10). After the attack is complete, the Coach calls out **"Counter-press"** and all 10 players make counter-pressing movements in relation to the position of the new ball.

Source: Jürgen Klopp's Liverpool training session at AXA Training Centre, Liverpool - 17th August 2021

Jürgen Klopp Practices: Attacking Positional Patterns of Play + Counter-pressing

3. Attacking Pattern of Play, Counter-pressing, and Fast Break Attack in a 2-Ball Practice

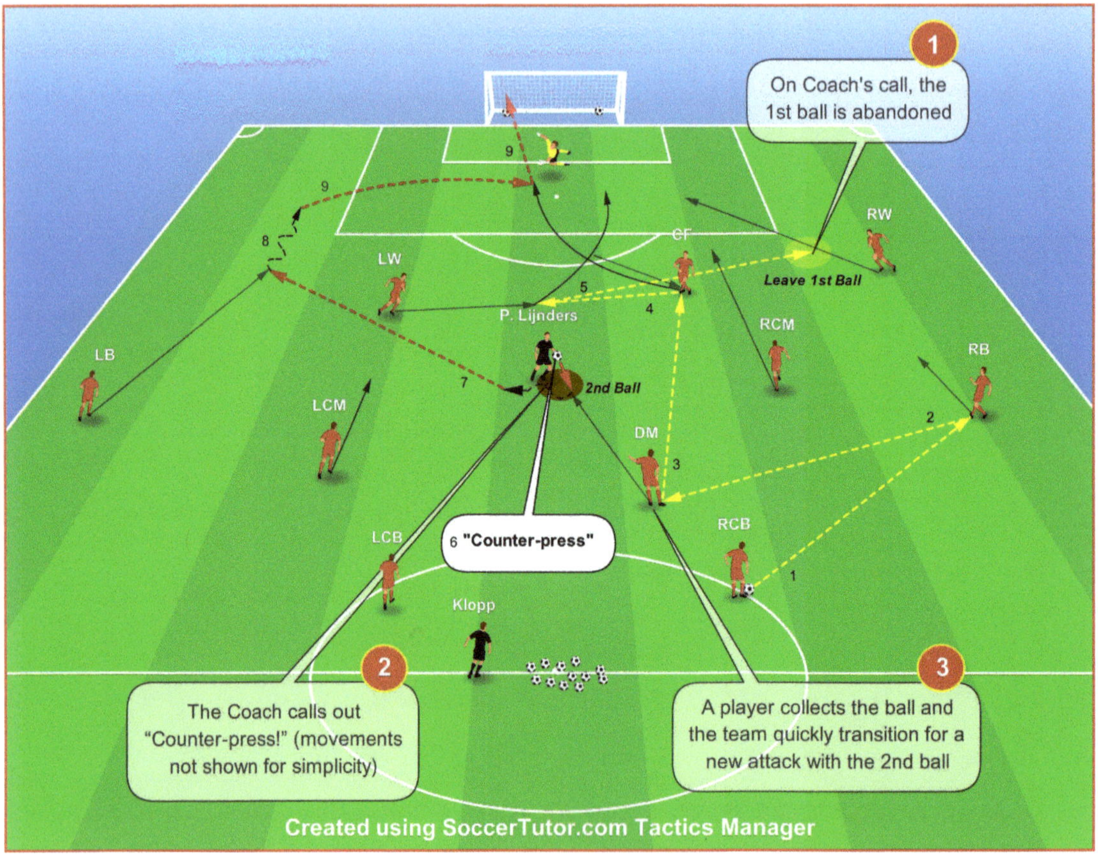

Practice Description

The players perform a set pattern of play and once the attack is complete, they react to the Coach's call and where the ball is to counter-press in relation to the position of the ball. This is followed by a fast break attack to complete the sequence.

1-2. The right centre back (**RCB**) passes to the right back (**RB**), who passes inside to the defensive midfielder (**DM**).

3-5. The **DM** passes to the forward (**CF**), who lays the ball off to the left winger (**LW**). The **LW** moves inside to receive and passes wide to the winger (**RW**).

Counter-press (6). At any point, the Coach can call out **"Counter-press"**, and all 10 players make counter-pressing movements in relation to the position of the new ball (1st ball is abandoned).

Fast Break Attack (7-9). The players try to score as quickly as possible (red arrows).

Source: Jürgen Klopp's Liverpool training session at AXA Training Centre, Liverpool - 7th July 2022

Positional Patterns of Play with 2nd/3rd Ball Attacks

Direct from
Jürgen Klopp's
Training Sessions

Jürgen Klopp Practices: Positional Patterns of Play with 2nd/3rd Ball Attacks

1. Play Through Midfield, then Wide for the Winger to Cross + 2nd Ball Attack

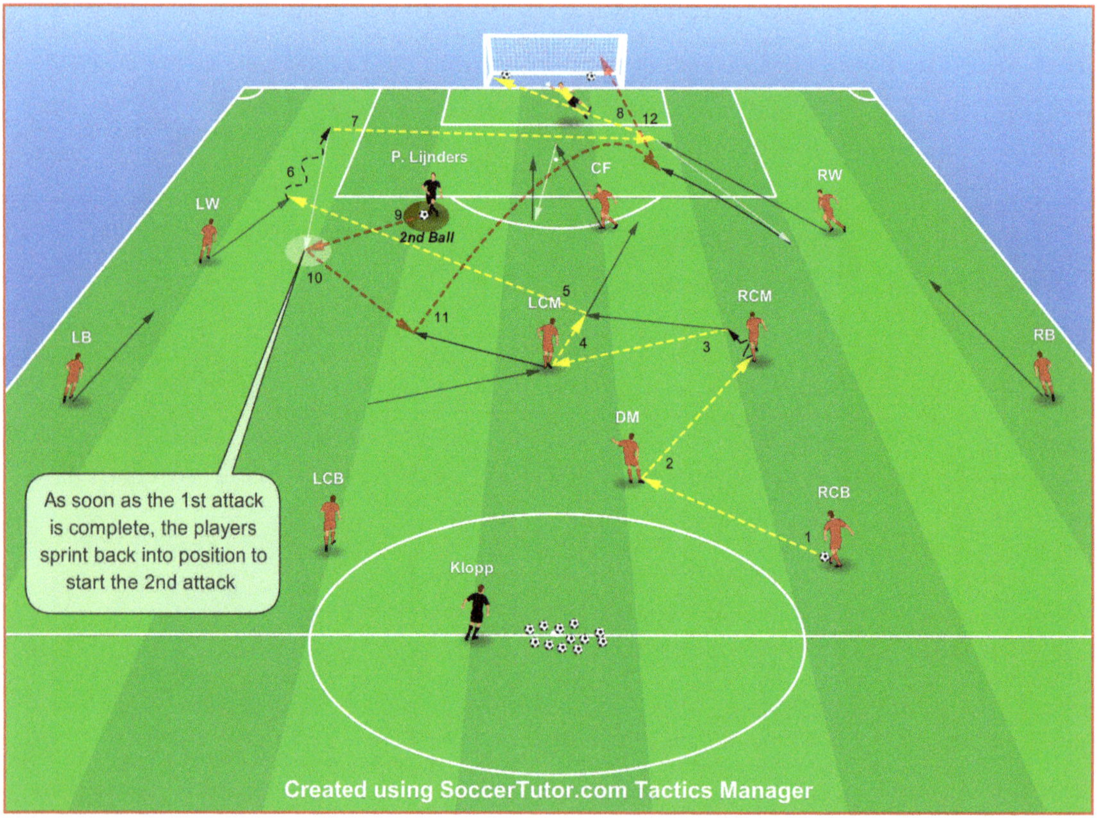

Practice Description

In the first practice displayed of this type, the Liverpool players perform 2 quick phases (2 balls) within the pattern of play practice format.

1. The right centre back (**RCB**) starts with a pass to the defensive midfielder (**DM**).

2. The **DM** passes forward to the right central midfielder (**RCM**).

3-4. The **RCM** moves forward with the ball and passes inside to the left central midfielder (**LCM**), who has moved across to receive. The **LCM** returns the ball to the **RCM** via a lay-off.

5-8. The **RCM** passes wide to the left winger (**LW**), who moves forward with the ball and delivers a ground cross for the opposite winger (**RW**) to score.

2nd Ball (9-12). As soon as the first attack is complete, the players sprint back into position to start the 2nd attack from the Coach. In this example, he passes the ball to the **LW** → **LCM** → Lofted pass to **RW**.

Source: Jürgen Klopp's Liverpool training session at AXA Training Centre, Liverpool - 18th March 2021

Jürgen Klopp Practices: Positional Patterns of Play with 2nd/3rd Ball Attacks

2. Through Pass for Left Winger's Cut Back + 2nd Ball Attack on Right Side

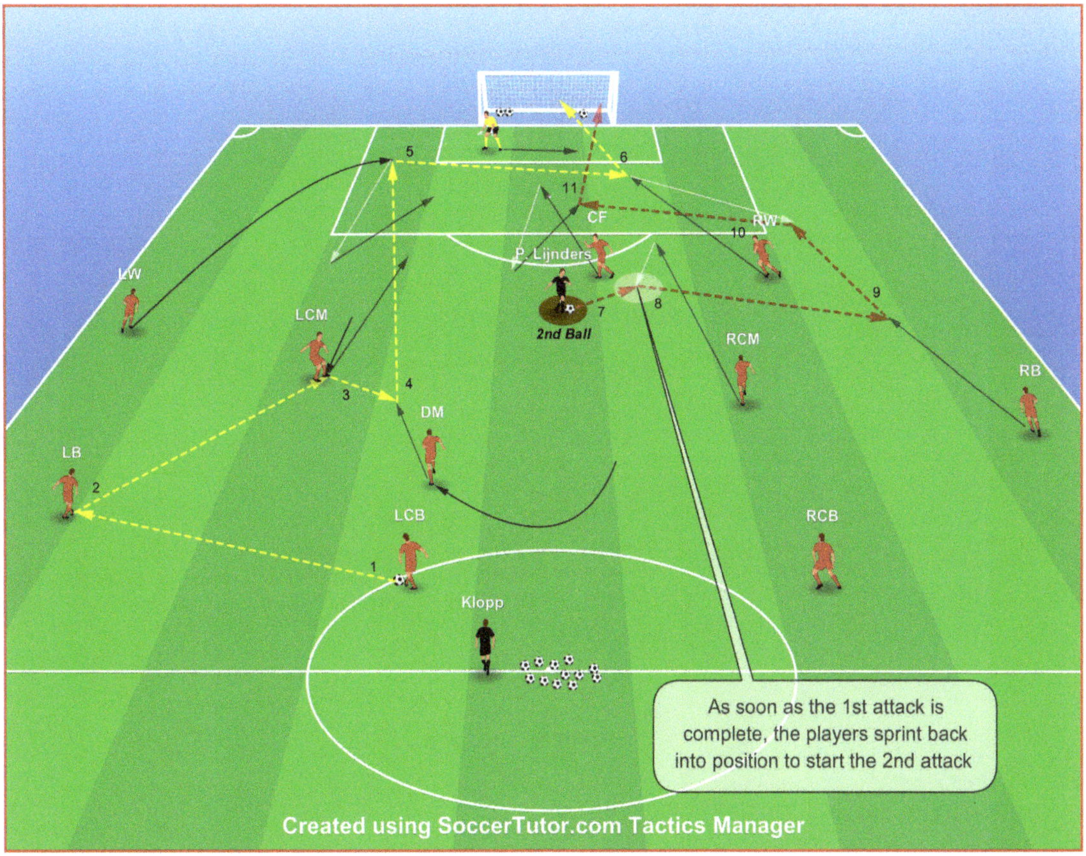

As soon as the 1st attack is complete, the players sprint back into position to start the 2nd attack

Practice Description

This is a variation of the previous practice with a different pattern of play displayed:

1-2. The left centre back (**LCB**) starts with a pass to the left back (**LB**), who passes to the left central midfielder (**LCM**).

3-4. The **LCM** lays the ball off for the oncoming defensive midfielder (**DM**), who plays a through pass into the box timed for the run of the left winger (**LW**).

5-6. The **LW** passes across the box for the right winger (**RW**) to score.

2nd Ball (7-8). As soon as the first attack is complete, the players sprint back into position. The Coach passes to the right central midfielder (**RCM**), who passes wide to the oncoming right back (**RB**).

9-11. The **RB** passes to the right winger (**RW**), who passes into the centre of the box for the centre forward (**CF**) to score.

Source: Jürgen Klopp's Liverpool training session at AXA Training Centre, Liverpool - 18th March 2021

Jürgen Klopp Practices: Positional Patterns of Play with 2nd/3rd Ball Attacks

3. Possession in Midfield with Lay-offs, Play into Forward, and Lofted Pass in Behind to Winger + 2nd Ball Attack

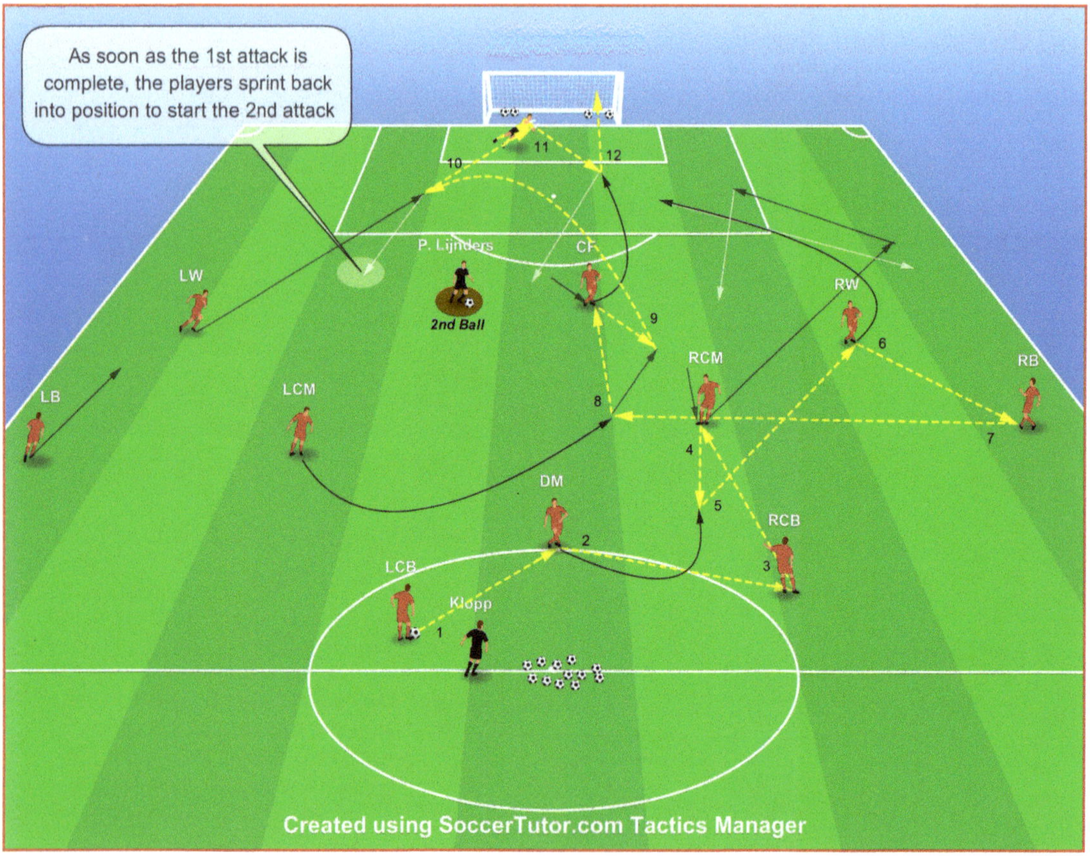

Practice Description

This is a variation of the previous practices with a different pattern of play displayed:

1-2. The left centre back (**LCB**) passes to the defensive midfielder (**DM**), who passes to the right centre back (**RCB**).

3-6. The **RCB** passes to the right central midfielder (**RCM**), who lays the ball off to the **DM**. The **DM** passes wide to the right winger (**RW**), who passes back to the **RB**.

7. The right back (**RB**) passes inside to the left central midfielder (**LCM**), who has made a big movement to receive.

8-12. **LCM** plays a one-two with the forward (**CF**) and plays a lofted pass to the left winger (**LW**) into the box. The **LW** shoots and the **CF** scores on the rebound.

2nd Ball. As soon as the first attack is complete, the players sprint back into position. The Coach passes to one of the players and they try to score again.

Source: Jürgen Klopp's Liverpool training session at AXA Training Centre, Liverpool - 18th March 2021

Jürgen Klopp Practices: Positional Patterns of Play with 2nd/3rd Ball Attacks

4. Short Fast Combination Play Around the Box + Finishing Inside and Outside the Box

Part 1/3 (Variation 1)

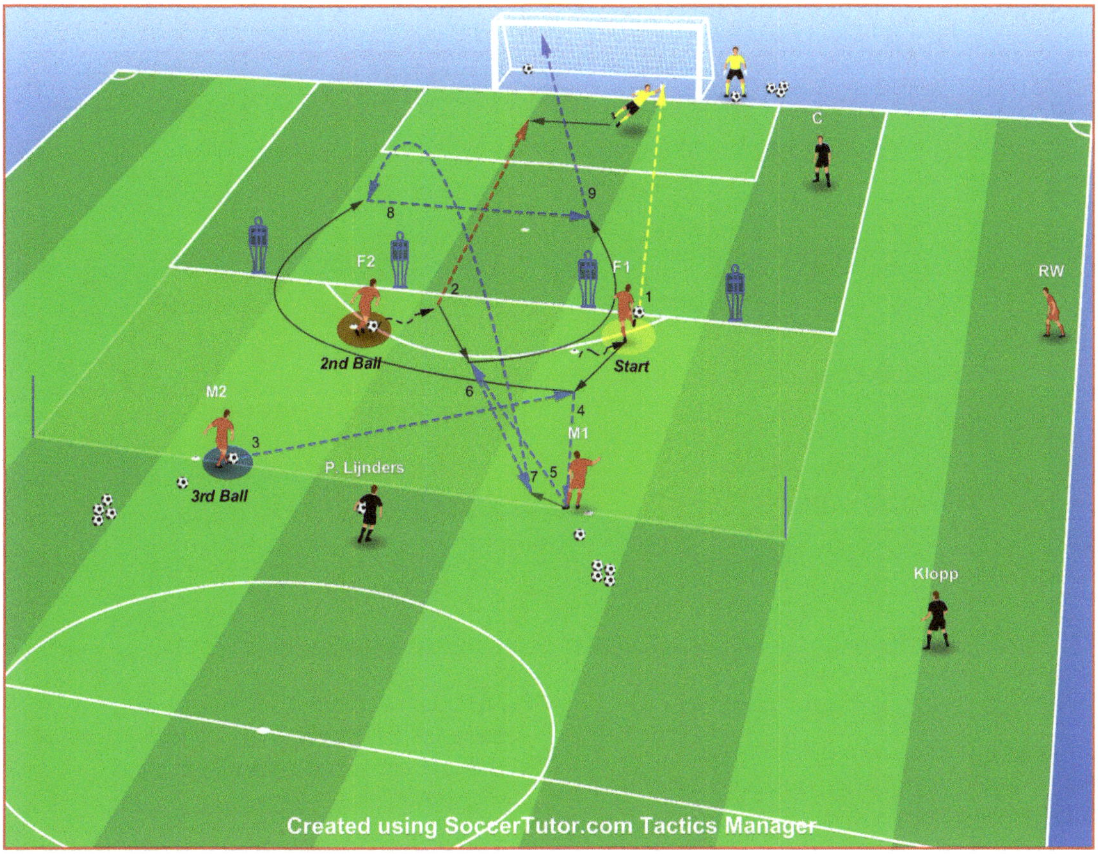

Practice Description (Variation 1)

M = Midfielder / F = Forward / RW = Right Winger

1st Ball (1) + 2nd Ball (2). F1 shifts the ball at an angle off the cone and shoots from outside the box, then **F2** does the same.

3rd Ball (3). M2 passes to **F1**, who drops back to receive.

4-5. F1 passes back to **M1**, and he passes to **F2**, who also drops back to receive.

6-7. F2 passes back to **M1**, who plays a lofted pass for the curved run of **F1** in between the blue centre back and right back mannequins.

8-9. F2 makes a curved run in the opposite direction (around the left centre back mannequin) to score from **F1's** final pass.

Source: Jürgen Klopp's Liverpool training session at AXA Training Centre, Liverpool - 18th July 2022

Jürgen Klopp Practices: Positional Patterns of Play with 2nd/3rd Ball Attacks

Part 1/3 (Variation 2)

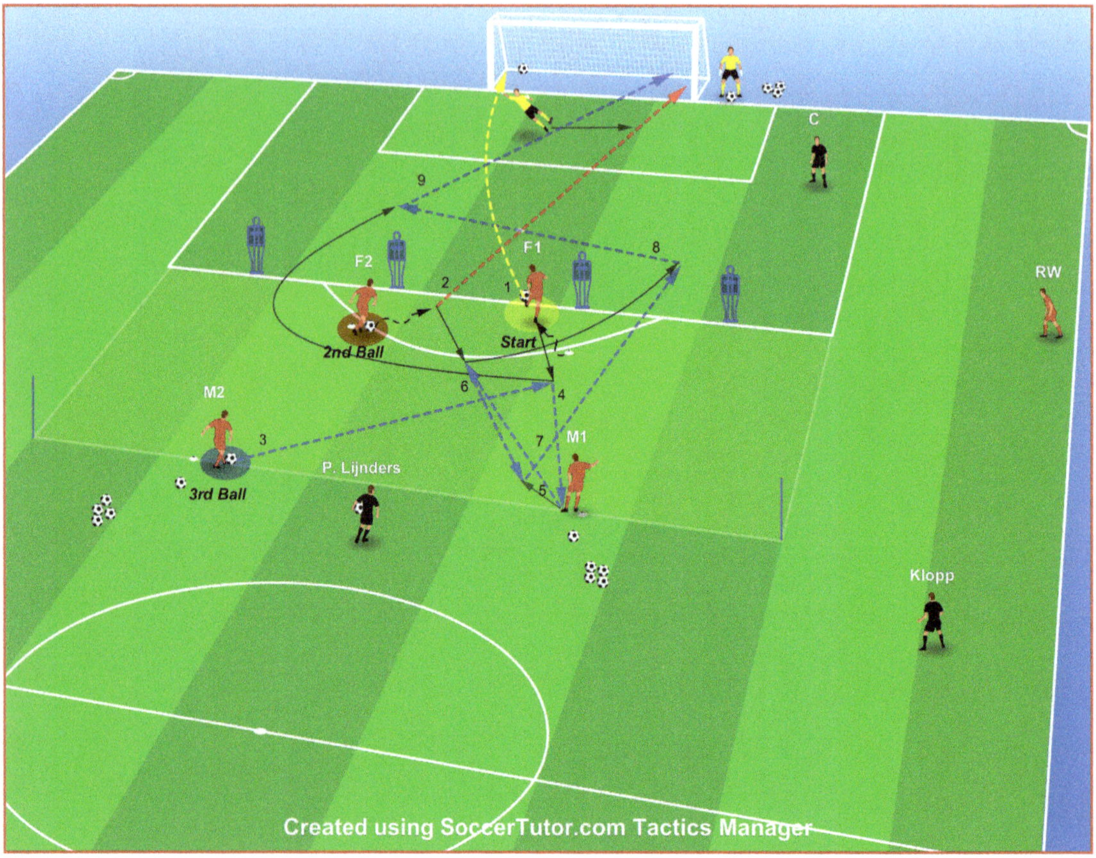

Practice Description (Variation 2)

This diagram shows a different variation of Part 1/3 which the Liverpool players used in this training session:

1st Ball (1). **F1** shifts the ball at an angle off the cone and shoots from outside the box.

2nd Ball (2). **F2** then does the same.

3rd Ball (3). **M2** passes to **F1**, who drops back to receive.

4-5. F1 passes back to **M1**, and he passes to **F2**, who also drops back to receive.

6-7. F2 passes back to **M1**, who plays a pass for the curved run of **F2** in between the left centre back and left back mannequins.

8-9. F1 makes a curved run in the opposite direction (in between the right centre back and right back mannequins) to score from **F2's** final pass.

Part 2/3 follows on the next page...

Source: Jürgen Klopp's Liverpool training session at AXA Training Centre, Liverpool - 18th July 2022

Jürgen Klopp Practices: Positional Patterns of Play with 2nd/3rd Ball Attacks

Part 2/3 - Wing Play (1v1), Cross & Finish

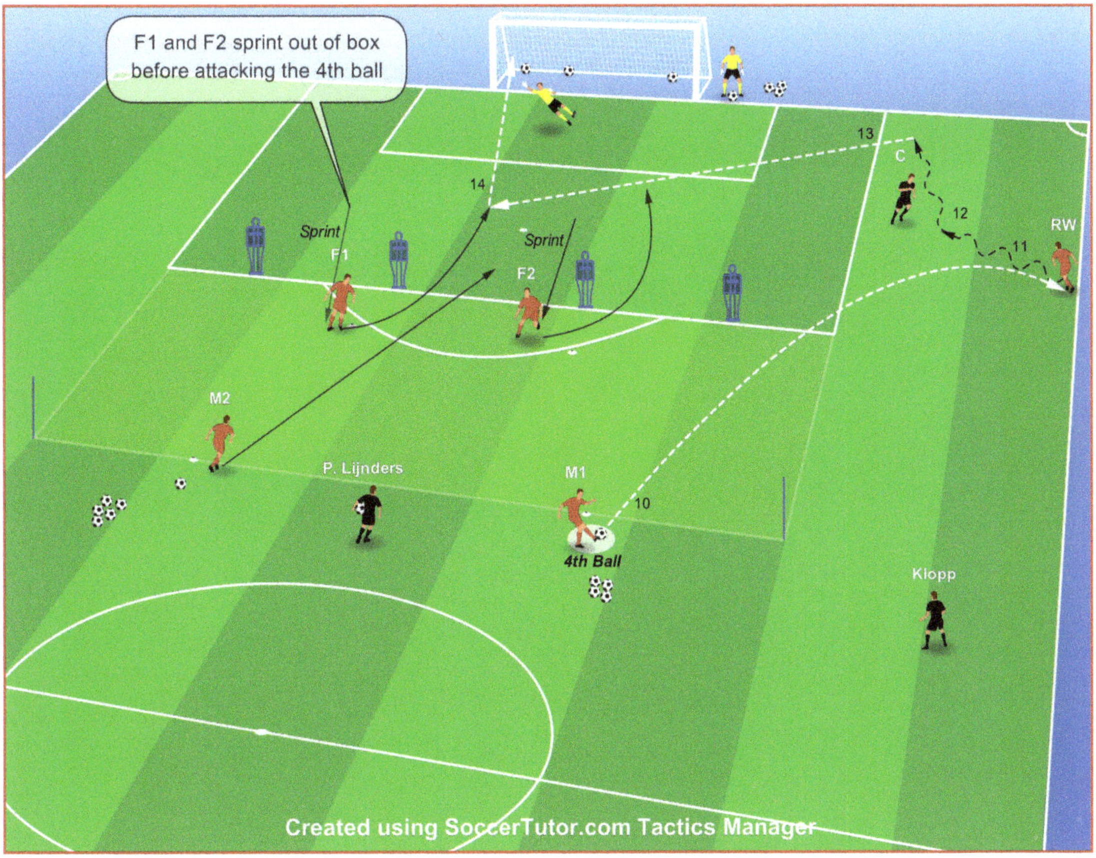

Practice Description (Part 2/3)

The players run back into position ready for the 4th ball:

- **4th Ball (10).** **M1** plays an aerial pass out to the right winger (**RW**) high up the pitch on the sideline.

- **11-12.** The **RW** uses his 1v1 skills to beat the Coach (passive defender) so he can then deliver a cross for one of his 3 teammates who make runs into the box.

- **13.** In this example, the **RW** decides to pass from the by-line into the centre of the box for **F1**. **F2** had made a run to the near post and **M2** was ready for a cut back.

- **14.** **F1** scores past the GK from close range.

Part 3/3 follows on the next page...

Source: Jürgen Klopp's Liverpool training session at AXA Training Centre, Liverpool - 18th July 2022

Jürgen Klopp Practices: Positional Patterns of Play with 2nd/3rd Ball Attacks

Part 3/3 - Lofted Pass, Cut Back & Finish

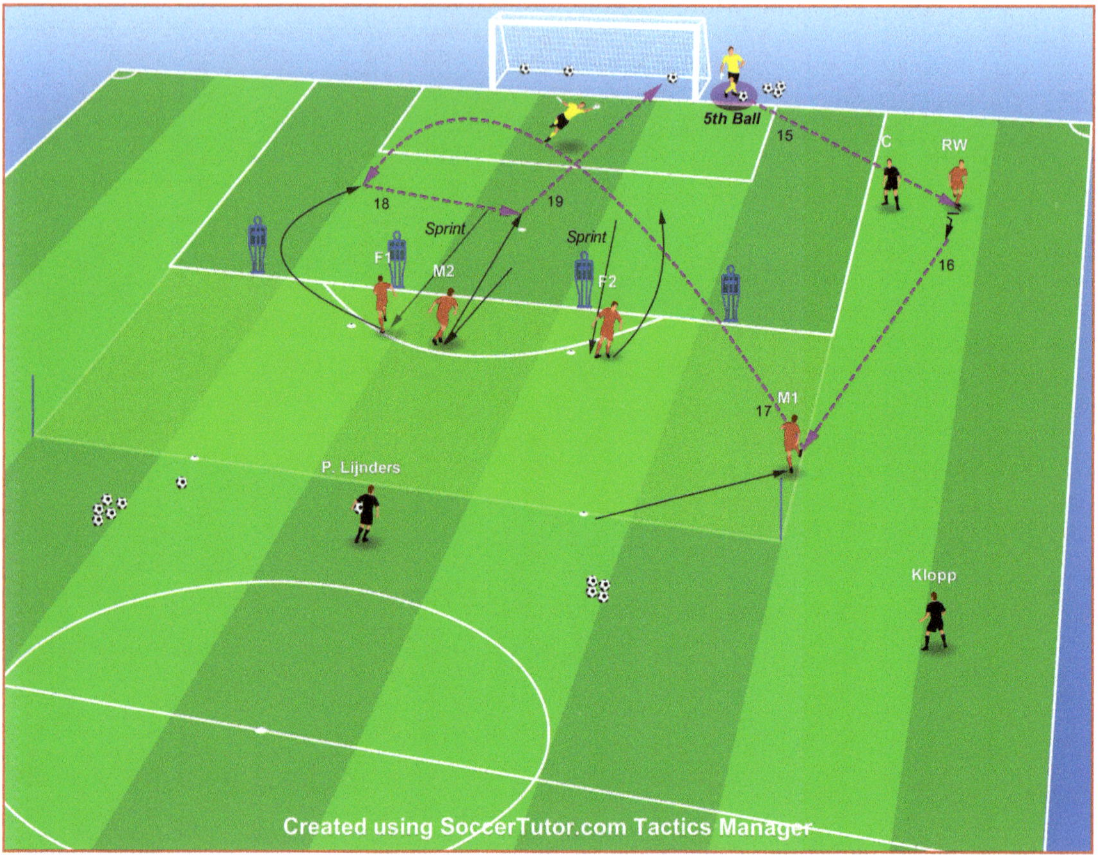

Practice Description (Part 3/3)

The players run back into position ready for the 5th ball:

5th Ball (15-16). The spare GK plays a new 5th ball to the right winger (**RW**), who moves back and passes to **M1**.

17. M1 moves off the cone to receive and **M2**, **F1**, and **F2** all make runs into the box. In this example, **M1** delivers a high cross towards the back post.

18-19. F1 cuts the ball back to the penalty spot for **M2** to score.

Source: Jürgen Klopp's Liverpool training session at AXA Training Centre, Liverpool - 18th July 2022

Jürgen Klopp Practices: Positional Patterns of Play with 2nd/3rd Ball Attacks

5. Pass and Move in Centre + Fast Attacks with 2nd/3rd Balls

Balls 1-2 (Possession + Fast Attack 1)

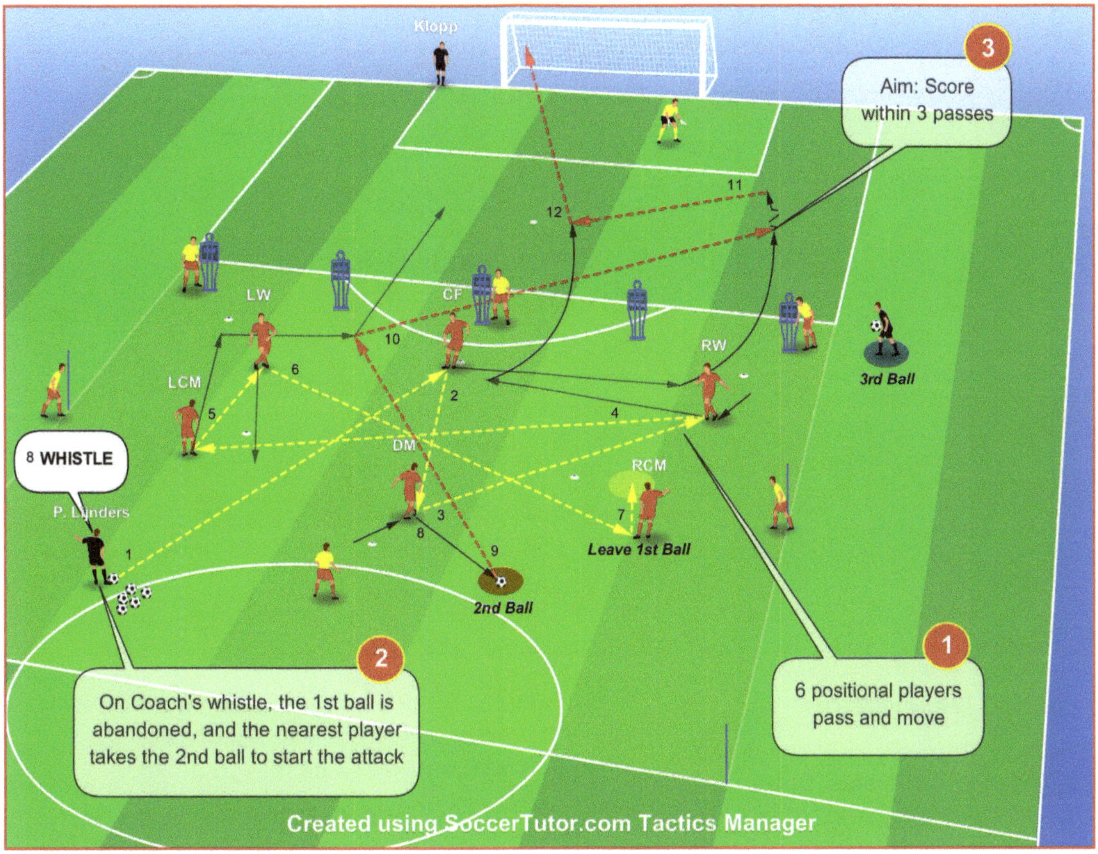

Practice Description

1-7. The practice starts from the Coach and the red players move the ball around within the central area shown. They make typical movements within their positional roles to pass and receive.

2nd Ball (8). The Coach blows his whistle and the 1st ball is abandoned. The 2nd ball is collected for a fast attack.

Fast Attack (9-12). The aim is to quickly attack and score using a **maximum of 3 passes** to do so.

The diagram example was observed during Liverpool's training session. The left winger (**LW**) plays a diagonal through pass to the right winger (**RW**), who cuts the ball back for the centre forward (**CF**) to score.

Source: Jürgen Klopp's Liverpool training session at AXA Training Centre, Liverpool - 18th July 2022

Jürgen Klopp Practices: Positional Patterns of Play with 2nd/3rd Ball Attacks

3rd Ball (Fast Attack 2)

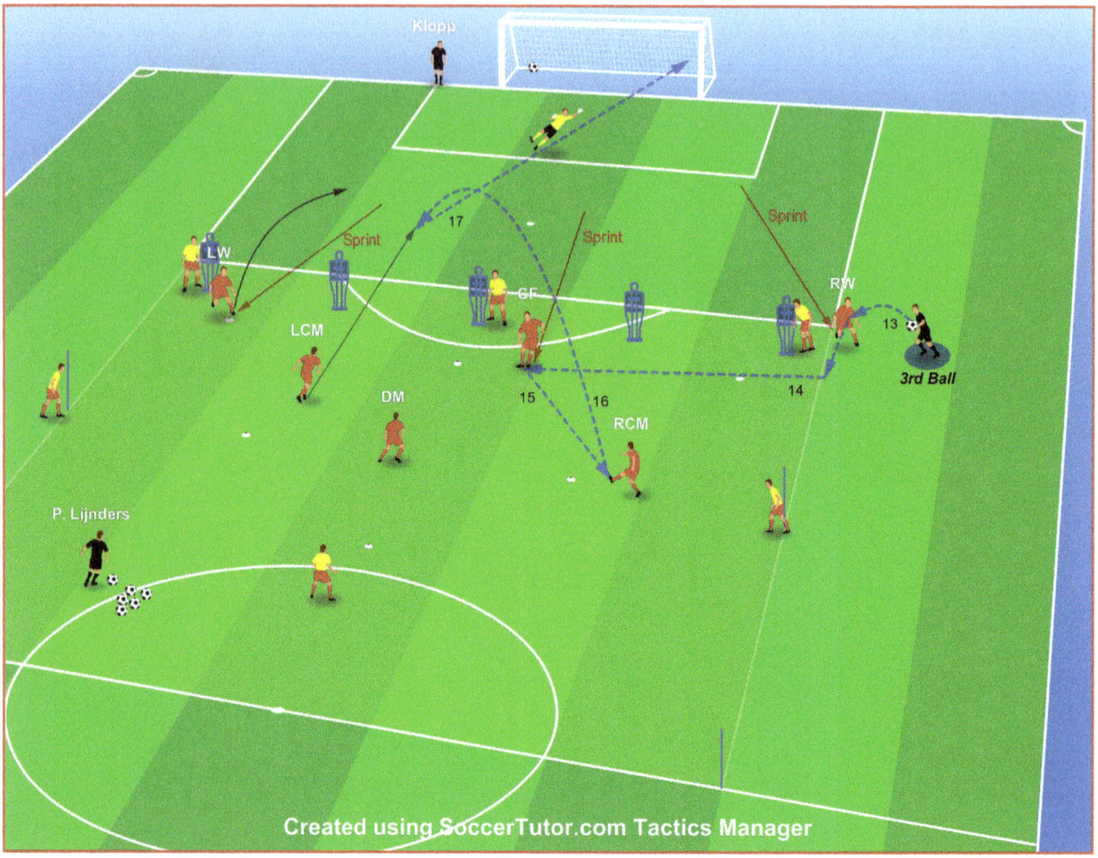

Practice Description

This is a continuation of the practice from the previous page and diagram (1st and 2nd Ball). After a set number of repetitions, the reds and yellows switch places.

3rd Ball (13). After the 2nd ball attack is finished, the players run back into position. The Coach then starts a 3rd ball attack. In this example, he gives the ball to the red right winger (**RW**).

Fast Attack (14-17). The aim again is to quickly attack and score using a **maximum of 3 passes** to do so.

The diagram example was observed during Liverpool's training session. The centre forward (**CF**) lays the ball off to the right central midfielder (**RCM**), who plays a lofted pass over the top and into the box for the left central midfielder (**LCM**) to score.

Source: Jürgen Klopp's Liverpool training session at AXA Training Centre, Liverpool - 18th July 2022

Attacking Combinations and Finishing

Direct from Jürgen Klopp's Training Sessions

"We want to attack the opponent non-stop."

Jürgen Klopp Practices: Attacking Combinations and Finishing

1. Pass Under Pressure, Curved Run into Box + Finish

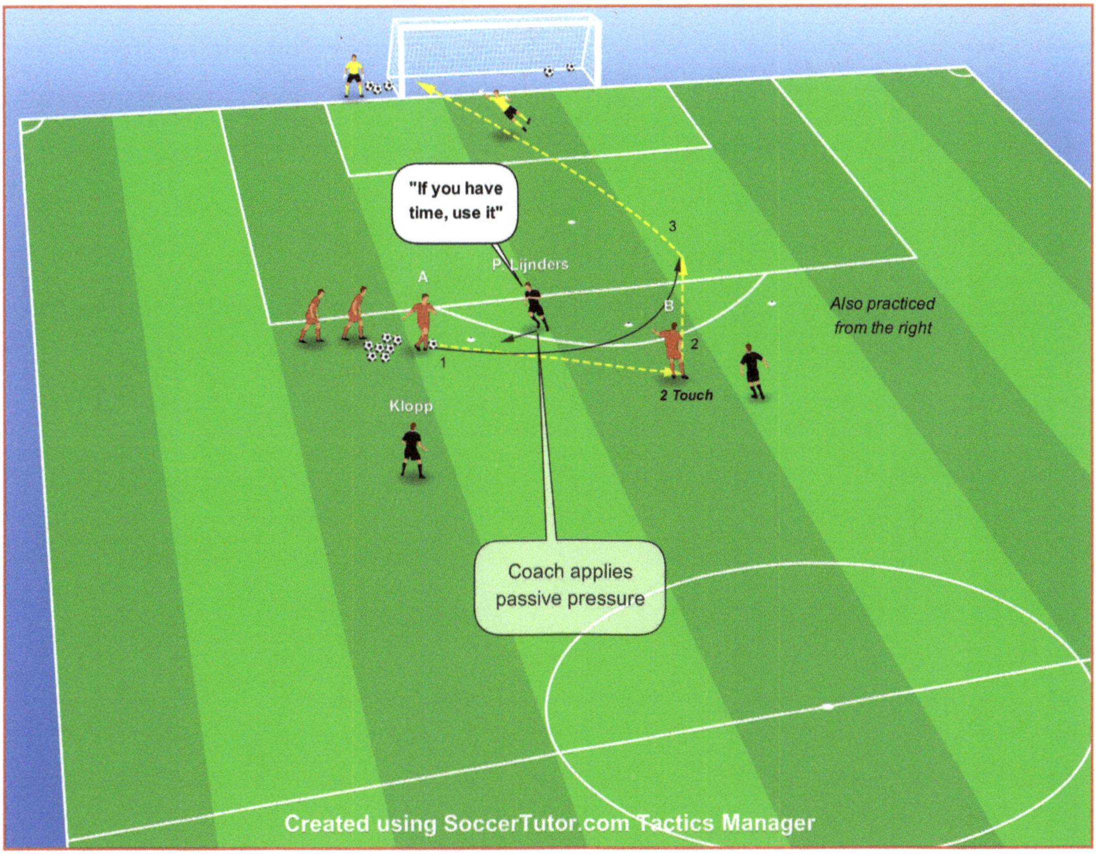

Practice Description

This was also practiced from the right side within the same training session, but we have only displayed the left side example.

1. The Coach *(P. Ljinders)* applies pressure as a passive defender and **Player A** passes to **Player B** in the centre.

2. **Player B** uses 2 touches to receive and then pass into the box for the curved run of **Player A**.

3. **Player A** *(Salah in this example)* must finish using <u>1 or 2 touches</u>. As the Coach says, if the players have time, they should use it (do not rush the finish).

A variation of this finishing practice is displayed on the next page...

Source: Jürgen Klopp's Liverpool training session at AXA Training Centre, Liverpool - 17th August 2021

Jürgen Klopp Practices: Attacking Combinations and Finishing

2. Short Passing Under Pressure, Movement + Finish

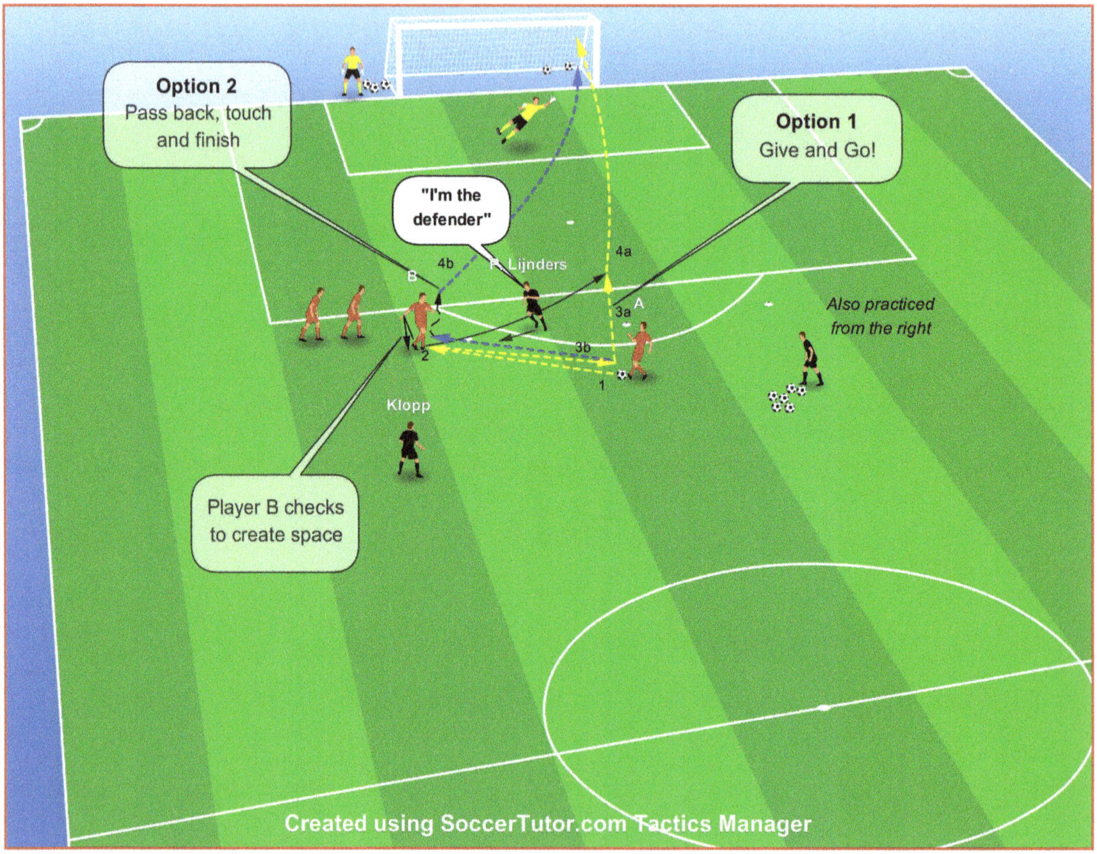

Practice Description

This was also practiced from the right side within the same training session but we have only displayed the left side example.

The Coach (P. Ljinders) applies pressure as a passive defender for the initial passes.

Option 1 - Give and Go (1-4a). Player A
plays a one-two with **Player B**, and then plays the 3rd pass into the box timed for the run of **Player B**, who then finishes

Option 2 - Pass back, touch & finish (1-4b).
Player A plays a one-two with **Player B**, and then plays the 3rd pass back to **B**. **Player B** opens up, takes a touch into the box and tries to finish past the GK.

A variation of this finishing practice is displayed on the next page...

Source: Jürgen Klopp's Liverpool training session at AXA Training Centre, Liverpool - 17th August 2021

Jürgen Klopp Practices: Attacking Combinations and Finishing

3. One-two, Lateral Third Man Run for Through Pass + Finish

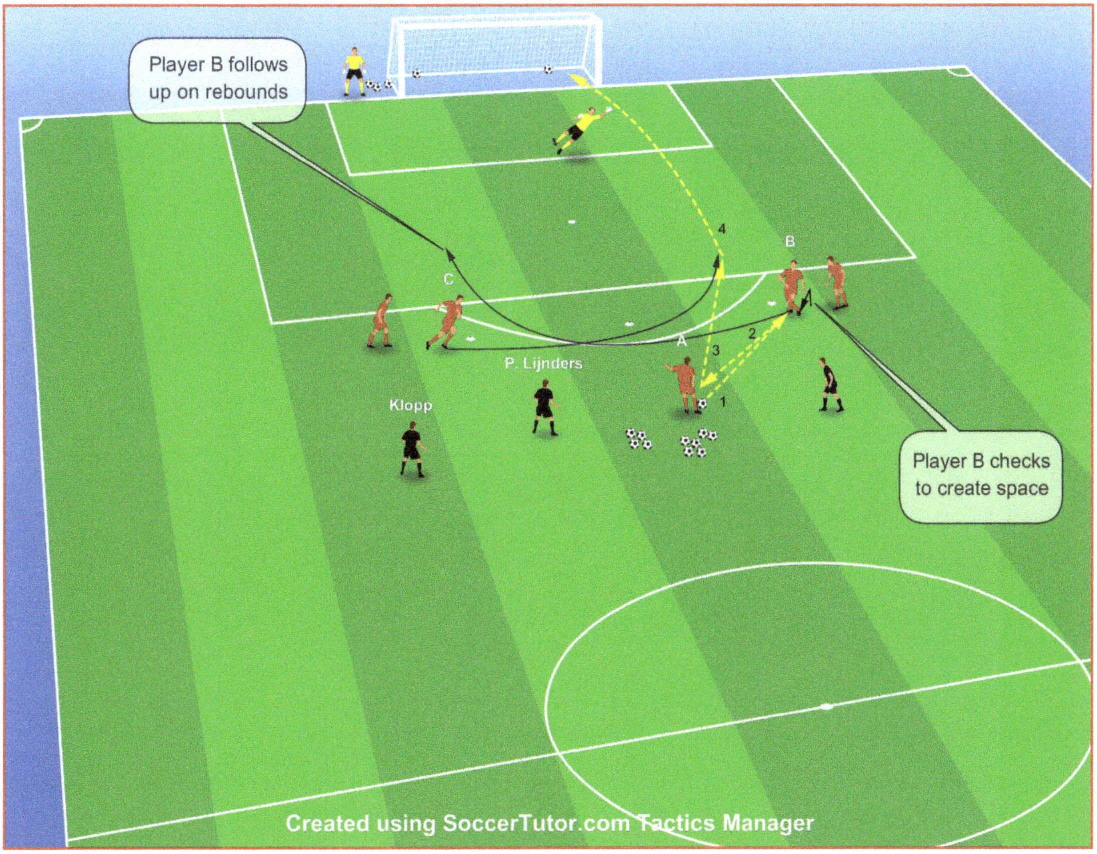

Practice Description

1. **Player A** passes to **B** (or **C**), who checks off the cone before moving to receive.

2. **Player B** plays a return pass to **Player A** (to complete a one-two combination).

3. **Player A** then plays a pass into the box for the well timed (curved) third man run of **Player C**.

4. **Player C** must finish using 1 or 2 touches, trying to score past the GK.

Player B has made a parallel run and follows up on any rebounds in case the GK makes a save.

* If the first pass is from A → C, then Players B and C simply switch roles for the same combination (opposite).

A variation of this finishing practice is displayed on the next page...

Source: Jürgen Klopp's Liverpool training session at AXA Training Centre, Liverpool - 17th August 2021

Jürgen Klopp Practices: Attacking Combinations and Finishing

4. Double One-two and Through Pass for Lateral Third Man Run + Finish

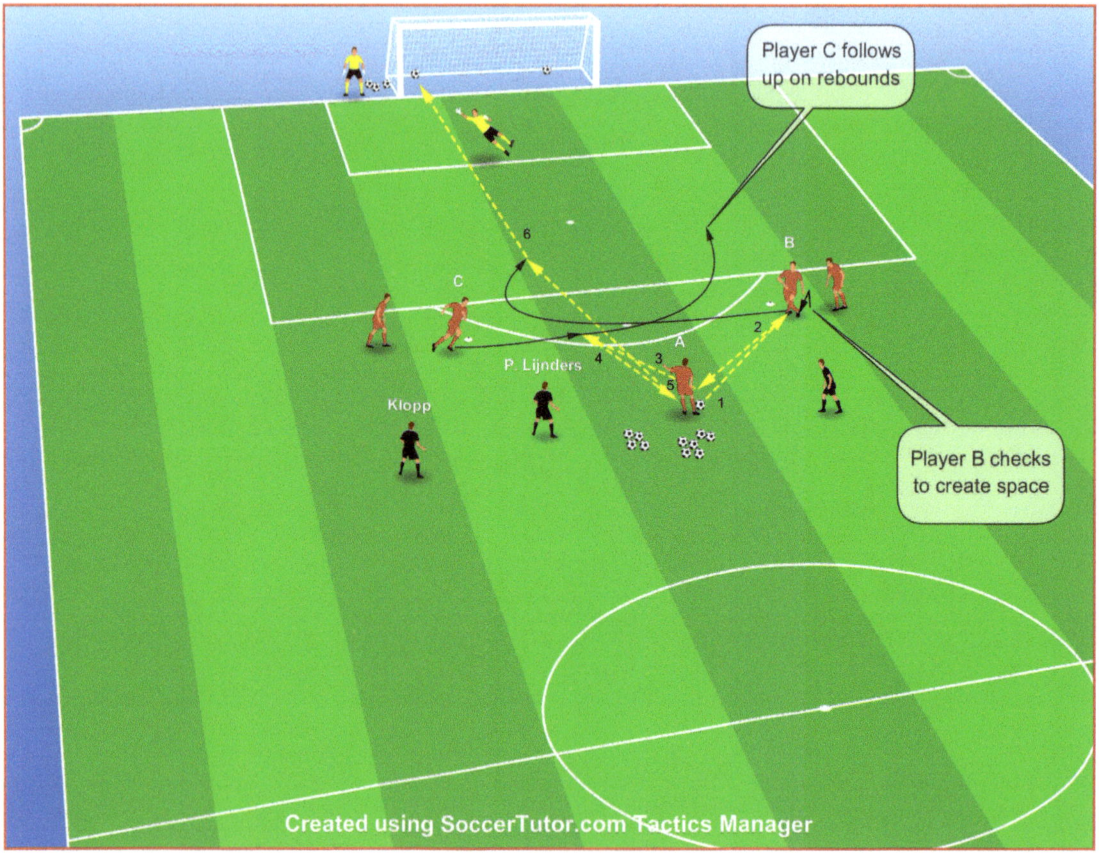

Practice Description

1. **Player A** passes to **Player B**.
2. **Player B** plays a return pass to **Player A** (to complete a one-two combination).
3. **Player A** passes to **Player C**.
4. **Player C** plays a return pass to **Player A** (to complete another one-two).
5. **Player A** then plays a pass into the box for the third man run of **Player B**.
6. **Player B** must finish using <u>1 or 2 touches</u>, trying to score past the GK. **Player C** has made a parallel run and follows up on any rebounds in case the GK makes a save.

* If the first pass is from A → C, then Players B and C simply switch roles for the same combination (opposite).

A variation of this finishing practice is displayed on the next page...

Source: Jürgen Klopp's Liverpool training session at AXA Training Centre, Liverpool - 17th August 2021

Jürgen Klopp Practices: Attacking Combinations and Finishing

5. One-two, Open Up to Receive and Finish + 2nd Ball Finish

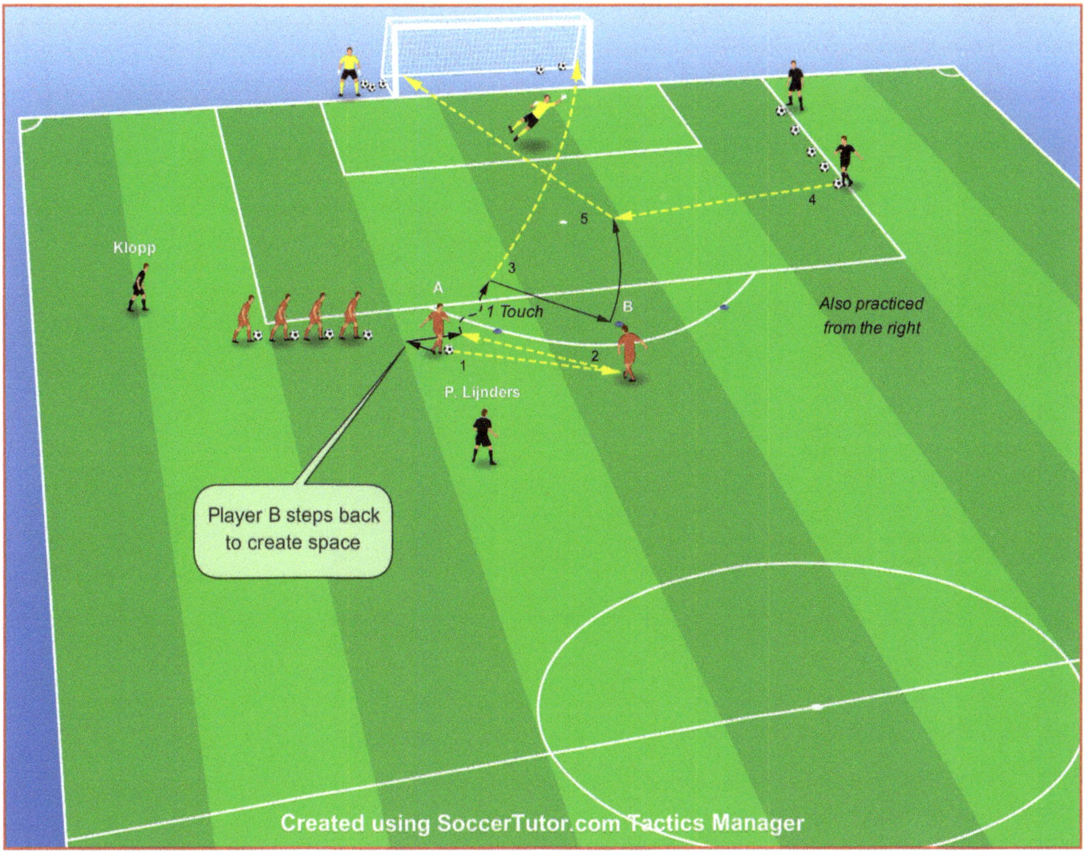

Practice Description

This was also practiced from the right side within the same training session, but we have only displayed the left side example.

1. **Player A** passes to **Player B** in the centre.

2. **Player B** plays a return pass to **Player A** (to complete a one-two combination).

3. **Player A** steps back to create space and then moves again to receive. He takes a touch forward into the box and then tries to finish past the GK.

4. **Player A** sprints back to the central blue cone and turns back towards goal very quickly. One of the Coaches passes a ball into the centre of the box.

5. **Player A** times his movement to try and meet the pas and finish first time (1 touch) past the GK again.

Source: Jürgen Klopp's Liverpool training session at AXA Training Centre, Liverpool - 17th August 2021

Jürgen Klopp Practices: Attacking Combinations and Finishing

6. Diagonal Lofted Pass in Behind with Fast Supporting Runs into the Box

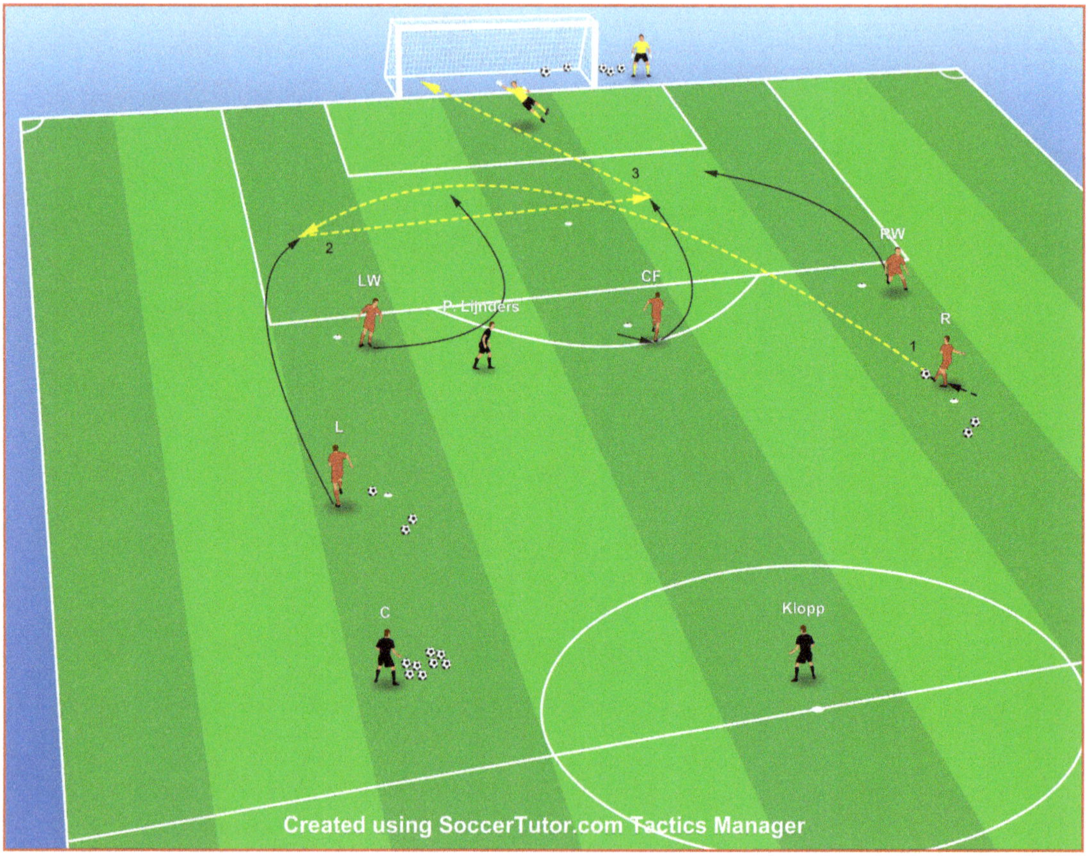

Practice Description

1. The player on the right side (**R**) plays a diagonal lofted pass to the far side of the box, timed and weighted well for the run of the player on the left side.

2. The left side player (**L**) plays the ball across the box. The left winger (**LW**), the centre forward (**CF**), and the right winger (**RW**) have all made runs into the box to the near post, centre, and far post respectively, as shown.

3. In this example, the **CF** scores past the GK.

The same pattern is repeated starting with a left side cross from Player L.

Source: Jürgen Klopp's Liverpool training session at Civitas Metropolitan Stadium, Madrid - 30th May 2019

Jürgen Klopp Practices: Attacking Combinations and Finishing

7. 3-Player Combination + Cross for Timed Runs into the Box

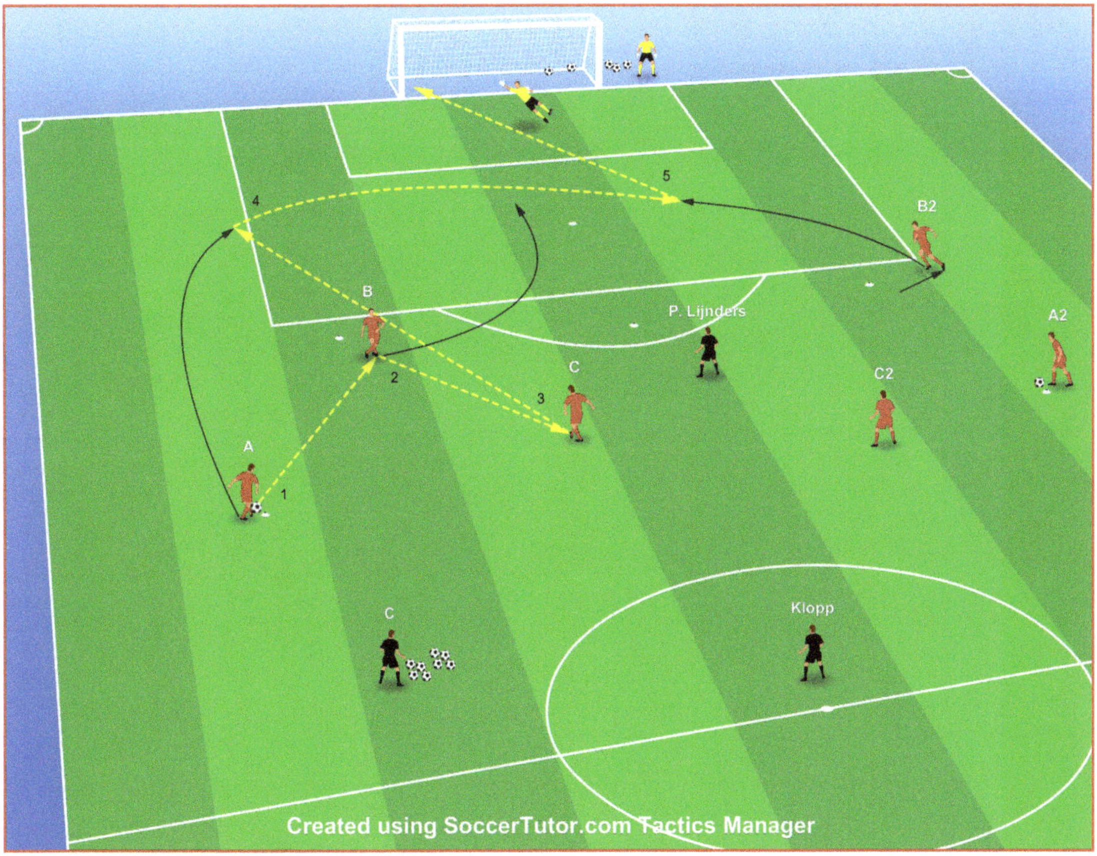

Practice Description

1. **Player A** passes to **Player B**.
2. **Player B** has his back to goal and passes back to **Player C**.
3. **Player C** plays a diagonal forward pass for the run of **Player A** in behind.
4. **Player A** delivers a cross into the box. **Player B** and **Player B2** on the opposite side make runs into the centre of the box to meet the cross.
5. In this example, **B2** scores past the GK.

The same pattern is repeated starting on the right side with Player A2.

Source: Jürgen Klopp's Liverpool training session at Civitas Metropolitan Stadium, Madrid - 30th May 2019

Jürgen Klopp Practices: Attacking Combinations and Finishing

8. Switch Play Wide, Give & Go, and Cross for Timed Runs / Box Finishing

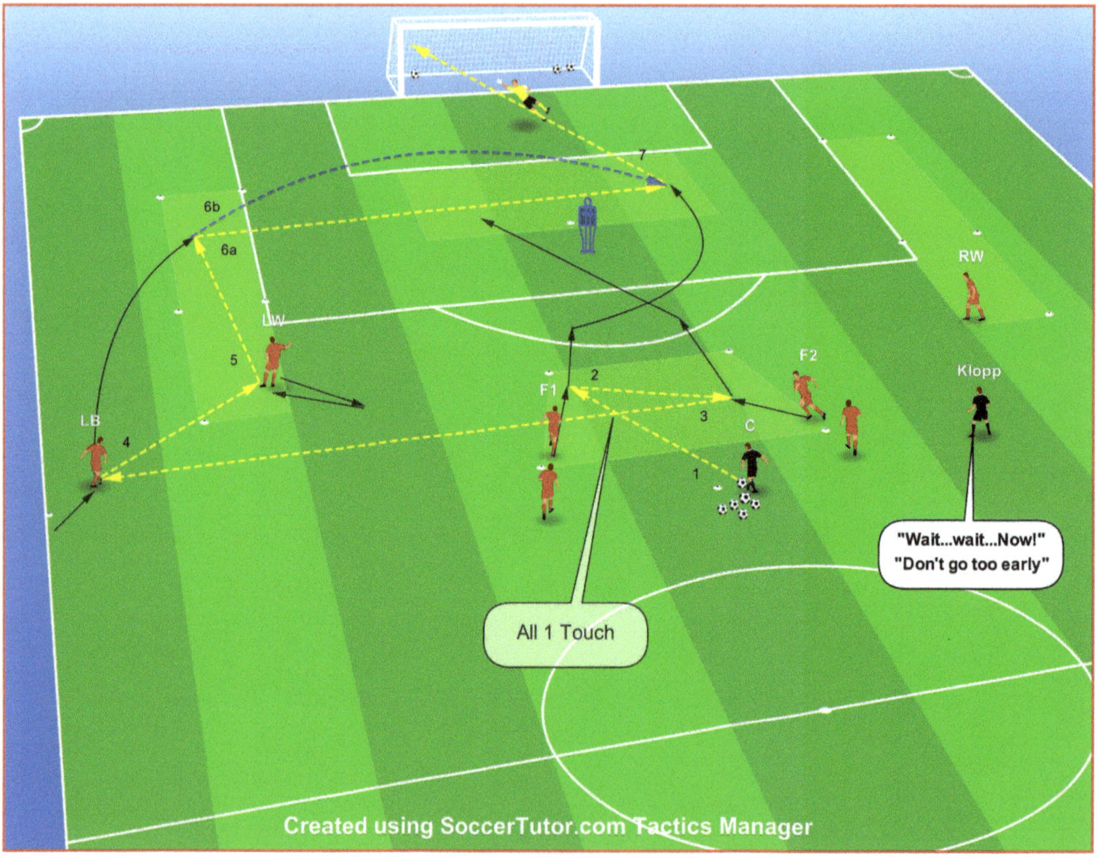

Practice Description

1. The Coach passes for the first forward (**F1**) to run onto.

2. **F1** passes back to **F2**, who also moves forward off his cone to receive.

3. **F2** plays a firm pass (ground or aerial) out wide to the left back (**LB**), who moves off his cone to receive.

4. The **LB** passes to the left winger (**LW**), who checks before moving to receive.

5. The **LW** plays a return pass for the advanced run of the **LB** on the outside.

6-7. The **LB** delivers a cross into the centre of the box (highlighted area). This can be a ground cross **(6a)** or aerial cross **(6b)**. Both forwards (**F1** & **F2**) make opposite runs to the near and far post areas. In this example, **F1** scores at the back post.

The same pattern is repeated on the right side with the right back (out of the picture on diagram) and the right winger.

Source: Jürgen Klopp's Liverpool training session at Melwood Training Ground, Liverpool - 13th July 2016

Jürgen Klopp Practices: Attacking Combinations and Finishing

9. 4-Ball Long Range Finishing Drill with Support Play

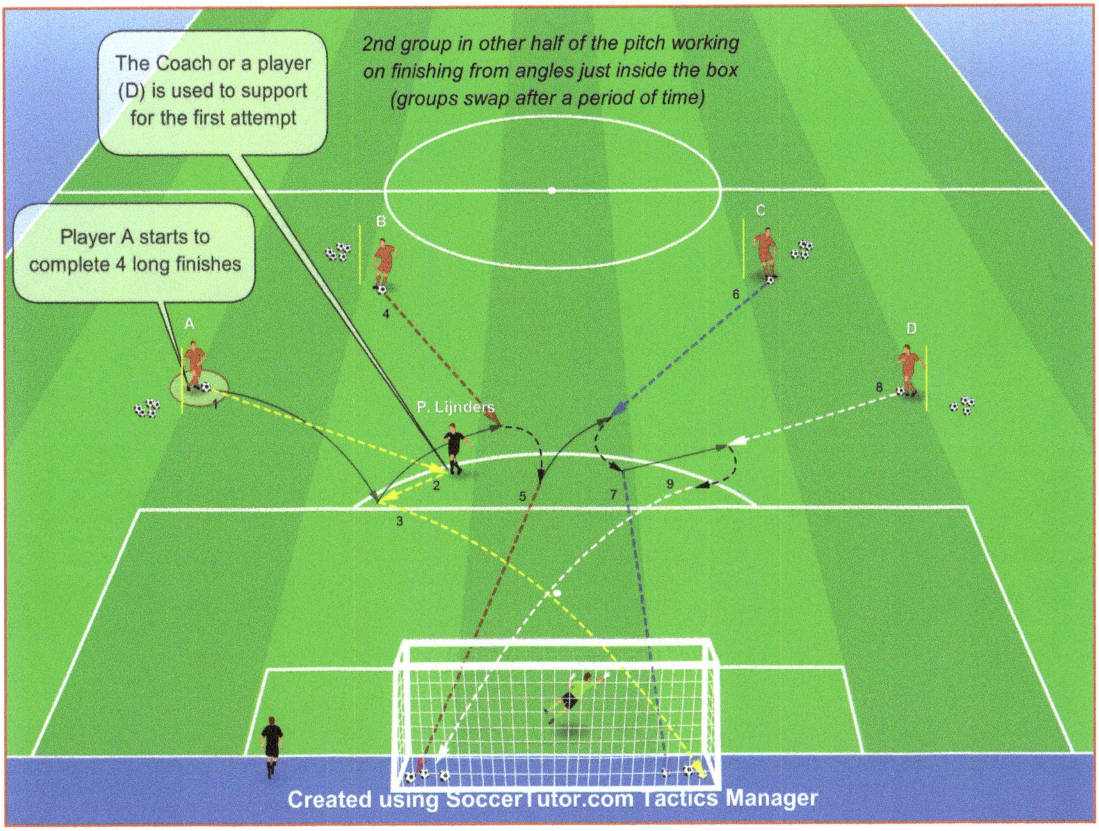

Practice Description

This drill enables the players to practice receiving and shooting/finishing from 4 different angles.

1st Ball (1-3). Player A passes to the Coach, who lays the ball of for **A** to shoot/finish using 1 or 2 touches.

2nd Ball (4-5). Player A moves to receive the next pass from **Player B**, takes a good directional touch and shoots again.

3rd Ball (6-7). Player A moves to receive the next pass from **Player C**, takes a good directional touch and shoots again.

4th Ball (8-9). Player A moves to receive the next pass from **Player D**, takes a good directional touch and shoots again.

The players then rotate their roles (A → B → C → D → A), and the practice continues with a new player completing 4 finishes.

Source: Jürgen Klopp's Liverpool training session at AXA Training Centre, Liverpool - 25th August 2022

Jürgen Klopp Practices: Attacking Combinations and Finishing

10. Quick Combination Play to Set the Ball Back to Finish from Different Positions

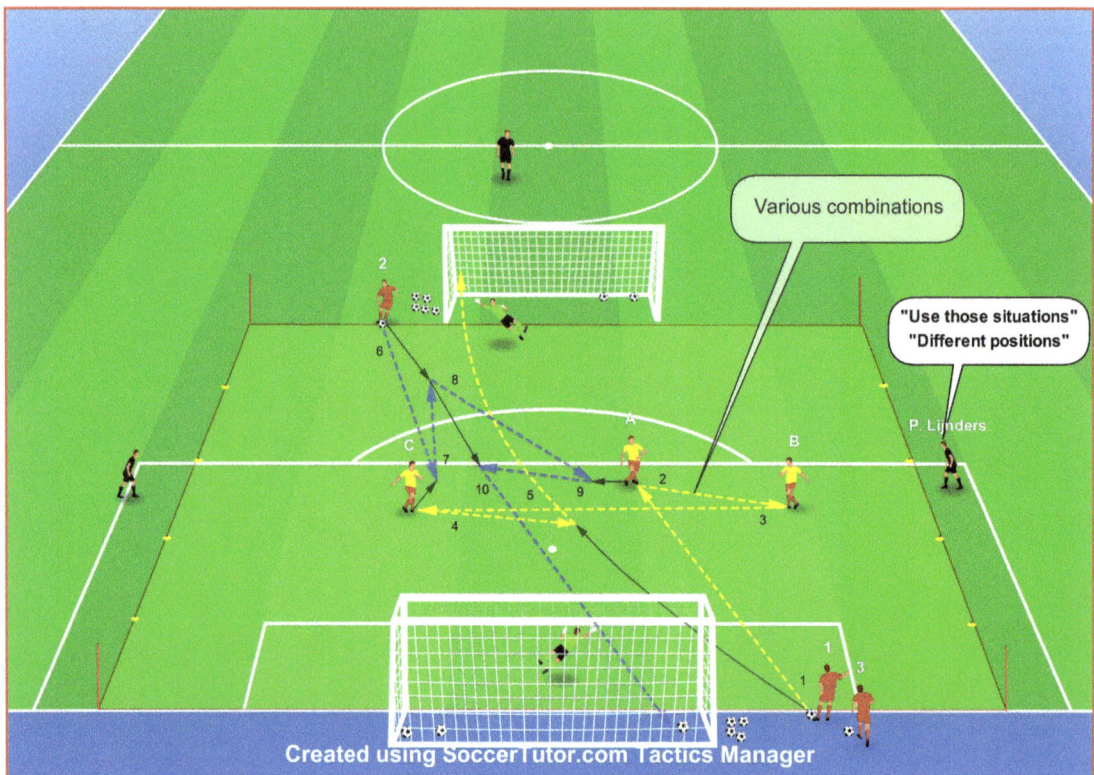

Practice Description

This practice starts with 3 players on the inside of the area (A-C) and 3 players waiting with a ball outside (1-3). It produced a number of different variations and we have displayed 2 of them:

1-2. **Player 1** passes to **Player A**, who sets the ball for **Player B**.

3-5. **B** passes across to **Player C**, who sets the ball back for the oncoming **Player 1** to shoot and try to score past the GK. **Player 1** moves to the opposite end (where Player 2 is).

6-7. **Player 2** passes to **Player C**, who passes back to **Player 2** and completes a one-two combination.

8-10. **Player 2** passes to **Player A**, who sets the ball back (another one-two) for the oncoming **Player 2** to shoot and try to score past the other GK.

Player 2 moves to the opposite end and **Player 3** continues with a new ball...

After a set period of time, the 3 inside players (A-C) switch roles with the 3 outside players (1-3).

Source: Jürgen Klopp's Liverpool training session at AXA Training Centre, Liverpool - 2nd March 2021

Jürgen Klopp Practices: Attacking Combinations and Finishing

11. Moving to Receive and Finish from Different Angles + Finishing in a 1v1 Duel (Multiple Balls)

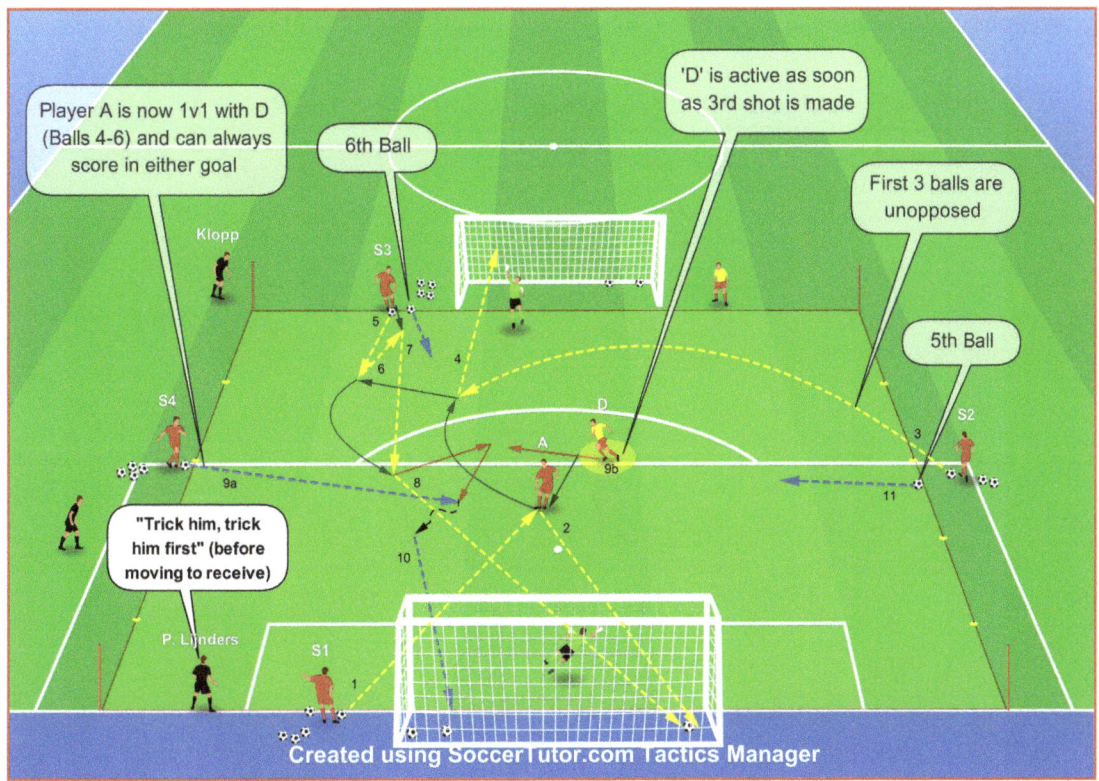

Practice Description

The first 3 balls are delivered for the central Player A (Salah in this observed practice) to receive and score unopposed. For the next 3 balls (4-6), Salah had to evade his maker (defender), receive, and score.

1-2. Outside **Player S1** feeds the 1st ball for **Player A** to finish (unopposed).

3-4. **Player S2** feeds the 2nd ball for **Player A** to finish (unopposed).

5-8. **Player S3** feeds the 3rd ball for **Player A** to finish (unopposed).

9-10. The defender (**D**) is now active, so **Player A** must try to evade his marker to receive. **Player S4** feeds a 4th ball for **Player A**, who takes a touch and scores.

11 → End. **Player S2** feeds a 5th ball for **Player A** to finish (not shown in diagram for simplicity).

Player S3 feeds a 6th ball for **Player A** to finish (also not shown).

NOTE: *Player A can receive from any outside player (S1-S4) and creates space for the best option. The outside players are doing active recovery waiting for their turn in the centre.*

Source: Jürgen Klopp's Liverpool pre-season training session in Salzburg, Austria - 23rd July 2022

Jürgen Klopp Practices: Attacking Combinations and Finishing

12. Simultaneous 3-Player End to End Mixed Combination Play with Long Range Finishing

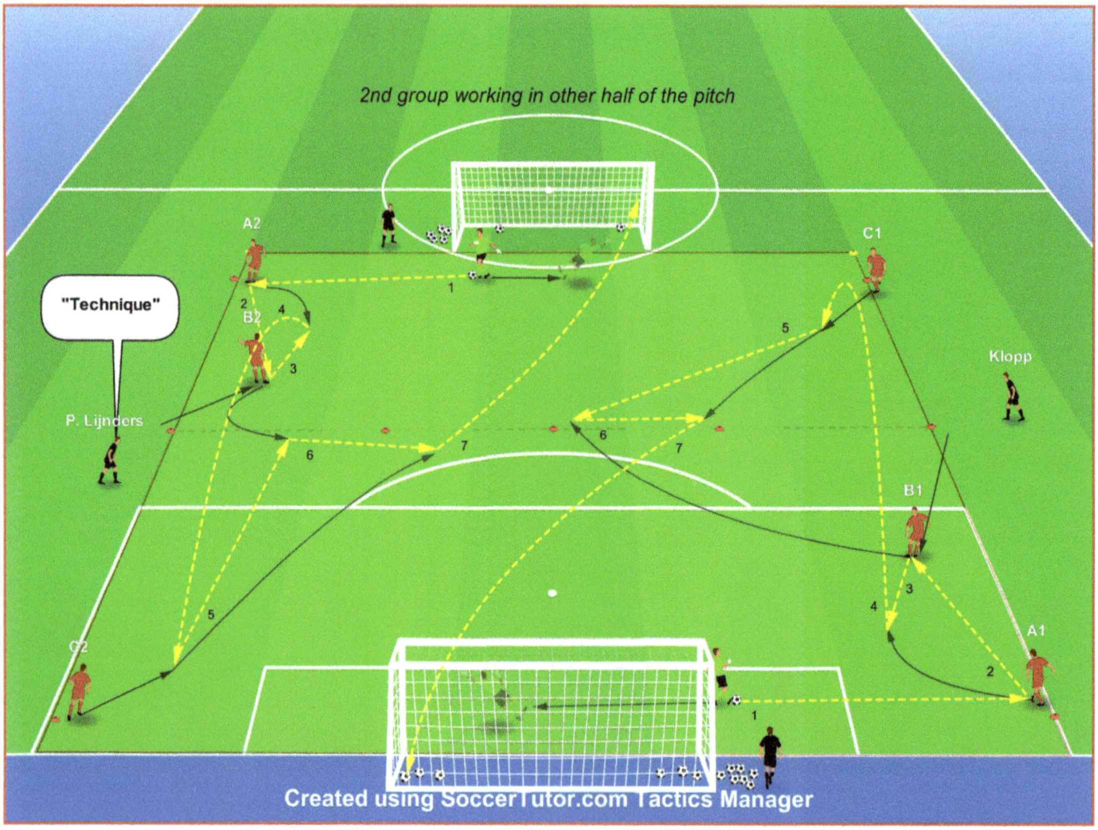

Practice Description

The practice runs on both sides simultaneously.

1-3. The GK starts by passing to **Player A**, who plays a short and quick one-two with **Player B**.

4. Player A hits a medium length aerial pass towards **Player C**, who moves forward off his cone to receive.

5. Player C passes into the centre, where **Player B** has moved to receive.

6-7. Player B sets the ball for **Player C** to shoot from long range, and try to score past the GK.

The players rotate their positions and the practice continues: A → B → C → A.

Source: Jürgen Klopp's Liverpool training session at AXA Training Centre, Liverpool - 25th August 2022

Jürgen Klopp Practices: Attacking Combinations and Finishing

13. Simultaneous 3-Player Combination Play with Overlap Third Man Run + Cross and Finish

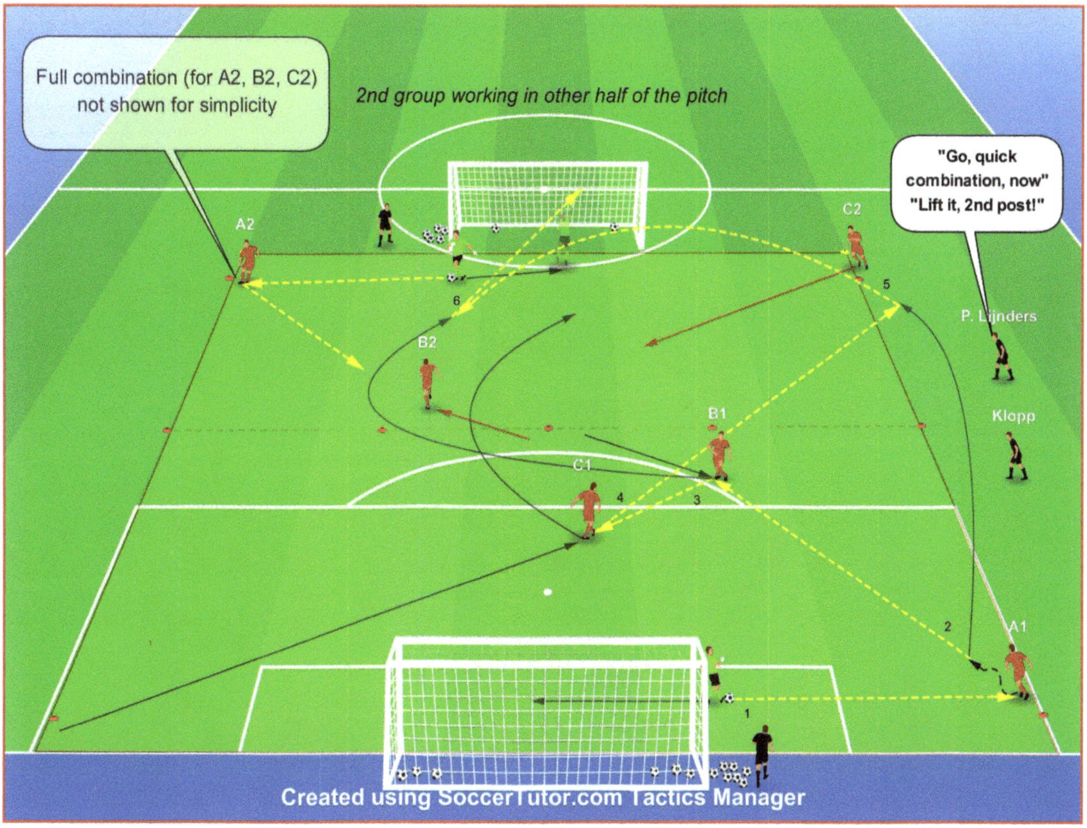

Practice Description

This is a variation of the previous practice and again runs on both sides simultaneously. The A1, B2, C2 combination isn't displayed for diagram simplicity.

1-2. The GK passes to **Player A** and he passes into the centre for **Player B**, who drops back to receive.

3-4. B lays the ball off for **Player C**, who plays a firm ground pass for the run of **A** on the outside.

5. A delivers a cross as **B** and **C** both make runs towards the goal.

6. In this example, it is **B** who meets the cross towards the back post to try and score past the GK.

The players rotate their positions and the practice continues: **A → B → C → A.**

Source: Jürgen Klopp's Liverpool training session at AXA Training Centre, Liverpool - 25th August 2022

Jürgen Klopp Practices: Attacking Combinations and Finishing

14. Fast Break Attack from Centre Circle with Deep Forward Runs

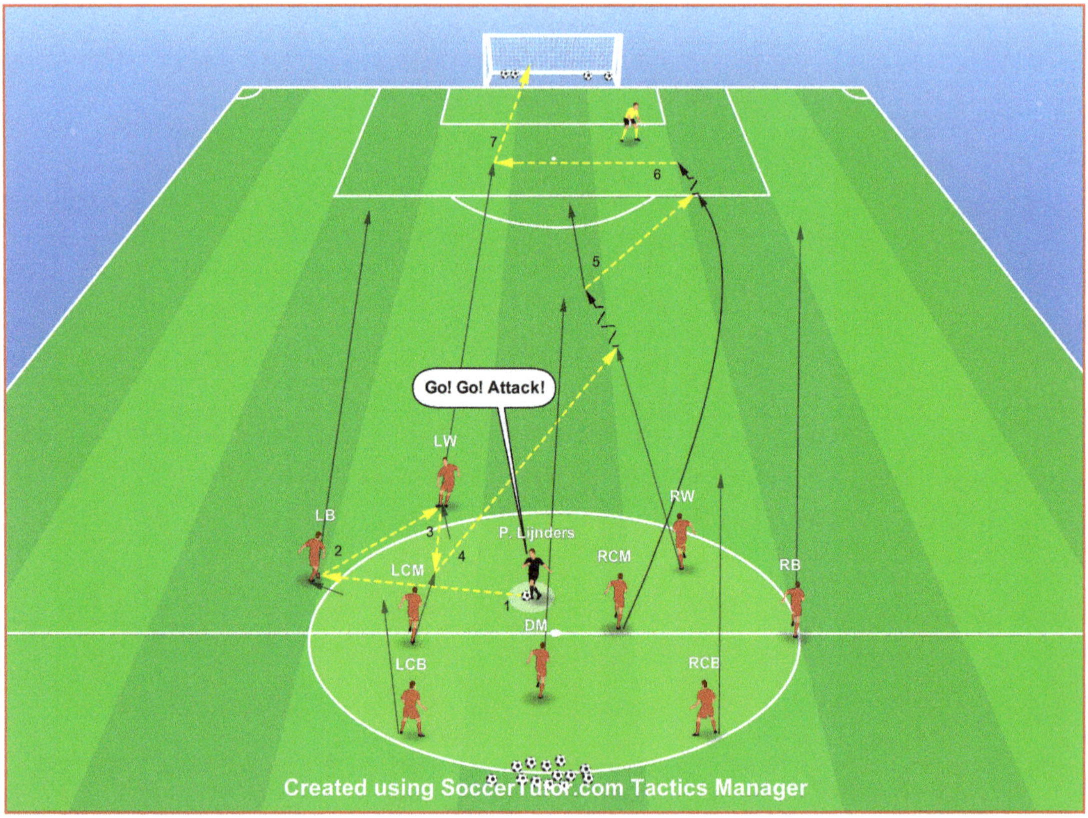

Practice Description

The practice starts with all 9 players inside the centre-circle. As soon as the Coach plays the ball to one of the players, they launch a fast break attack with simple combination play and lay-offs.

1. In this example, Liverpool's Coach Pep Ljinders plays the ball to the left back (**LB**) on the edge of the centre-circle.

2. The **LB** plays forward to the left winger (**LW**). Players start to make forward runs.

3. The **LW** lays the ball back for the oncoming left central midfielder (**LCM**).

4. The **LCM** plays the first forward pass for a runner (to the right winger - **RW**).

5. The **RW** receives, dribbles the ball forward, and passes outside to his right for the overlapping run of the right central midfielder (**RCM**).

6-7. The **RCM** enters the box and passes it across for his teammate (**LW**) to score into an empty net.

Source: Jürgen Klopp's Liverpool training session at AXA Training Centre, Liverpool - 18th March 2021

Jürgen Klopp Practices: Attacking Combinations and Finishing

15. One-two Set to Shoot + Sprint to Receive for 1v1 vs the Goalkeeper Circuit

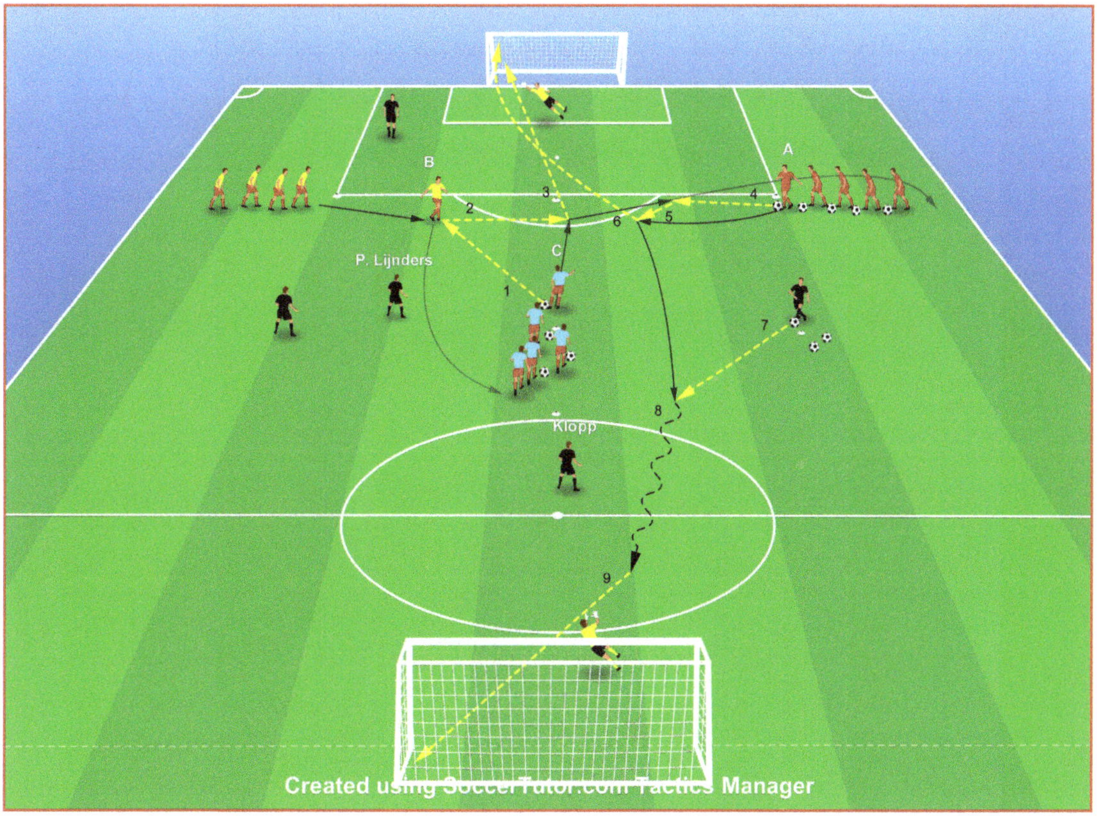

Practice Description

The practice starts with 3 groups of 5 players in 3 different stations.

1. **Player C** passes to **Player B**, who moves inside off their cone.

2-3. **Player B** sets the ball for **Player C** to shoot from outside the box.

4. **Player B** moves across to meet **Player A's** pass (new 2nd ball).

5-6. **Player B** sets the ball for **Player A** to shoot from outside the box.

7-9. **Player A** sprints towards the opposite goal, receives from the Coach, and then tries to score in a 1v1 versus the GK.

The players rotate to the next station:
A → B → C → A.

Source: Jürgen Klopp's Liverpool training session at Melwood Training Ground, Liverpool - 3rd September 2020

Jürgen Klopp Practices: Attacking Combinations and Finishing

16. Attacking Runs and Finishing in Pairs with Double Switch of Play and Wide Crossing Zones

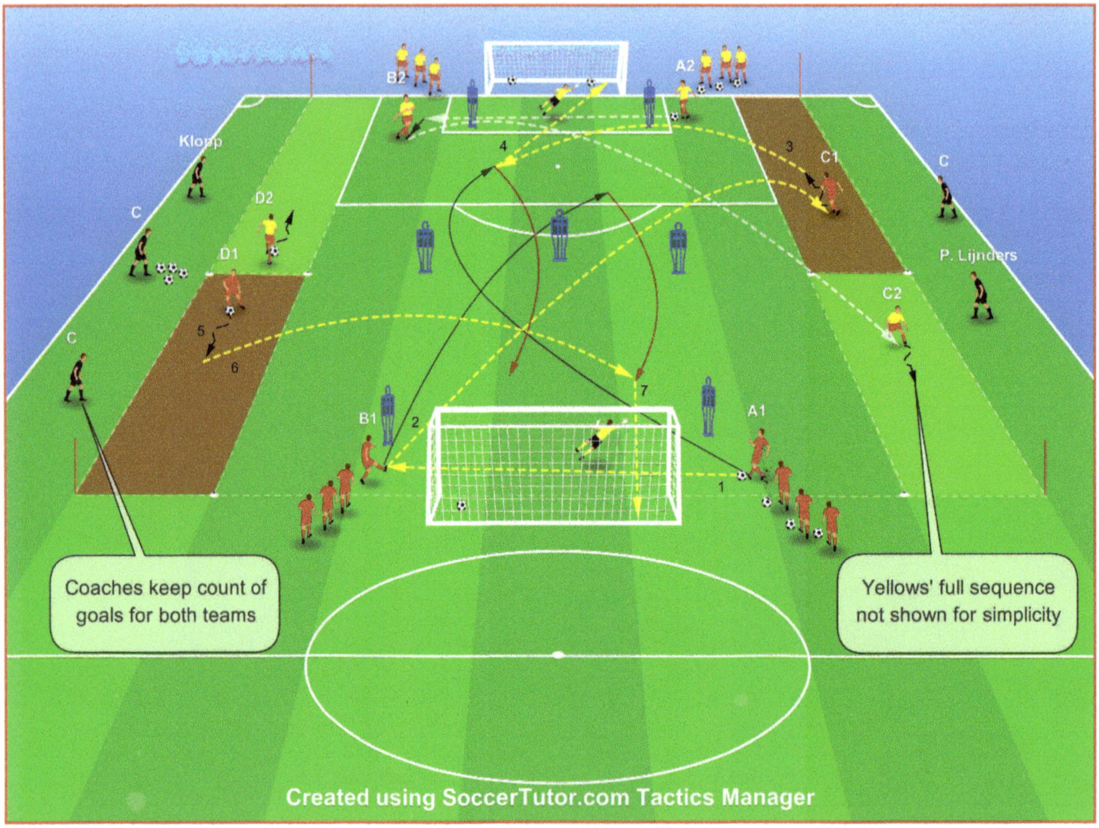

Coaches keep count of goals for both teams

Yellows' full sequence not shown for simplicity

Practice Description

Both sides run simultaneously with the players in pairs (A & B). The full A2, B2, C2, D2 sequence isn't displayed for simplicity.

1-2. **Player A** passes to **Player B**, who hits a diagonal switch of play into **Player C's** side zone.

3-4. **C** receives within the side zone and deliverers a cross. Both **A** and **B** have made forward runs to provide support. In this example, **A** scores.

5-7. Both **A** and **B** quickly sprint back in the opposite direction (*red movement arrows*). **Player D** has a new ball and waits for the right moment to deliver a cross for **A** or **B** to score in the opposite goal. This time, **B** scores.

Once these 2 phases are complete, the next pairs waiting repeat the same sequence.

Source: Jürgen Klopp's Liverpool training session at AXA Training Centre, Liverpool - 25th August 2022

Jürgen Klopp Practices: Attacking Combinations and Finishing

17. 4-Player Attacking Wave Break Aways with Multiple 1-Touch Overlaps + 2nd Ball Fast Break Attack

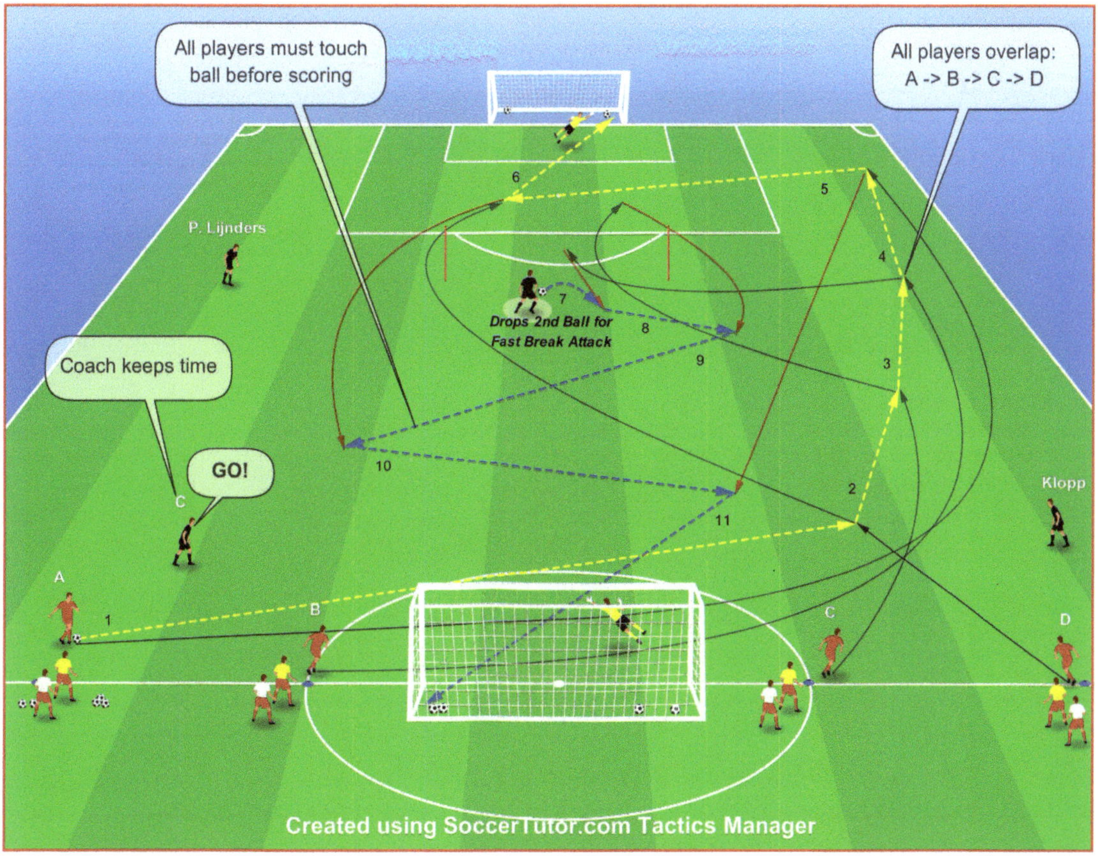

Practice Description

The players perform attacking waves in groups of 4 (A-D). In the first phase, they sprint at full speed to receive on the overlap.

1. **Player A** passes across the pitch for **Player D**, who moves forward at an angle to receive.

2. **D** uses <u>1 touch</u> to pass the ball to **Player C** on the overlap.

3-4. **C** uses <u>1 touch</u> to pass the ball to **Player B** on the overlap. **B** uses <u>1 touch</u> to pass the ball to **Player A** on the final overlap.

5-6. **A** crosses the ball for the 3 players (B, C & D) who have made runs towards the box. In this example, **D** scores.

7-11. The Coach feeds a new ball in (to B in diagram example) and all 4 players launch a fast break attack to score at the opposite end. Once complete, the next group of 4 repeat the same sequence.

Source: Jürgen Klopp's Liverpool pre-season training session in Singapore - 13th July 2022

Jürgen Klopp Practices: Attacking Combinations and Finishing

18. Various End to End Attacking Combinations and Finishing in Groups of 3

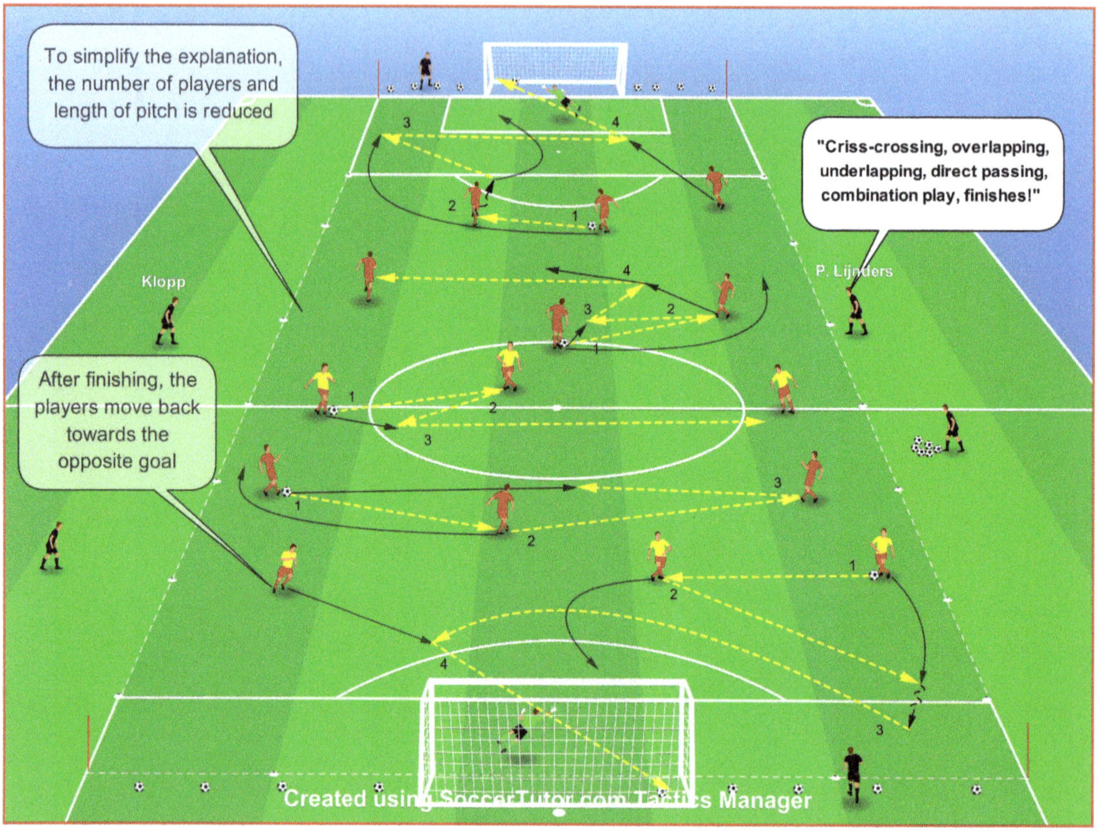

Practice Description

This practice was observed using the full length of the pitch, but the pitch length and number of players has been reduced for the diagram to simplify the explanation.

- The players are all in groups of 3 and move up and down the full length of the area.
- As they progress up the pitch, they use various different combinations to combine with each other.
- Coach Pep Ljinders says "Criss-crossing, overlapping, underlapping, direct passing, combination play, finishes!"
- When they reach the final area of the pitch, they use combination play to create a goal scoring chance and score past the GK.
- Once they have finished their attack, they receive a new ball from the Coach and repeat the practice back towards the opposite goal.

Source: Jürgen Klopp's Liverpool training session at AXA Training Centre, Liverpool - 25th August 2022

Jürgen Klopp Practices: Attacking Combinations and Finishing

19. Possession Play in Zones + Fast Break Attack Combinations and Finishing

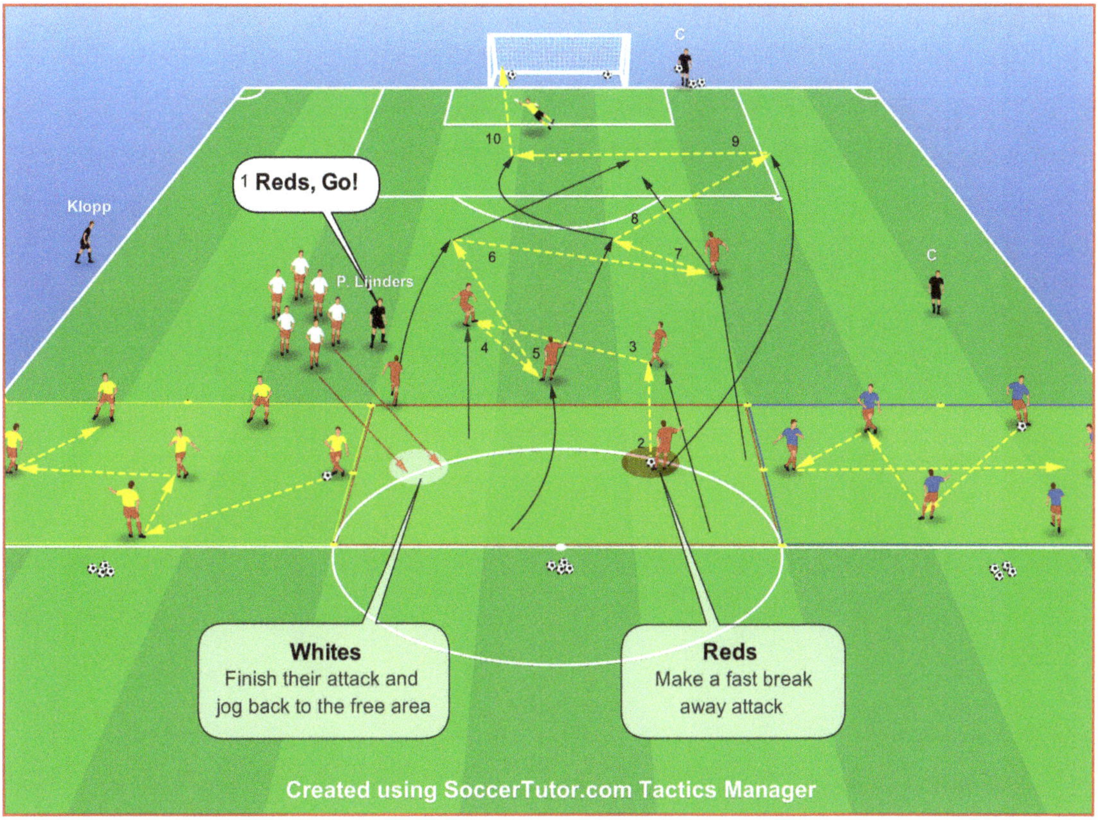

Practice Description

- The players are in 4 groups of 4 (white, yellow, red, and blue).

- The white group starts with an attacking combination and tries to score (this is not shown in the diagram for simplicity).

- The other 3 groups start within the 3 marked out zones near the halfway line. Each group has 1 ball and simply pass the ball between each other, waiting for the Coach's call.

- The Coach calls out the colour of one of the groups (**"Reds, Go!"**) - That group must launch a fast break attack.

- In this example, the reds use short and fast combination play to progress up the pitch including an overlapping run, pass into the box and finish.

- The white team have jogged back into the free area and the practice continues in the same way with the players waiting for the Coach's next call.

Source: Jürgen Klopp's Liverpool training session at Melwood Training Ground, Liverpool - 22nd August 2018

©SOCCERTUTOR.COM   JÜRGEN KLOPP VOL.2: PRACTICES FROM KLOPP'S SESSIONS

Multi-Ball Attacking Combinations and Finishing

Direct from Jürgen Klopp's Training Sessions

JÜRGEN KLOPP VOL.2: *PRACTICES FROM KLOPP'S SESSIONS*

Jürgen Klopp Practices: Multi-Ball Attacking Combinations and Finishing

KLOPP'S MULTI-BALL FINISHING DRILLS

Jürgen Klopp: "We want to attack the opponent non-stop."

LIVERPOOL'S ATTACKING PRESSURE STYLE

During the **2018-2019 and 2019-2020 Premier League seasons** combined (76 matches), Liverpool recorded **62 wins**, 10 draws, with only 4 losses, and scored an incredible **174 goals (2.29 per match)**.

Their "attacking pressure" style is admired around the world, and they are able to create chances and score goals repeatedly against the best teams in world football, best displayed by their miraculous 4-0 comeback win over Barcelona in May 2019, and their recent 7-0 win over Manchester United in March 2023.

The multi-ball finishing drills included in this section are taken directly from observed Liverpool training sessions, and are a **fundamental training element for the attacking intensity** they have displayed in the extremely successful last few seasons.

This relentless effort to attack and recycle the ball to attack again, and again is what has helped them to apply great pressure on their opponents and overwhelm them.

Using these drills gives you the opportunity to **replicate Klopp and Liverpool's all-action high tempo attacking and constant pressure style of play**.

These drills also enable the Liverpool players to practice specific combinations repetitively in various different scenarios in the final third.

This means that they are **fully prepared with solutions for all the different attacking situations** which occur during a match. All the players know what passes and crosses to deliver, and what runs and finishes they can make. They are constantly challenged to score from a variety of different finishes.

NOTE BEST: *Every action in these multi-ball drills is planned precisely so the players are never waiting around, which replicates the intensity and speed of a competitive match.*

DIAGRAM FORMAT

To best display these multi-ball finishing drills, we have colour-coded each ball on the diagrams and descriptions as follows:

- **Ball 1**
- **Ball 2**
- **Ball 3**
- **Ball 4**
- **Ball 5**
- **Ball 6**
- **Ball 7**
- **Ball 8**

Jürgen Klopp Practices: Multi-Ball Attacking Combinations and Finishing

1. 3-Balls: Two Player Central Finishing, Cut Back & Finish + 3v2 Attack

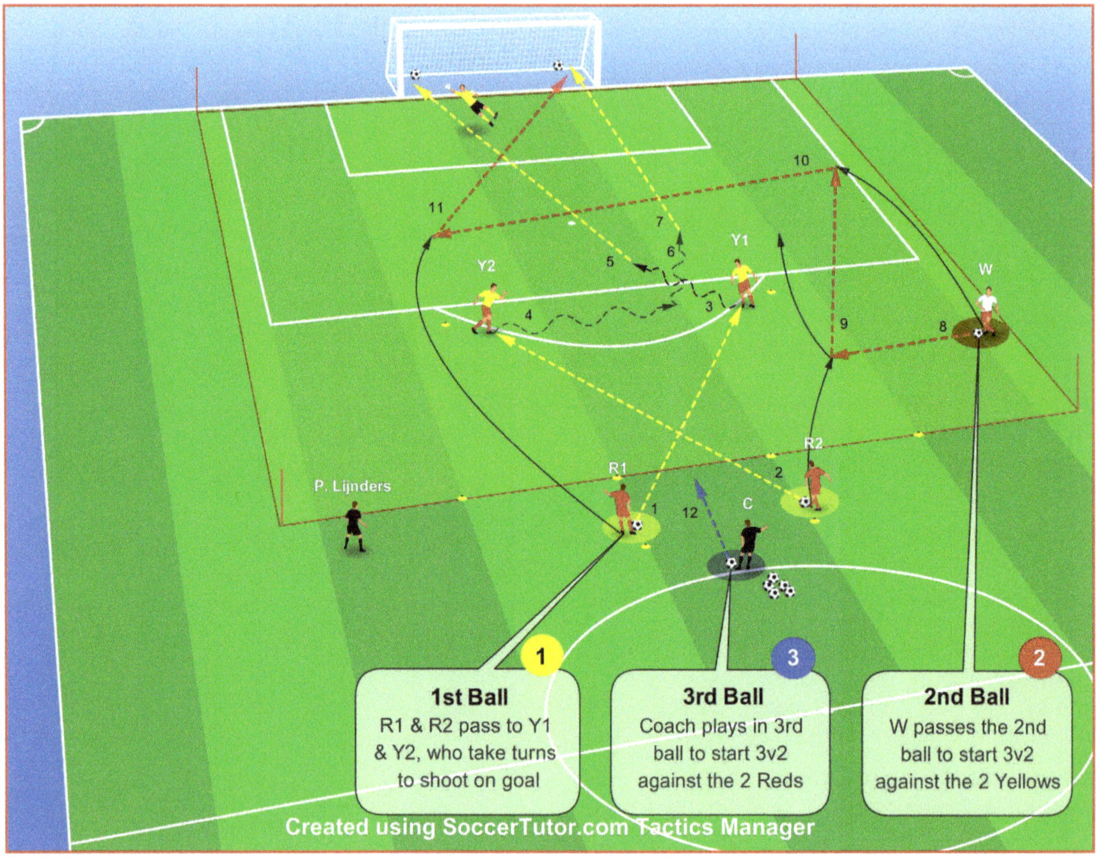

1st Ball
R1 & R2 pass to Y1 & Y2, who take turns to shoot on goal

3rd Ball
Coach plays in 3rd ball to start 3v2 against the 2 Reds

2nd Ball
W passes the 2nd ball to start 3v2 against the 2 Yellows

Practice Description

1st Ball (1-7). Players R1/R2 start by passing diagonally to **Players Y1/Y2**, who receive on the half turn, carry the ball into the box in different ways as shown, and try to score.

2nd Ball (8-11). The winger (**W**) passes a 2nd ball to a red player to start a 3v2 attack against the 2 yellow players. In this example, **W** plays a give & go with **R2** and squares it for **R1** to score.

3rd Ball (12 →). After the 2nd ball attack is complete, the Coach passes a 3rd ball to a yellow player. The 2 yellows (**Y1** & **Y2**) + the white winger (**W**) play 3v2 against the 2 red players, who transition to become defenders.

Source: Jürgen Klopp's Liverpool training session at Melwood Training Ground, Liverpool - November 2019

©SOCCERTUTOR.COM   JÜRGEN KLOPP VOL.2: PRACTICES FROM KLOPP'S SESSIONS

Jürgen Klopp Practices: Multi-Ball Attacking Combinations and Finishing

2. Through Passes to the Wingers for Runs into the Box in a 3-Ball Finishing Drill

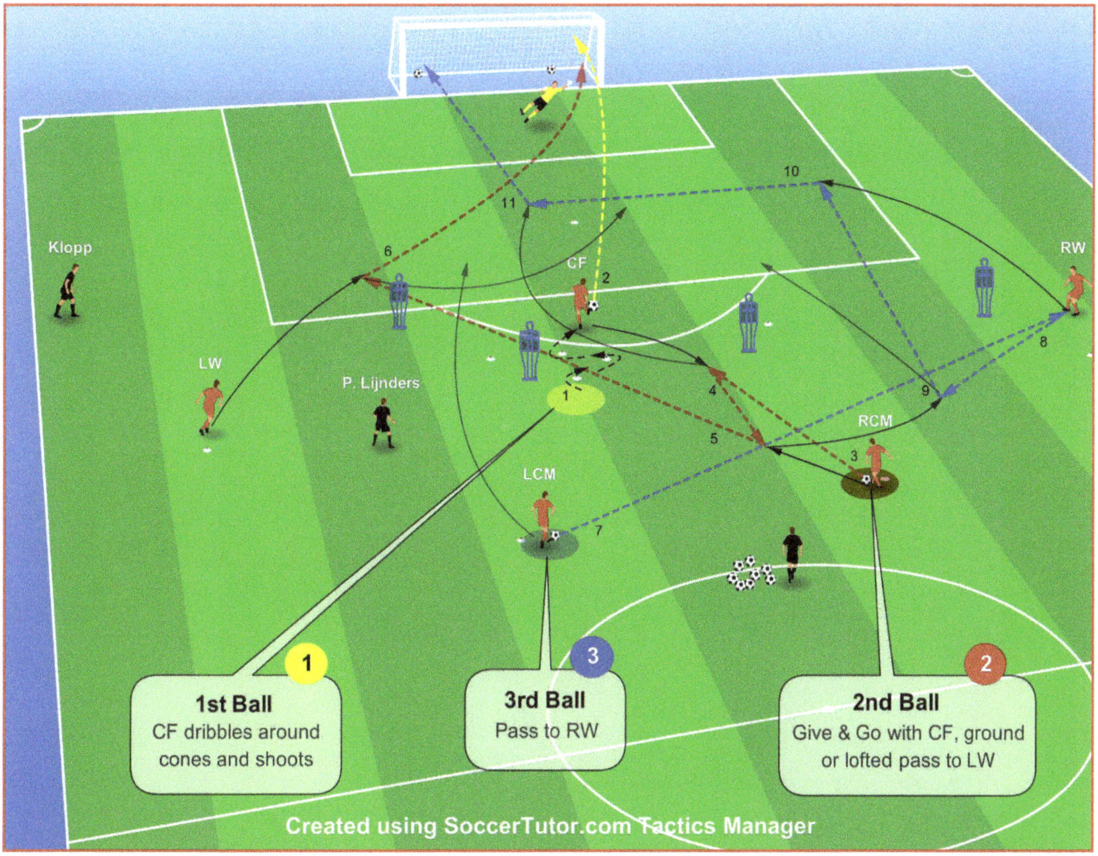

1st Ball
CF dribbles around cones and shoots

3rd Ball
Pass to RW

2nd Ball
Give & Go with CF, ground or lofted pass to LW

Practice Description

1st Ball (1-2). The centre forward (**CF**) dribbles the ball through the cones as shown, and then shoots from the edge of the box.

2nd Ball (3-6). The right central midfielder (**RCM**) passes a 2nd ball to the **CF**, who drops back after shooting.

The **CF** lays the ball off for the **RCM** to complete the one-two.

The **RCM** plays a final pass through the mannequins and into the box for the well-timed run of the left winger (**LW**). The **LW** tries to score.

3rd Ball (7-11). The left central midfielder (**LCM**) passes a 3rd ball out wide to the right winger (**RW**). The **RW** lays the ball off for the **RCM**, who plays a through pass into the box for the well-timed run of the **RW**. The **RW** passes into the box for either the **LW** or the **CF** to score.

Source: Jürgen Klopp's Liverpool training session at Melwood Training Ground, Liverpool - 5th June 2020

Jürgen Klopp Practices: Multi-Ball Attacking Combinations and Finishing

3. Crossing and Finishing + Receive and Shoot in a 4-Ball Finishing Drill

Balls 1-2 (Finishing)

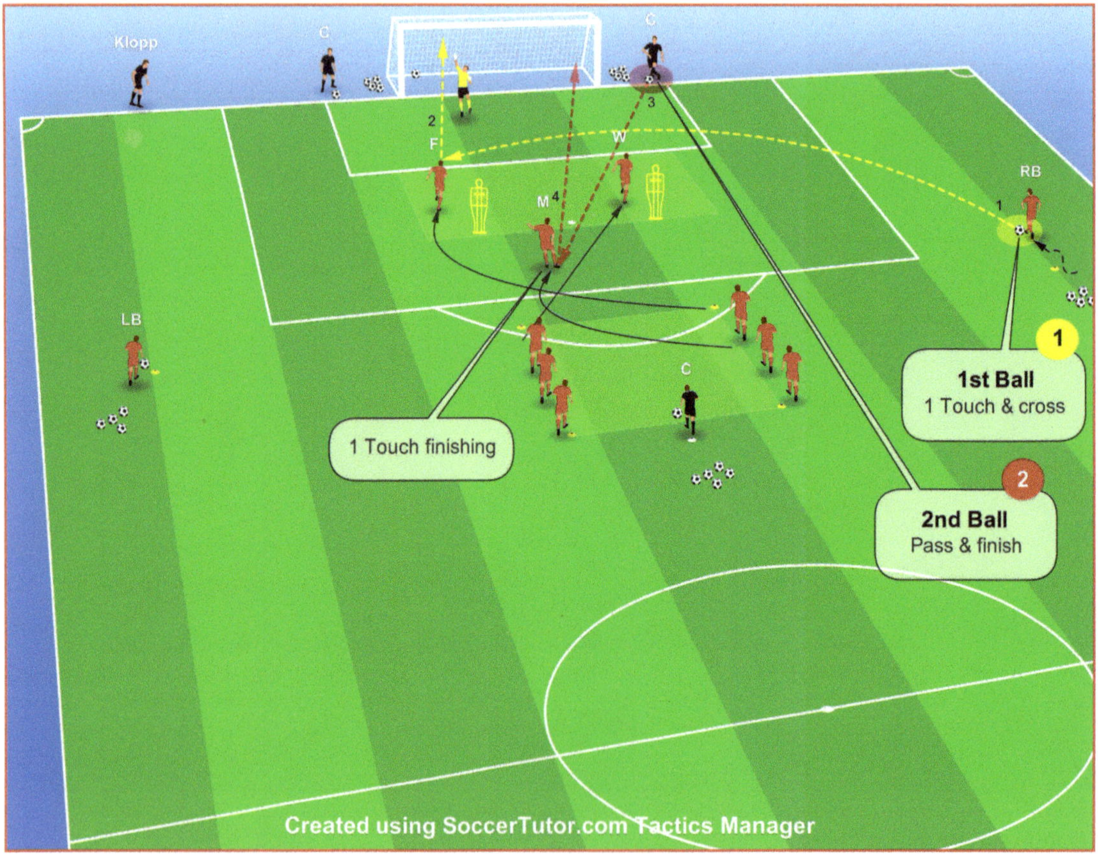

Practice Description

1st Ball (1-2) - 1 Touch & Cross. The forward (**F**), the winger (**W**), and the midfielder (**M**) all make runs from the centre into the box. The right back (**RB**) takes a touch forward and delivers a cross into the box *(mainly into central area highlighted)*. In this example, **F** scores at the back post (1 touch finishing).

Note: The **RB** practices all types of crosses including a pull back for **M**.

2nd Ball (3-4) - Pass & Finish. The Coach passes a 2nd ball in from the by-line. In this example, he passes to **M** for another 1 touch finish to score.

The 3rd and 4th ball diagram and description follows on the next page...

Source: Jürgen Klopp's Liverpool training session at Melwood Training Ground, Liverpool - 11th April 2019

Jürgen Klopp Practices: Multi-Ball Attacking Combinations and Finishing

Balls 3-4 (Finishing)

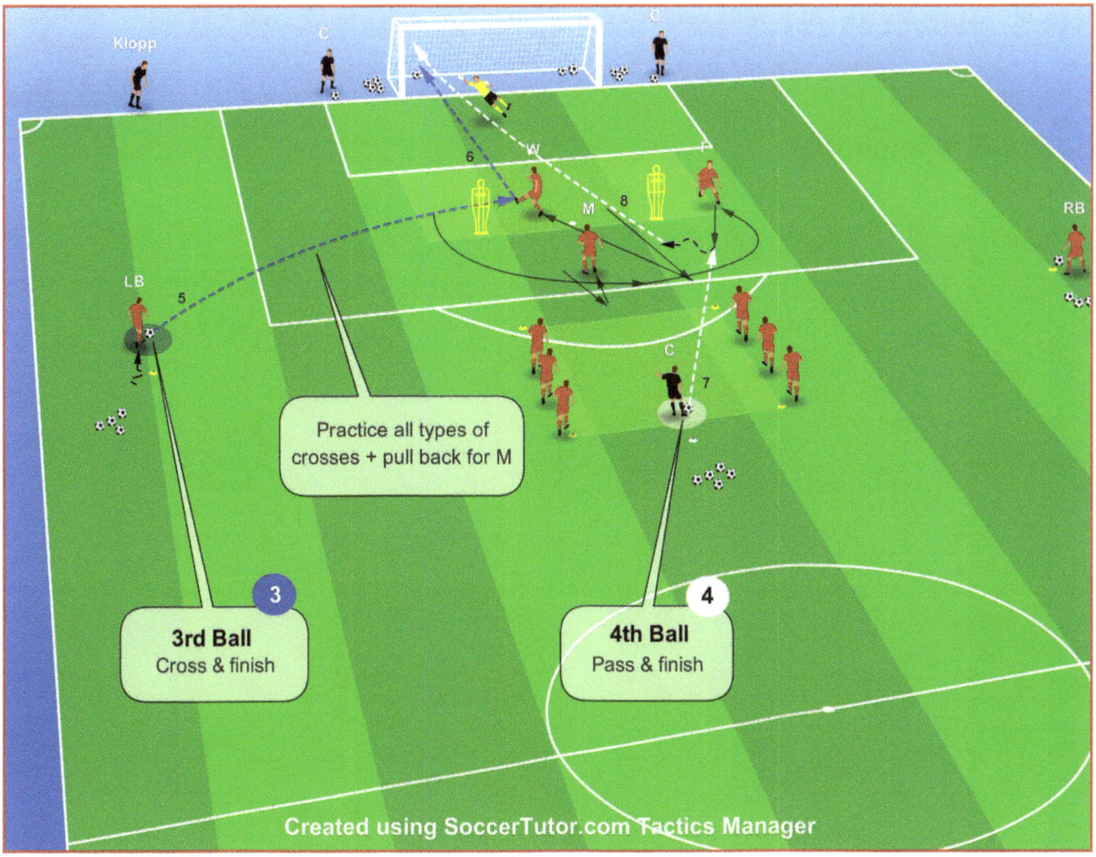

[Diagram: Practice all types of crosses + pull back for M. 3rd Ball - Cross & finish. 4th Ball - Pass & finish.]

3rd Ball (5-6) - Cross & Finish. The forward (**F**), the winger (**W**), and the midfielder (**M**) all make movements in the box, as shown. The left back (**LB**) takes a touch forward and delivers a cross into the box.

In this example, **W** scores at the near post (1 touch finishing).

Note: The **LB** practices all types of crosses including a pull back for **M**.

4th Ball (7-8) - Pass & Finish. The Coach passes a 4th ball in from the centre. In this example, he passes to **F**, who drops back after the 3rd ball phase. He receives on the half-turn to open up, move inside, and tries to score (final finish).

Source: Jürgen Klopp's Liverpool training session at Melwood Training Ground, Liverpool - 11th April 2019

Jürgen Klopp Practices: Multi-Ball Attacking Combinations and Finishing

4. Different Finishes + Quick Passes and Switch of Play for Cross in a 4-Ball Finishing Drill

Balls 1-3 (Finishing)

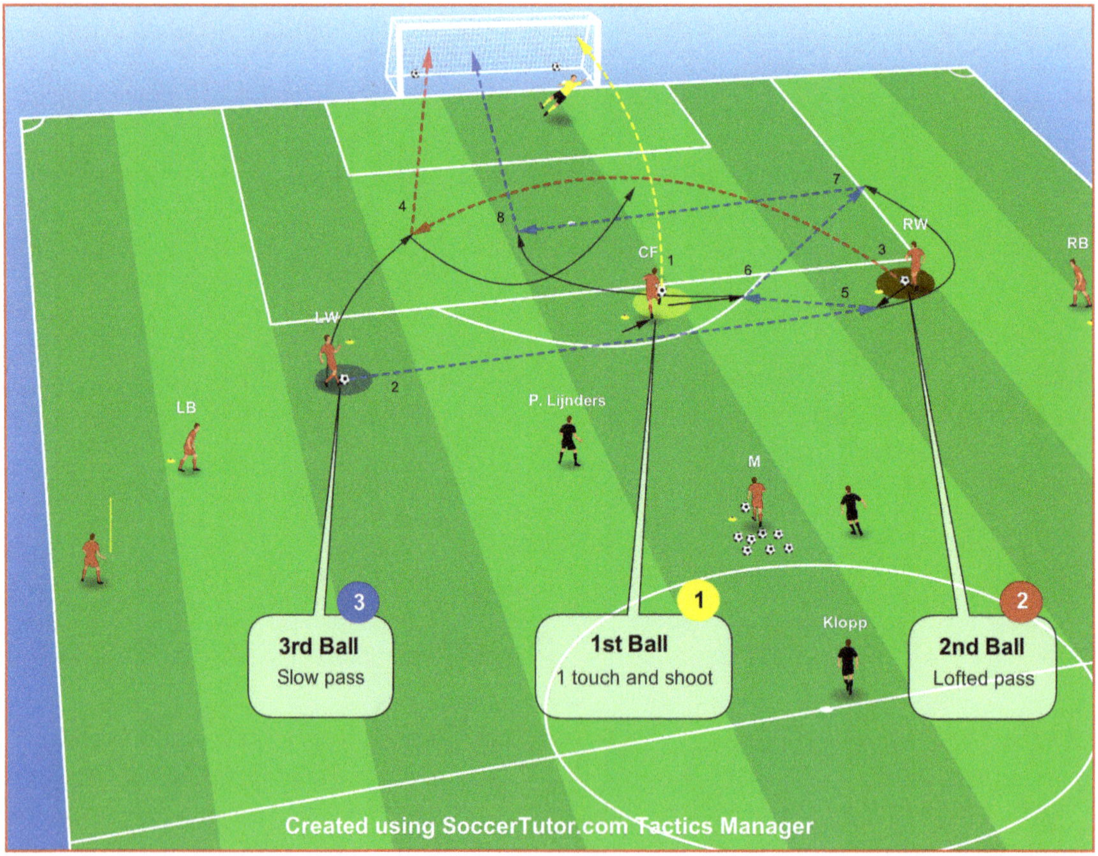

Practice Description

1st Ball (1). The centre forward (**CF**) has a ball, takes a touch forward, and shoots.

2nd Ball (3-4). The right winger (**RW**) plays a lofted pass into the box for the opposite left winger (**LW**) to score.

3rd Ball (2). The <u>slow pass</u> from the **LW** is played before the **RW's** lofted pass.

5-8. After the lofted pass, the **RW** steps back and plays a give & go with the **CF**, who moves across. The **RW** delivers a ground cross into the box for either the **LW** or **CF** to score.

The 4th ball diagram and description follows on the next page...

Source: Jürgen Klopp's Liverpool pre-season training session in Salzburg, Austria - 15th July 2021

Jürgen Klopp Practices: Multi-Ball Attacking Combinations and Finishing

4th Ball (Return Passes + Cross & Finish)

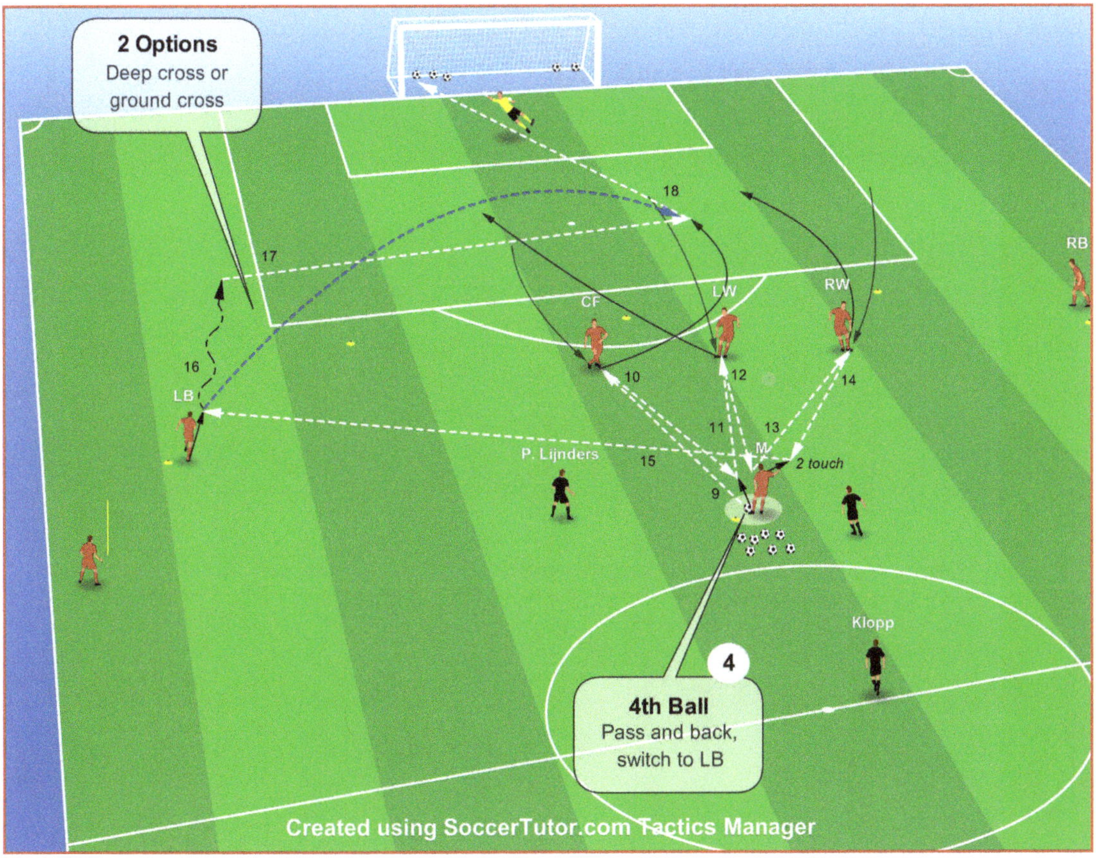

[Diagram: 4th Ball practice showing midfielder M starting with the 4th ball, exchanging passes with CF, LW, RW (positions 9-14), then passing wide to LB (15-18) who has 2 options: deep cross or ground cross. Labels include "2 Options - Deep cross or ground cross", "2 touch", "P. Lijnders", "Klopp", "4th Ball - Pass and back, switch to LB".]

4th Ball (9-14). The midfielder (**M**) starts with the 4th ball and exchanges passes with the centre forward (**CF**), the left winger (**LW**), and the right winger (**RW**).

During this phase *(pass and back)*, the players use 2 touches to pass and receive.

15-18. The midfielder (**M**) then passes out wide to the left back (**LB**), who moves off his cone to receive, and runs forward with the ball.

The **CF**, **LW**, and the **RW** all make different runs into the box and the **LB** has 2 options: Deep cross (blue arrow) or dribble forward + ground cross.

In this example, it is the **CF** who scores after a curved run into the central area of the box.

This was also practiced using the right back within the same training session, but we have only displayed the left side example.

Source: Jürgen Klopp's Liverpool pre-season training session in Salzburg, Austria - 15th July 2021

Jürgen Klopp Practices: Multi-Ball Attacking Combinations and Finishing

5. Positional One-touch Combination Play in and Around the Box in a 4-Ball Finishing Drill

Balls 1-3 (Short Interplay + Finishing)

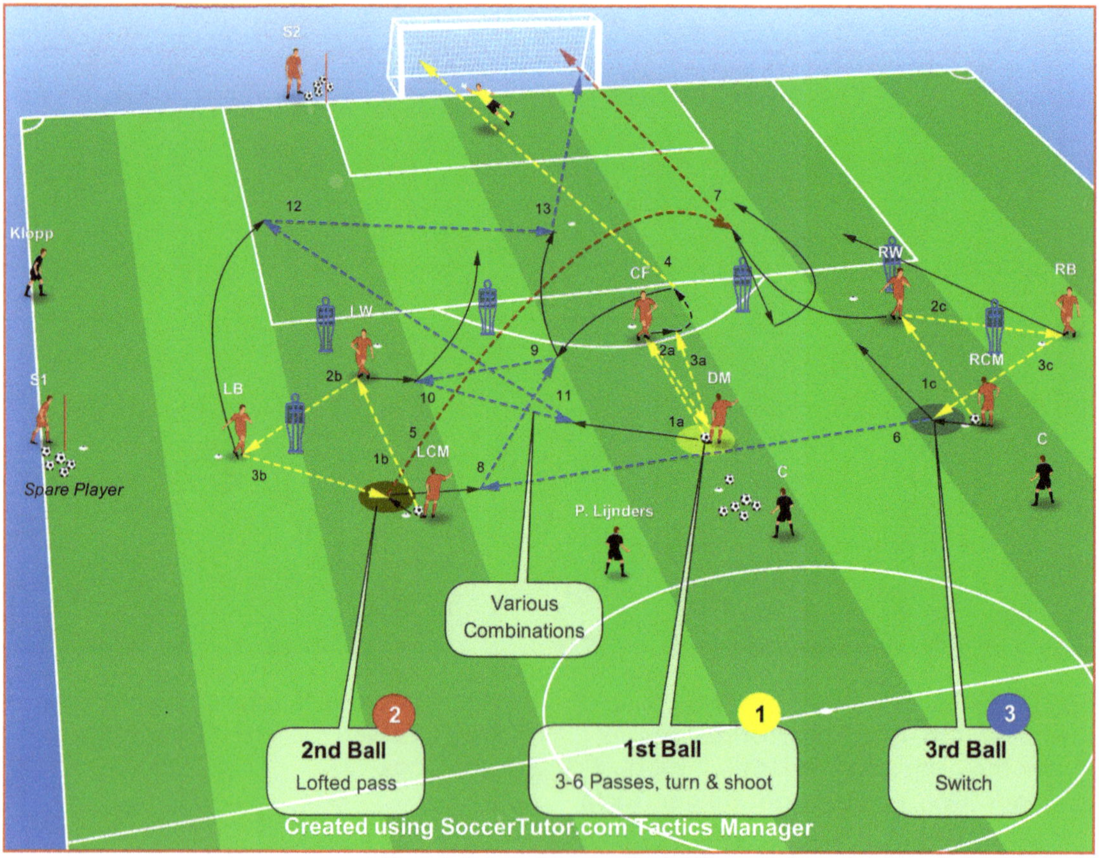

Practice Description

1st Ball (1-4). The defensive midfielder (**DM**) exchange passes, then the centre forward (**CF**) turns and shoots.

On both sides, the central midfielders (**L/RCM**), wingers (**L/RW**), and full backs (**L/RB**) pass around the mannequin.

2nd Ball (5+7). The **LCM** plays a lofted pass into the box for the **RW** to score.

3rd Ball (6). Before **LCM's** lofted pass, the **RCM** passes the ball across the pitch towards the **LCM**.

8-13. From here, the players can perform various combinations which result in the left back (**LB**) receiving on the overlap.

The **LB** delivers a cut back for one of the oncoming runners to score (the **CF** in the diagram example).

Source: Jürgen Klopp's Liverpool training session at AXA Training Centre, Liverpool - 22nd April 2022

Jürgen Klopp Practices: Multi-Ball Attacking Combinations and Finishing

4th Ball (Various Combinations)

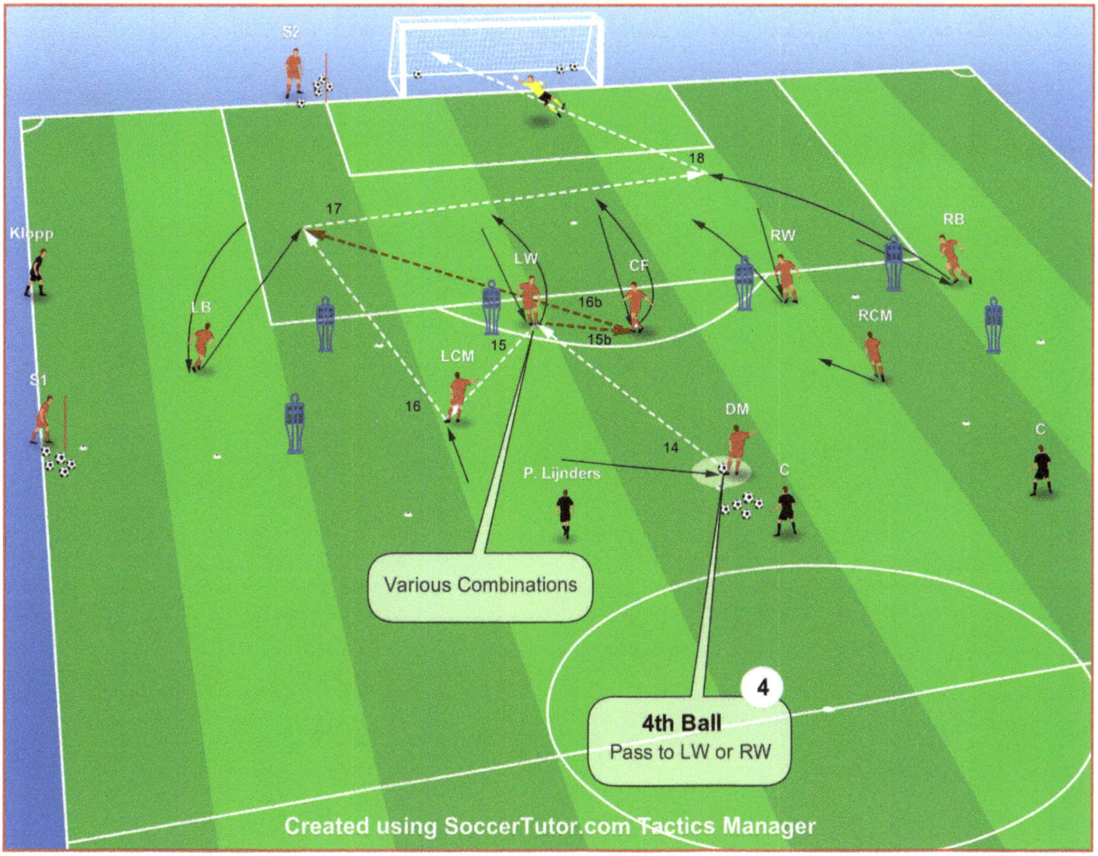

4th Ball (14-18). As soon as the 3rd ball phase is complete, the defensive midfielder passes to one of the wingers (**LW** *in diagram example*) with the 4th ball.

The **LW** lays the ball off for the oncoming central midfielder (**LCM**), who plays a through pass for the run of the left back (**LB**) into the box.

Th **LB** passes across the box for any of the following runners: **LW**, **CF**, right winger (**RW**), or right back (**RB**).

In the diagram example, the **RB** scores at the back post.

Option 2 (15b-18). The **LW** lays the ball off to the **CF** instead, and he passes to the **LB** in the box.

The same pattern can be repeated on the right side, starting with a pass to the RW and the RB delivers the final ball.

Source: Jürgen Klopp's Liverpool training session at AXA Training Centre, Liverpool - 22nd April 2022

Jürgen Klopp Practices: Multi-Ball Attacking Combinations and Finishing

6. Centre Forward & Wingers Combine in and Around the Box in a 5-Ball Finishing Drill

Balls 1-4 (Finishing)

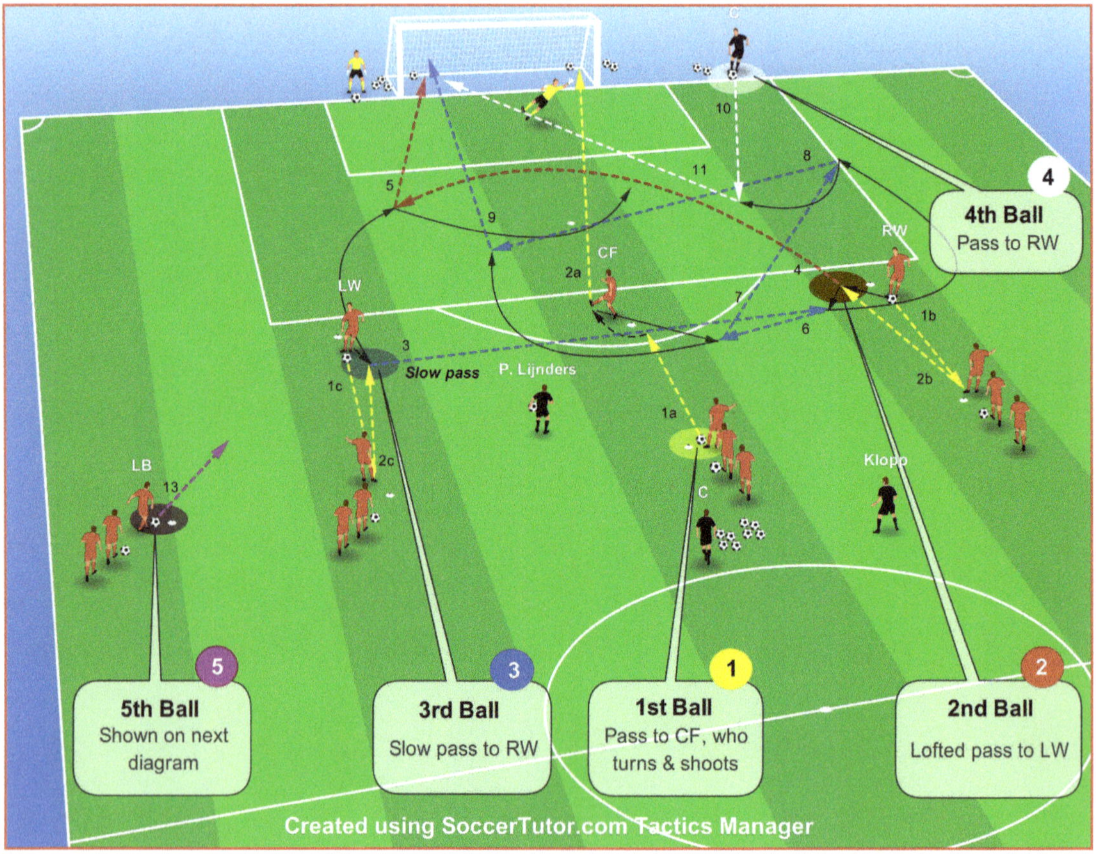

Practice Description

1st Ball (1-2). The centre forward (**CF**) receives, turns, and shoots.

The wingers (**LW** + **RW**) both play one-twos and receive back.

2nd Ball (4-5). The **RW** plays a lofted pass into the box for the opposite winger (**LW**) to score.

3rd Ball (3). The <u>slow pass</u> from the **LW** is played before the **RW's** lofted pass.

6-9. After the lofted pass, the **RW** plays a give & go with the **CF** and delivers a ground cross for either the **CF** or **LW**.

4th Ball (10-11). The Coach on the by-line passes for the **RW** to score with a first time finish.

Source: Jürgen Klopp's Liverpool training session at Vodafone Park Stadium (Besiktas), Turkey - August 13th 2019

Jürgen Klopp Practices: Multi-Ball Attacking Combinations and Finishing

5th Ball (Combination Play)

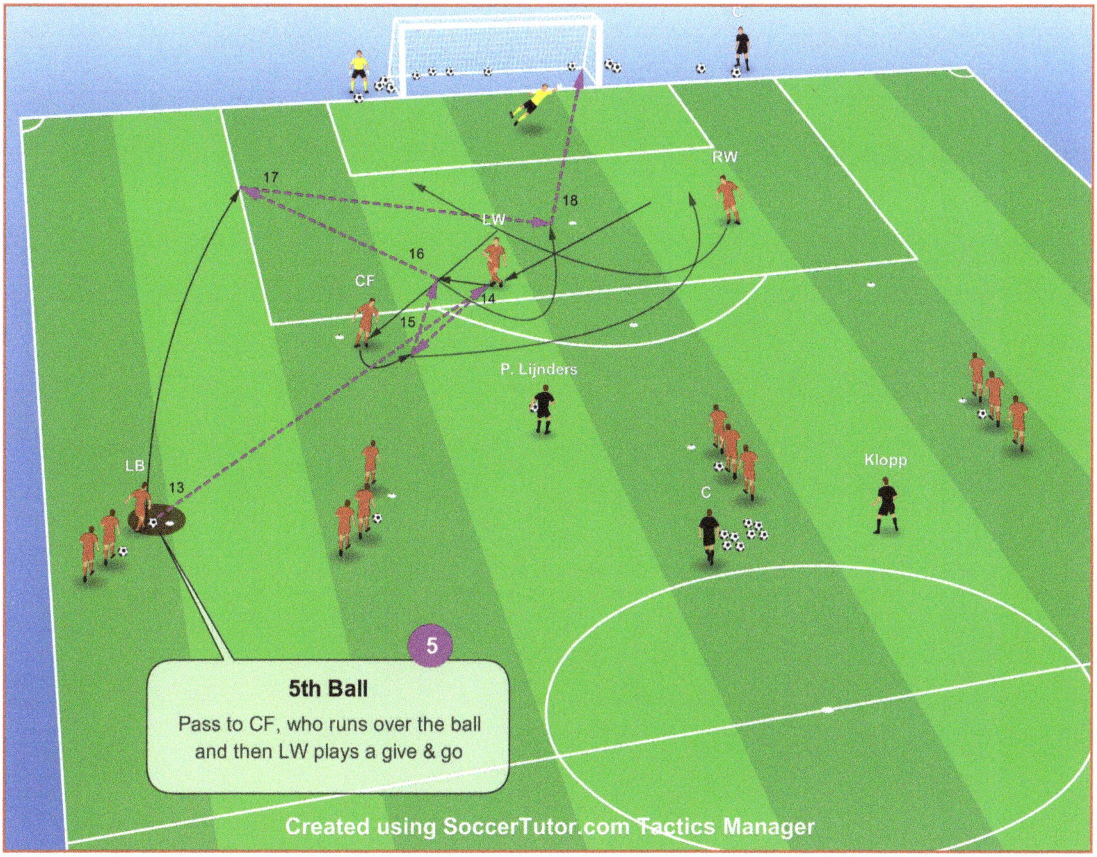

5th Ball
Pass to CF, who runs over the ball and then LW plays a give & go

5th Ball (13). The left back (**LB**) plays a new 5th ball in towards the centre forward (**CF**). The **CF** runs over the ball (dummy), and it reaches the left winger (**LW**).

14-15. The **LW** plays a one-two with the **CF**, and receives the return pass inside the box.

16-17. The **LW** plays the next pass for the oncoming advanced run of the **LB**, who delivers a cross for one of the 3 players who make movements in the box (**LW**, **RW**, or **CF**).

18. In this example, the **LW** scores from a cut back near the penalty spot.

Source: Jürgen Klopp's Liverpool training session at Vodafone Park Stadium (Besiktas), Turkey - August 13th 2019

Jürgen Klopp Practices: Multi-Ball Attacking Combinations and Finishing

7. 3 Forwards Continuous Finishing from Various Types of Assists (7-Balls)

Balls 1-4 (Finishing)

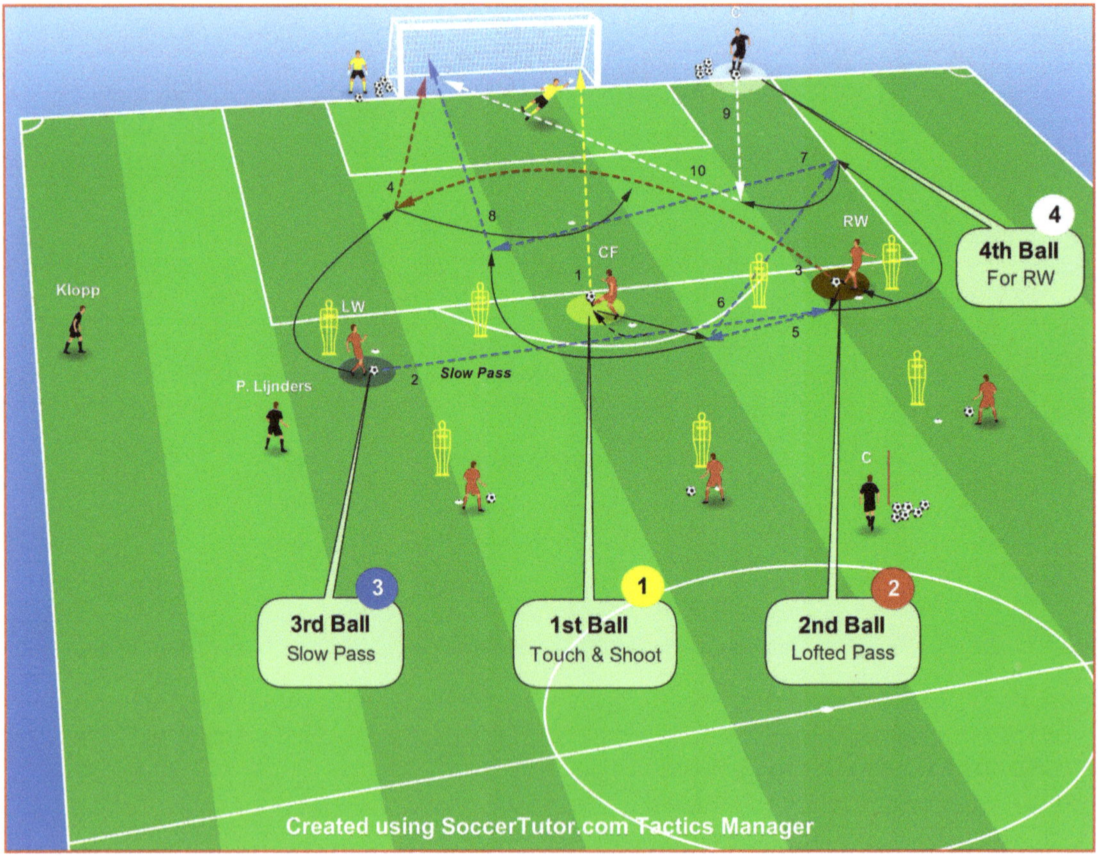

Practice Description

1st Ball (1). The centre forward (**CF**) takes a touch forward and shoots.

2nd Ball (3-4). The **RW** plays a lofted pass into the box for the left winger (**LW**), who runs around the mannequin.

3rd Ball (2). The slow pass from the **LW** is played before the **RW's** lofted pass.

5-8. After the lofted pass, the **RW** plays a give & go with the **CF**, runs around the mannequin to receive the return, and delivers a ground cross for either the **LW** or **CF** to score.

4th Ball (9-10). The Coach on the by-line passes for the **RW** to score with a first time finish.

Source: Jürgen Klopp's Liverpool training session at AXA Training Centre, Liverpool in 2022

Jürgen Klopp Practices: Multi-Ball Attacking Combinations and Finishing

Balls 5-7 (Varied Assists)

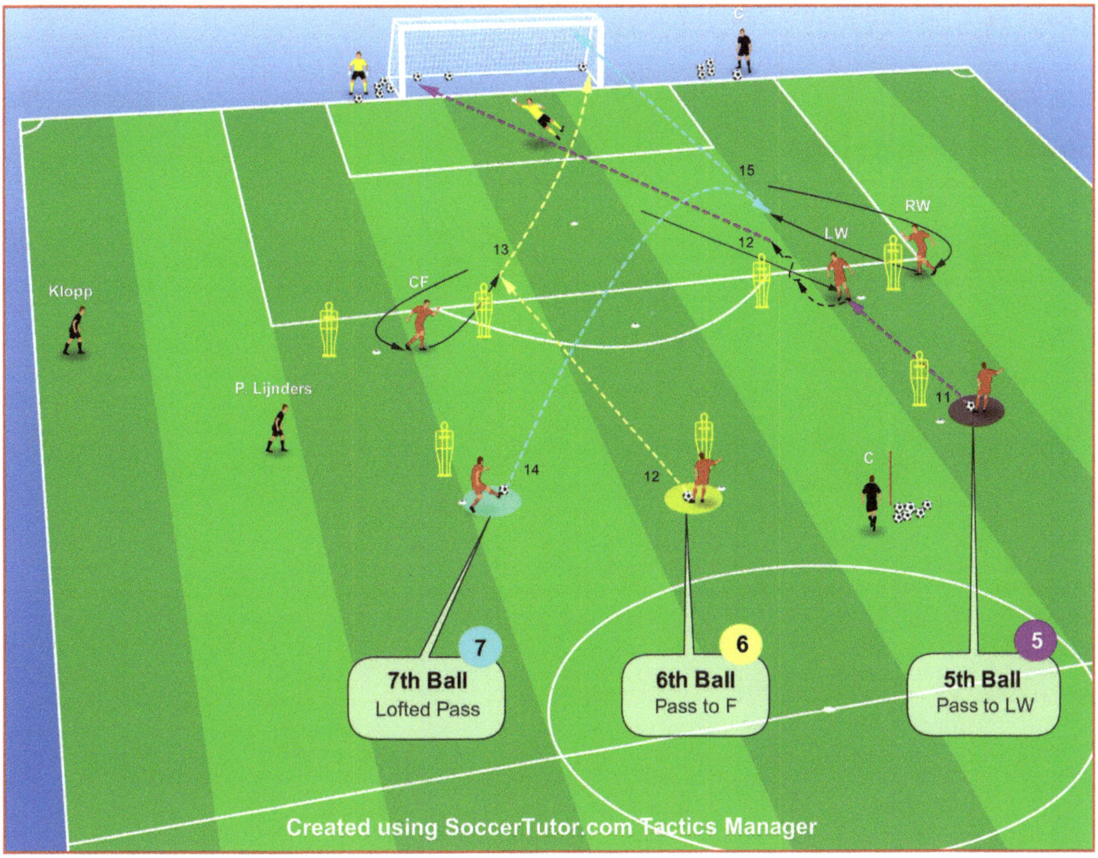

5th Ball (11-12). The left winger (**LW**) receives, turns into the box, and shoots.

6th Ball (12-13). The centre forward (**CF**) drops back at an angle, and then makes an opposite second movement forward. He moves to meet the next pass into the box and finishes on goal.

7th Ball (14-16). The right winger (**RW**) also drops back at an angle, and then makes an opposite second movement forward. He moves to meet the lofted pass into the box and finishes on goal.

Source: Jürgen Klopp's Liverpool training session at AXA Training Centre, Liverpool in 2022

Jürgen Klopp Practices: Multi-Ball Attacking Combinations and Finishing

8. Technical 8-Ball Finishing Variations from Central Positions

Balls 1-4 (Finishing)

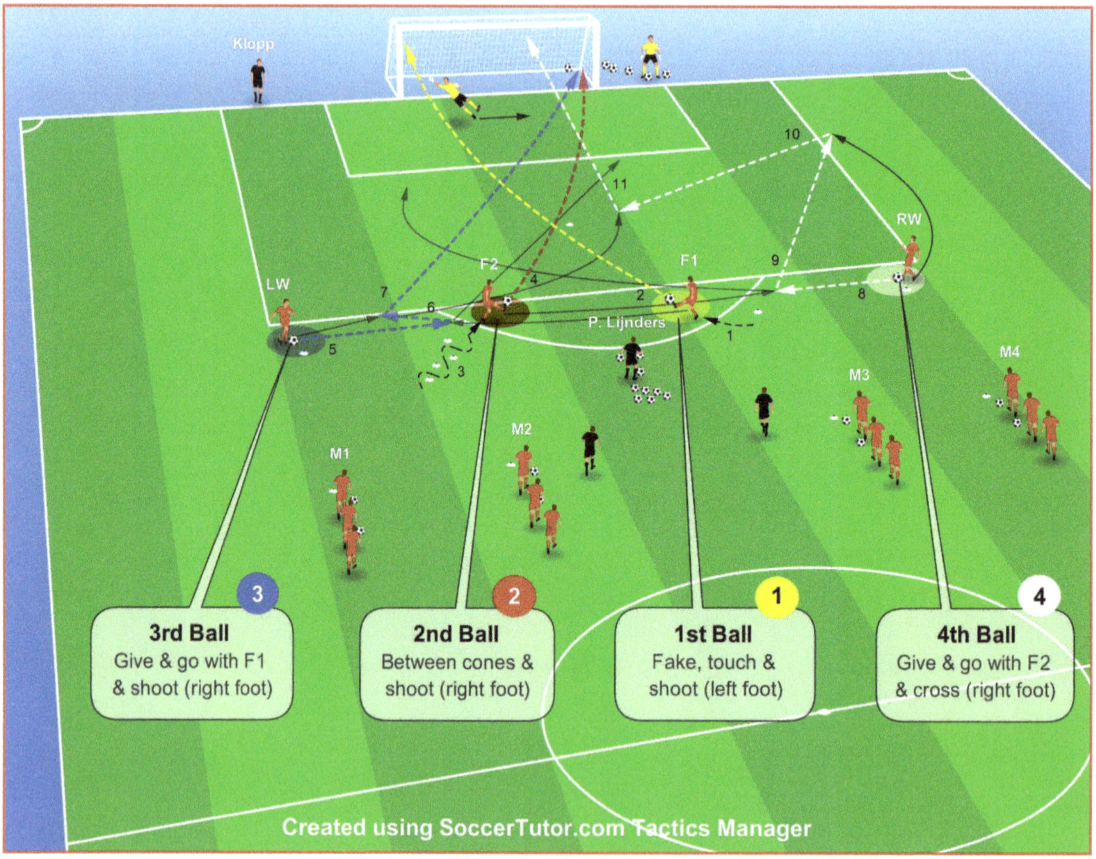

[Diagram: Practice setup showing goal, Klopp, P. Lijnders, F1, F2, LW, RW, and groups M1–M4 lined up with balls at stations 1 (yellow), 2 (red), 3 (blue), 4 (white)]

- **3rd Ball** — Give & go with F1 & shoot (right foot)
- **2nd Ball** — Between cones & shoot (right foot)
- **1st Ball** — Fake, touch & shoot (left foot)
- **4th Ball** — Give & go with F2 & cross (right foot)

Practice Description

1st Ball (1-2). The forward (**F1**) fakes to shoot, takes a touch, and shoots.

2nd Ball (3-4). **F2** dribbles the ball through the 4 cones and shoots.

3rd Ball (5-7). The left winger (**LW**) plays a give & go with **F1** who moves across. The **LW** shoots with his right foot.

4th Ball (8-11). The right winger (**RW**) plays a give & go with **F2** who moves across. The **RW** delivers a ground cross/cut back for either the **LW** or **F1** to score.

The diagram and description for Balls 5-8 follow on the next page...

Source: Jürgen Klopp's Liverpool training session at Melwood Training Ground, Liverpool - 11th April 2019

Jürgen Klopp Practices: Multi-Ball Attacking Combinations and Finishing

Balls 5-8 (Varied Serves for Box Finishing)

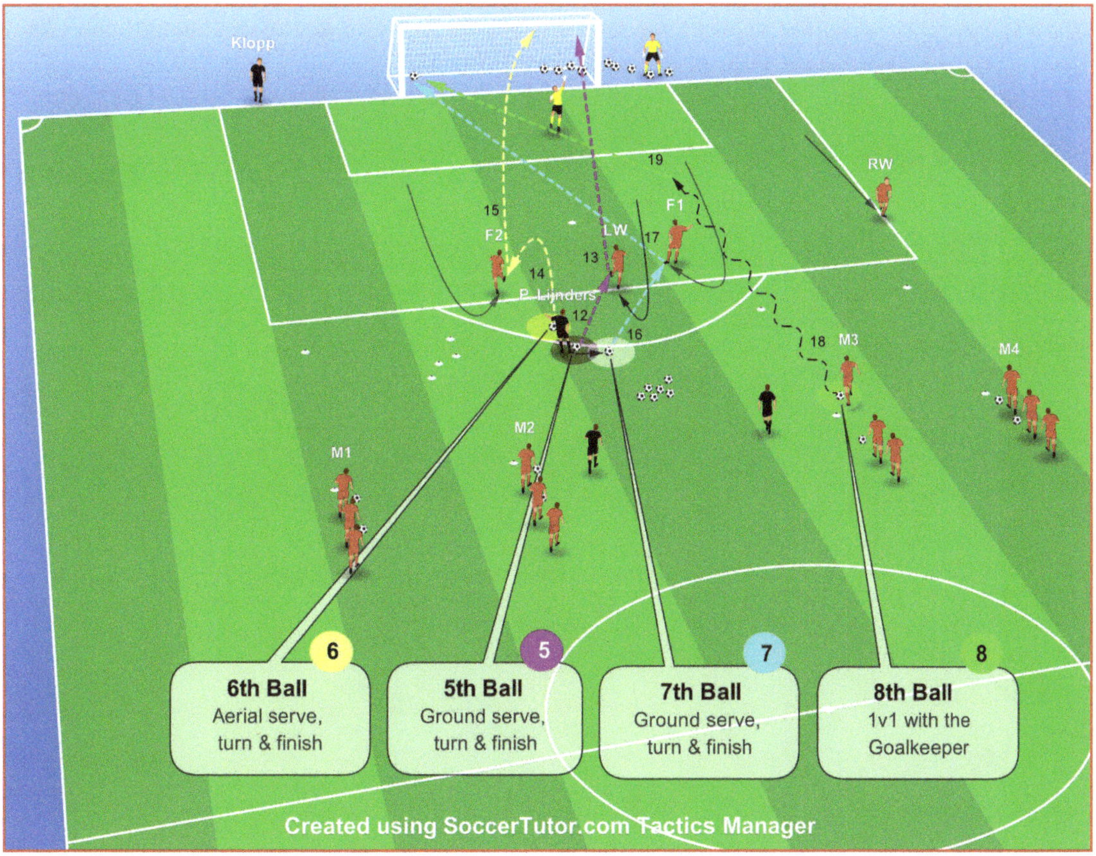

6th Ball — Aerial serve, turn & finish
5th Ball — Ground serve, turn & finish
7th Ball — Ground serve, turn & finish
8th Ball — 1v1 with the Goalkeeper

5th Ball (12-13). The Coach serves the ball to the left winger (**LW**) along the ground, who turns and finishes.

6th Ball (14-15). The Coach throws the ball up in the air (aerial serve) for the forward (**F2**), who moves to meet the ball and finishes.

7th Ball (16-17). The Coach serves the ball to the other forward (**F1**) along the ground, who moves to meet the ball and finishes.

8th Ball (18-19). Either central midfielder **M2** or **M3** *(in diagram)* dribbles forward into the box and finishes in a 1v1 with the GK.

→ **M1, M2, M2** & **M4** move to become the new **LW, RW, F1** & **F2** as the practice continues, and those players move to the back of the *4 x M queues*.

Source: Jürgen Klopp's Liverpool training session at Melwood Training Ground, Liverpool - 11th April 2019

Jürgen Klopp Practices: Multi-Ball Attacking Combinations and Finishing

9. Positional Attacking Combinations Around the Box in an 8-Ball Finishing Drill

Balls 1-4 (Finishing)

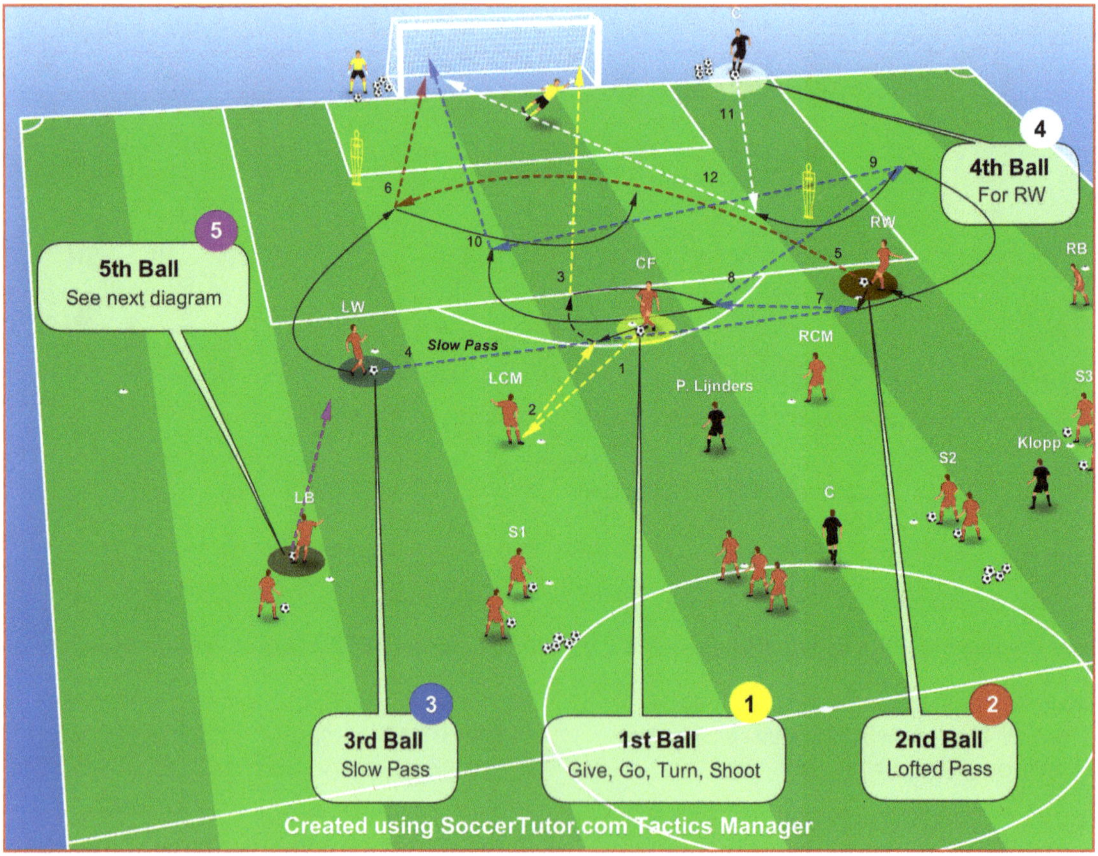

Practice Description

1st Ball (1-3). The centre forward (**CF**) plays a one-two with the left central midfielder (**LCM**), turns, and shoots.

2nd Ball (5-6). The right winger (**RW**) plays a lofted pass into the box for the left winger (**LW**) to score.

3rd Ball (4). The slow pass from the **LW** is played before the **RW's** lofted pass.

7-10. After the lofted pass, the **RW** plays a give & go with the **CF**, and delivers a ground cross for either the **LW** or **CF** to score.

4th Ball (11-12). The Coach on the by-line passes for the **RW** to score with a first time finish.

The diagram and description for Balls 5-6 follow on the next page...

Source: Jürgen Klopp's Liverpool training session at AXA Training Centre, Liverpool - 4th February 2022

Jürgen Klopp Practices: Multi-Ball Attacking Combinations and Finishing

Balls 5-6 (4-Player Combination)

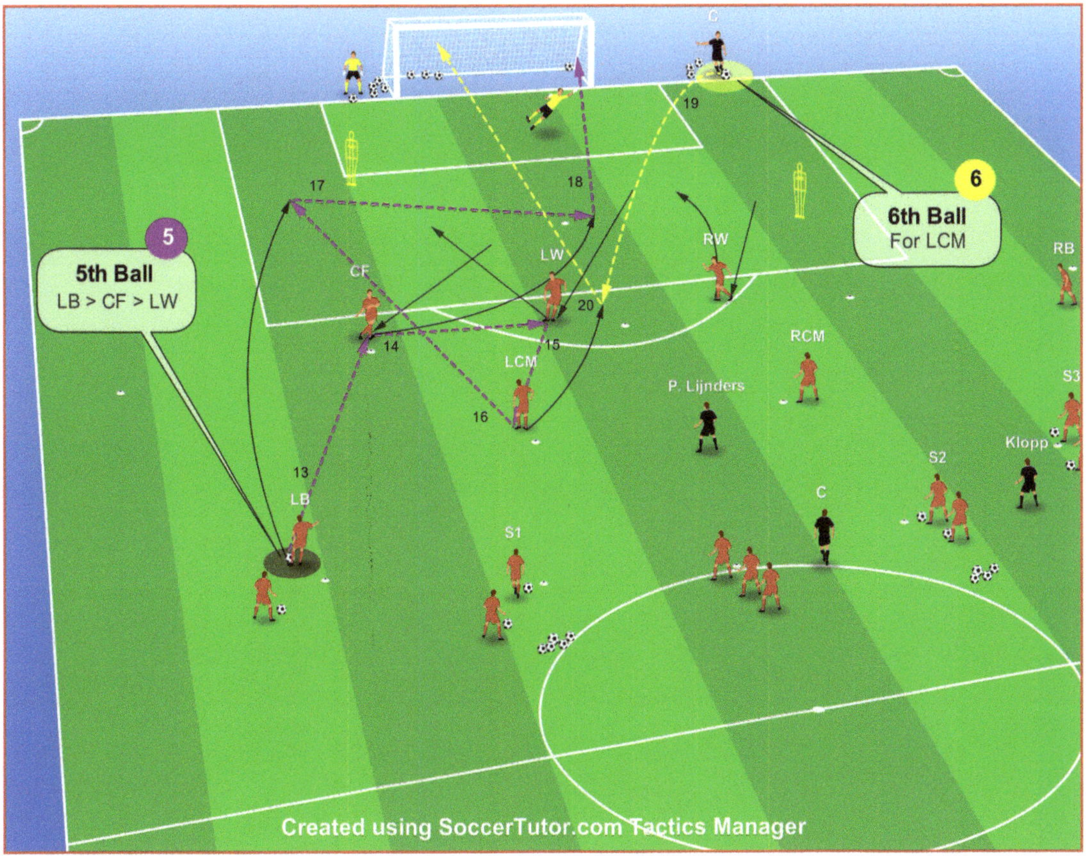

5th Ball (13-14). The left back (**LB**) passes to the centre forward (**CF**), who passes across to the **LW** in a central position.

15-16. The **LW** passes back to the left central midfielder (**LCM**), who plays a through pass for the overlapping run of the **LB** into the box.

17. The **LB** must evade the mannequin (defender) and cut the ball back for one of the oncoming runners into the box (**LW**, **RW**, or **CF**).

18. In this example, the **LB** cuts the ball back to the penalty spot for the **CF** to score.

6th Ball (19-20). The Coach chips the ball in from the by-line for the **LCM** to move forward and volley, half-volley, or receive and shoot.

The diagram and description for Balls 7-8 follow on the next page...

Source: Jürgen Klopp's Liverpool training session at AXA Training Centre, Liverpool - 4th February 2022

Jürgen Klopp Practices: Multi-Ball Attacking Combinations and Finishing

Balls 7-8 (Switch of Play + Dribble for 1v1)

7th Ball (21). The left centre back (**LCB**) switches the play with a long aerial pass to the right back (**RB**).

22-23. The **RB** dribbles inside and then passes for the run of the right central midfielder (**RCM**) on the overlap.

24-25. RB delivers a ground cross for one of the 3 players making runs into the box (**LW**, **RW**, or **CF**). In the diagram example, the **LW** scores coming in at the back post.

8th Ball (26-27). The **RB** drops back to receive **S3's** pass, dribbles forward into the box, and finishes in a 1v1 with the GK.

Source: Jürgen Klopp's Liverpool training session at AXA Training Centre, Liverpool - 4th February 2022

Jürgen Klopp Practices: Multi-Ball Attacking Combinations and Finishing

10. One-twos, Turn & Shoot, Give & Go, and Crossing in a 4-Ball Finishing Drill

Balls 1-3 (Various Set-ups for Finishing)

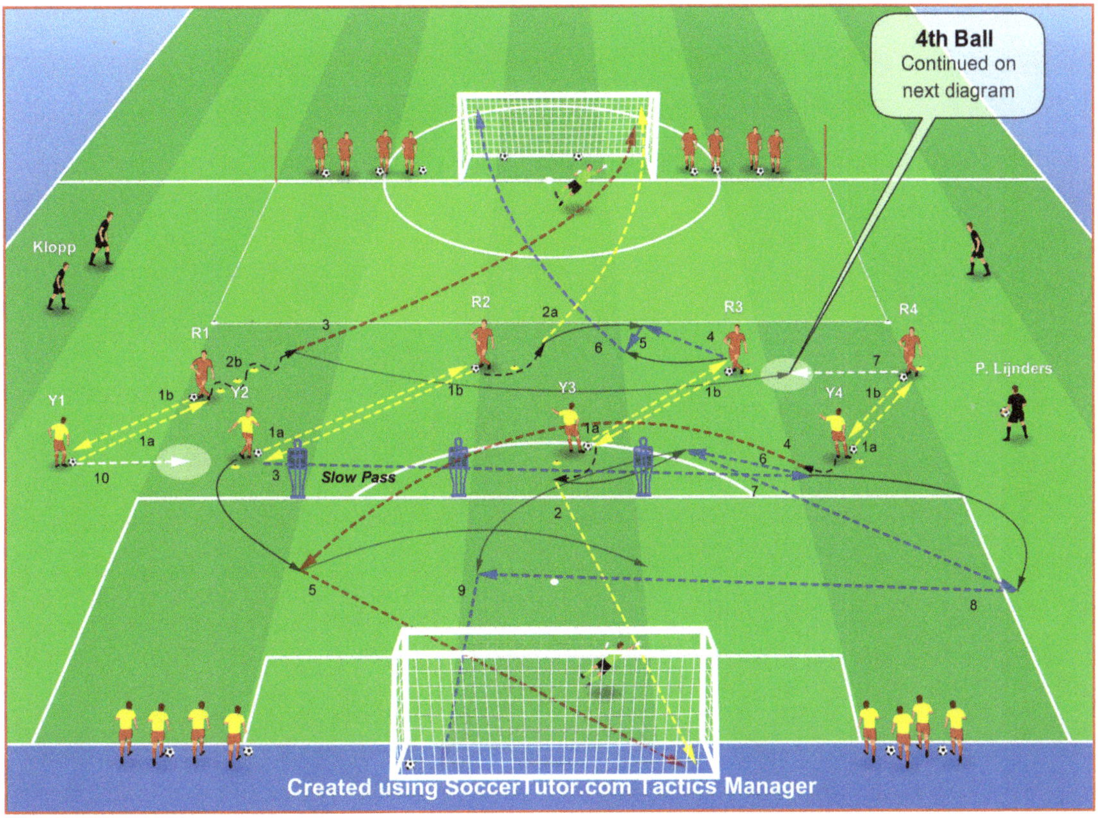

Red Players Description

1st Ball (1a-2a). R2 and **Y2** pass to each other. **R2** turns, and shoots.

1st Ball (1b-2b). R1 and **Y1** pass to each other. **R1** turns, and dribbles through the 3 cones. **R3** and **Y3** pass to each other, as do **R4** and **Y4**.

2nd Ball (3). R1 shoots from a wide angle.

3rd Ball (4-6). R3 passes to **R2**, who sets the ball for **R3** to shoot.

Yellow Players Description

1st Ball (2). Y3 turns and shoots.

2nd Ball (4-5). Y4 plays a lofted pass for the run of **Y2** to score.

3rd Ball (3). The slow pass from **Y2** is played before **Y4's** lofted pass.

6-9. After the lofted pass, **Y4** meets **Y2's** pass and plays a give & go with **Y3**, who moves across. **Y4** delivers a ground cross into the box for either **Y2** or **Y3** to score.

Source: Jürgen Klopp's Liverpool pre-season training session in Evian, France - 3rd August 2021

Jürgen Klopp Practices: Multi-Ball Attacking Combinations and Finishing

4th Ball (Give & Go Cross or Deep Cross)

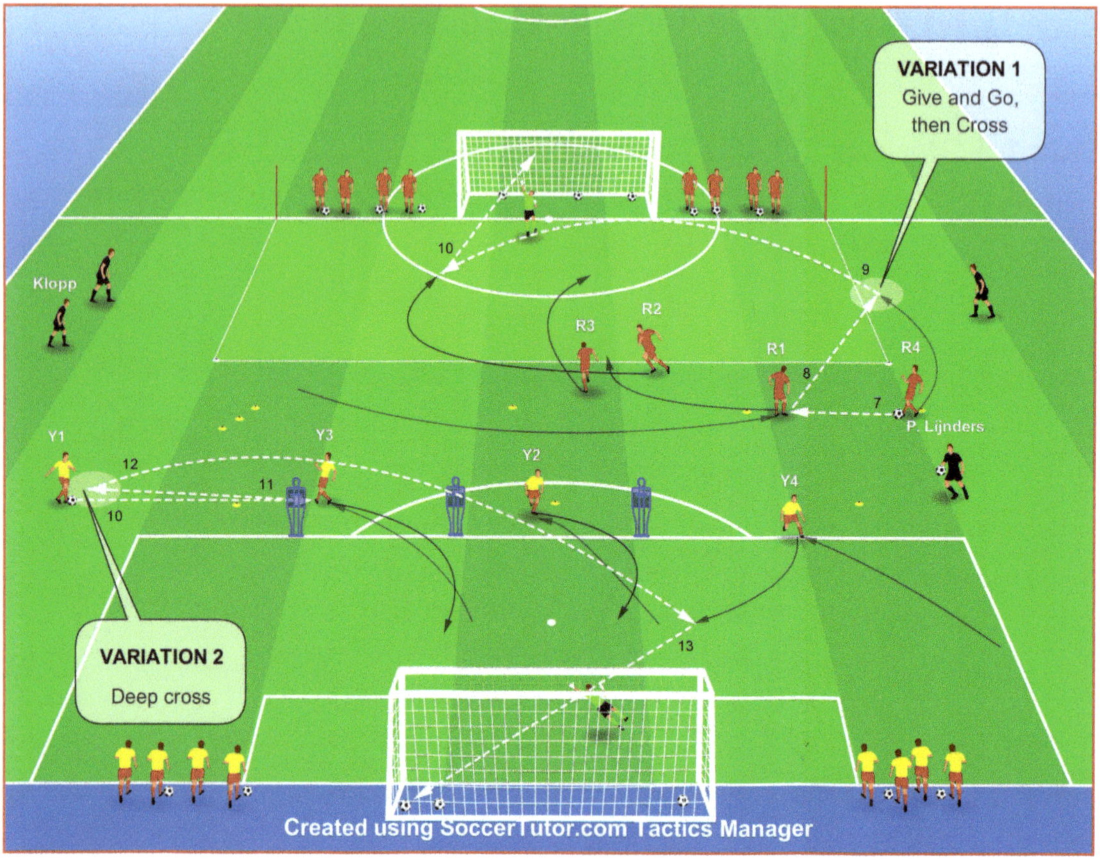

After the first 3 balls, the players run back into position.

Red Players Description

4th Ball (7-10). **R4** plays a give & go with **R1** and then delivers a cross into the box for either **R2** or **R3**, or cuts the ball back for **R1** to score.

In the diagram example, **R2** scores at the back post from an aerial cross.

Yellow Players Description

4th Ball (10-13). **Y1** plays a one-two with **Y3** and then delivers a deep cross into the box for any of **Y2** or **Y3**, or **Y4** to score.

In the diagram example, **Y4** scores at the back post.

Source: Jürgen Klopp's Liverpool pre-season training session in Evian, France - 3rd August 2021

Jürgen Klopp Practices: Multi-Ball Attacking Combinations and Finishing

11. Dynamic Wing Play, Dribbling, and 1v1s in a 5-Ball Finishing Drill

Balls 1-3 (Shooting & Finishing)

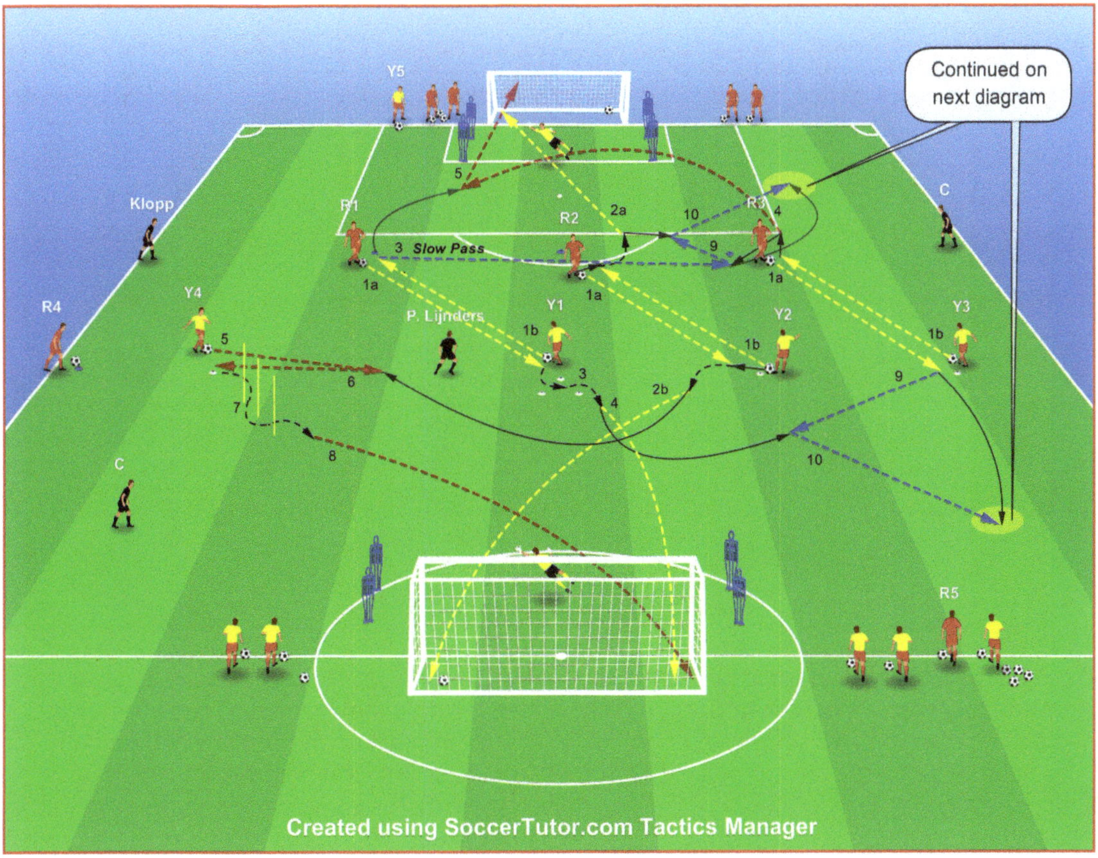

Practice Description

1st Ball (1-4). **R2** and **Y2** pass to each other. **R2** turns, and shoots.

R1 and **Y1** pass to each other. **Y1** turns, dribbles through the 3 cones, and shoots. **R3** and **Y3** also pass to each other.

2nd Ball (4-5). **R3** plays a lofted pass for the run of **R1** into the box to score.

6-8. **Y4** plays a one-two with **Y2**, who moves across to support after shooting. **Y4** then dribbles through the poles and shoots at goal.

3rd Ball (3). The **slow pass** from **R1** is played before **R3's** lofted pass (*2nd ball*).

9-10. **R3** plays a give & go with **R2**, and **Y3** plays a give & go with **Y1**. The sequence continues on the next page...

Source: Jürgen Klopp's Liverpool pre-season training session in Salzburg, Austria - 20th August 2020

Jürgen Klopp Practices: Multi-Ball Attacking Combinations and Finishing

4th Ball (Crossing & Finishing)

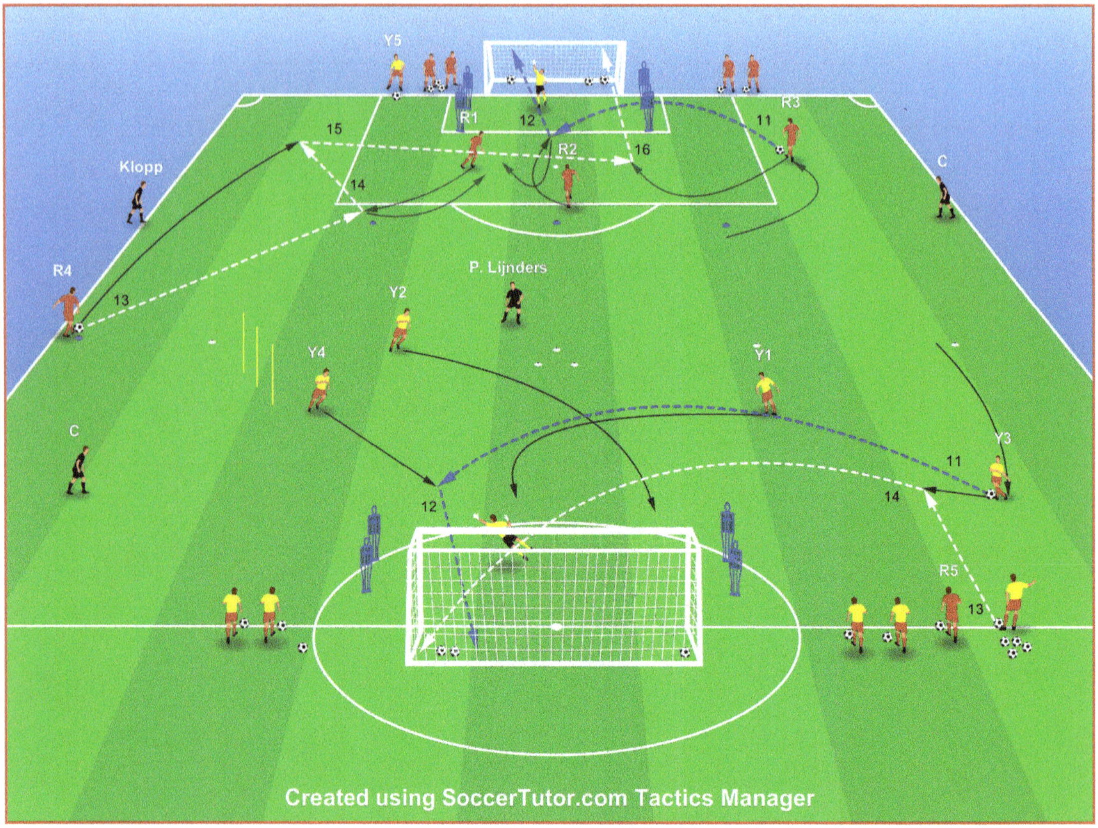

11-12. **R3** delivers a cross into the box for one of his 2 teammates to score. In the diagram example, **R2** scores after an aerial cross into the centre of the box (close range).

Y3 delivers a cross into the box for one of his 3 teammates to score. In this example, **Y4** scores after an aerial cross to the back post.

4th Ball (13-16). **R4** plays a give & go with **R1**, who plays the return pass for **R4's** advanced run on the flank. **R4** delivers a cross into the box for one of his 3 teammates to score. In the diagram example, **R3** scores after a ground cross.

An outside yellow player passes to **Y3**, and he shoots at goal from a wide angle to complete the practice sequence.

Source: Jürgen Klopp's Liverpool pre-season training session in Salzburg, Austria - 20th August 2020

Jürgen Klopp Practices: Multi-Ball Attacking Combinations and Finishing

5th Ball (Dribbling for 1v1)

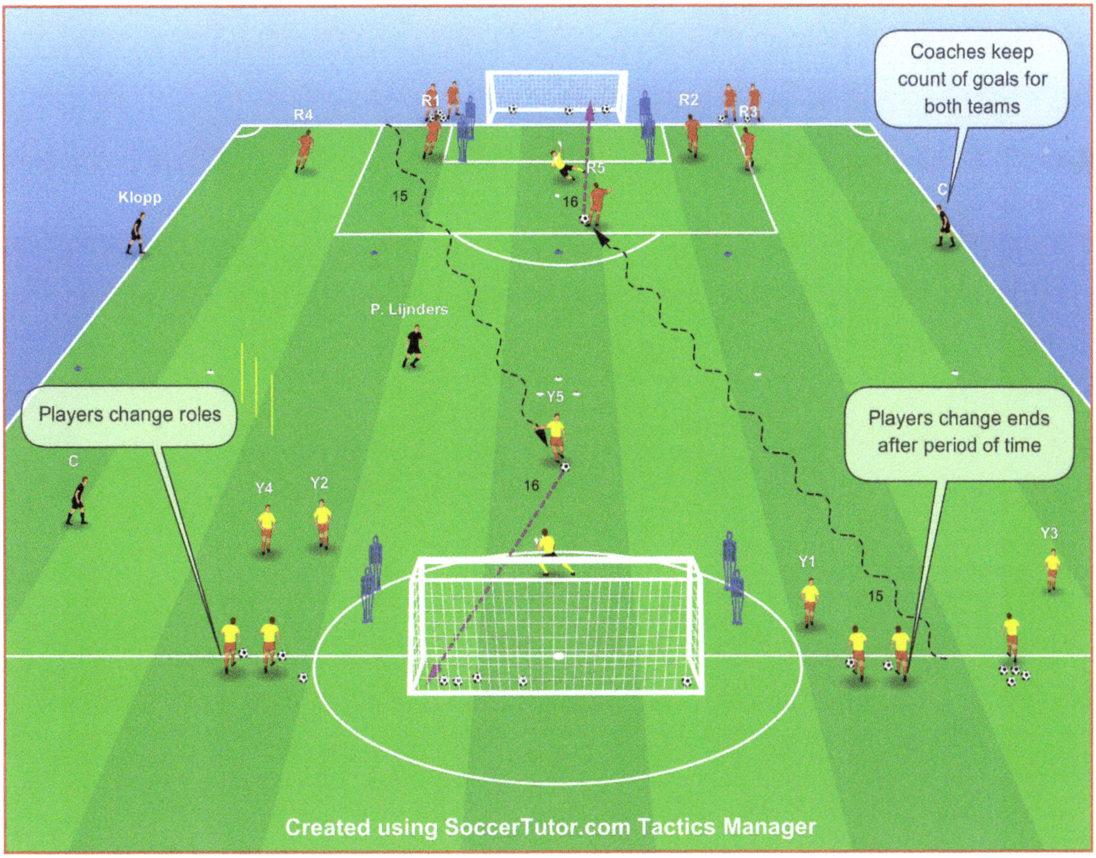

5th Ball (15). R5 and Y2 dribble a new ball in from opposite by-lines.

5th Ball (16). They both drive towards goal and finish in a 1v1 vs the GK.

The Coach keeps a count of total goals for both teams.

→ The players change roles, and the teams change ends after a period of time.

Source: Jürgen Klopp's Liverpool pre-season training session in Salzburg, Austria - 20th August 2020

Jürgen Klopp Practices: Multi-Ball Attacking Combinations and Finishing

12. Shoot, Lofted Pass Finish, Combination + Fast Counter Attack in a 4-Ball Finishing Drill

Balls 1-3 (Finishing)

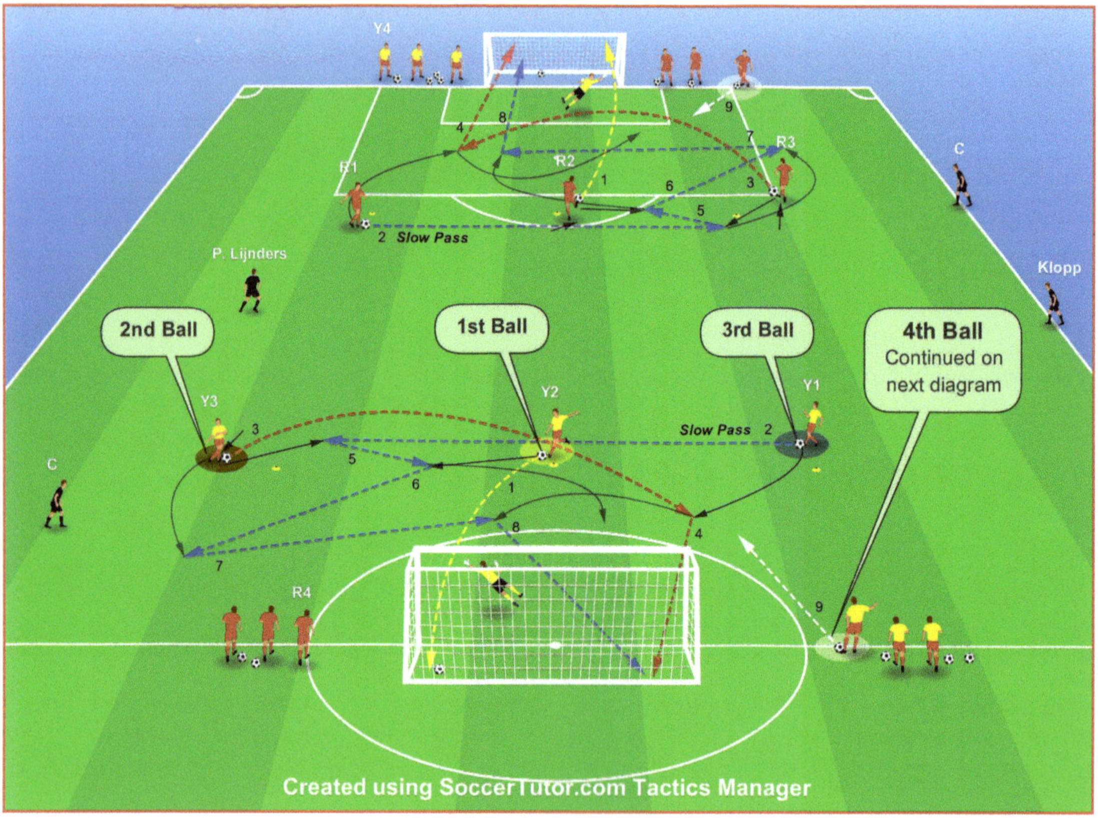

Practice Description

There are 2 groups of 3 players at each end and both carry out the same sequence:

1st Ball (1). Player 2 shoots.

2nd Ball (3-4). Player 3 plays a lofted pass for the run of **Player 1** to score.

3rd Ball (2). The <u>slow pass</u> from **Player 1** is played before **Player 3's** lofted pass.

5-8. After the lofted pass, **Player 3** meets **Player 1's** pass and plays a give & go with **Player 2**, who moves across.

Player 3 delivers a ground cross into the box for either **Player 1** or **Player 2** to score.

The 4th ball diagram and description follows on the next page...

Source: Jürgen Klopp's Liverpool pre-season training session in Salzburg, Austria - 15th July 2021

Jürgen Klopp Practices: Multi-Ball Attacking Combinations and Finishing

4th Ball (Fast Break Attack)

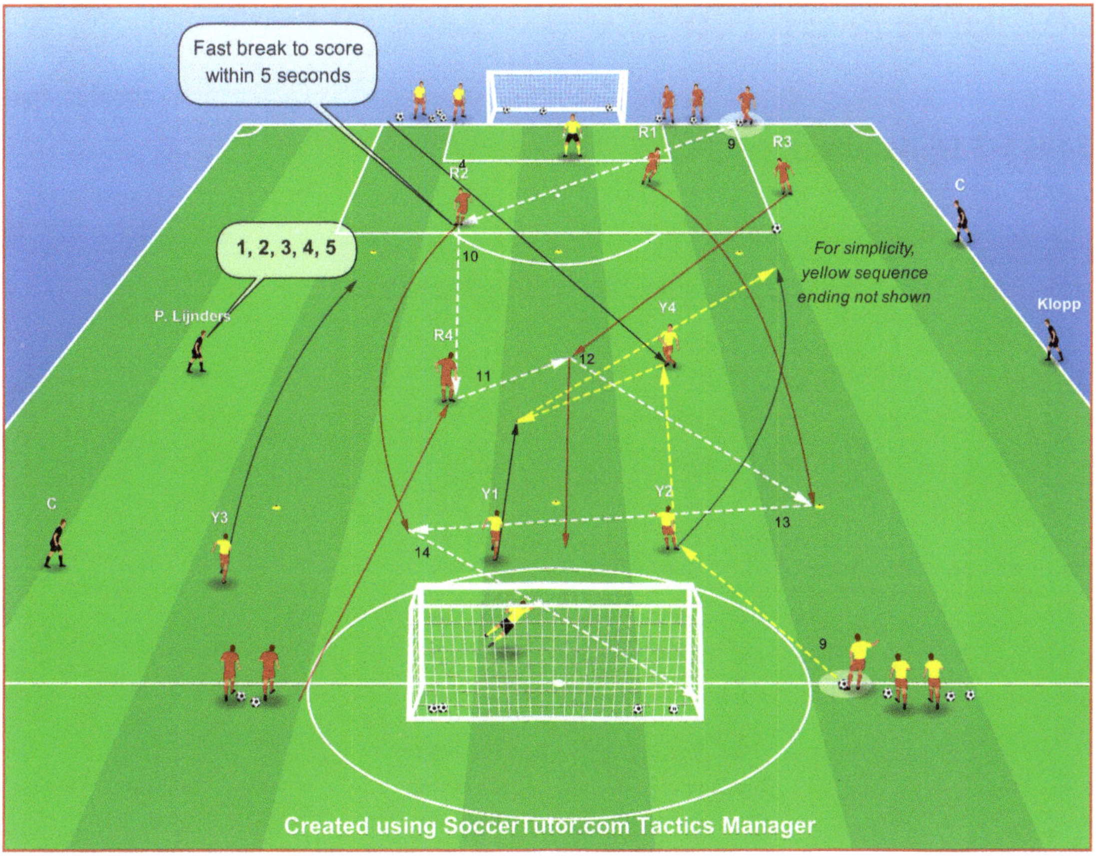

4th Ball (9-14). As soon as the 3rd ball phase is complete, we move into a fast break attack phase.

An outside red player (by-line) passes a new ball in for the reds and 1 player sprints inside from the halfway line (**R4**) to take part.

The reds **launch their 4-man fast break attack and must score within 5 seconds**.

At the same time, an outside yellow player (halfway line) passes a new ball in for the yellows and 1 player sprints inside from the by-line (**Y4**) to take part.

The yellows launch their 4-man fast break attack in the opposite direction to the reds, and also must score 5 seconds.

Source: Jürgen Klopp's Liverpool pre-season training session in Salzburg, Austria - 15th July 2021

Jürgen Klopp Practices: Multi-Ball Attacking Combinations and Finishing

13. Feint, Move & Shoot, Lofted Pass, and Give & Go Finishing + 3v2 Attack

Balls 1-3 (Finishing)

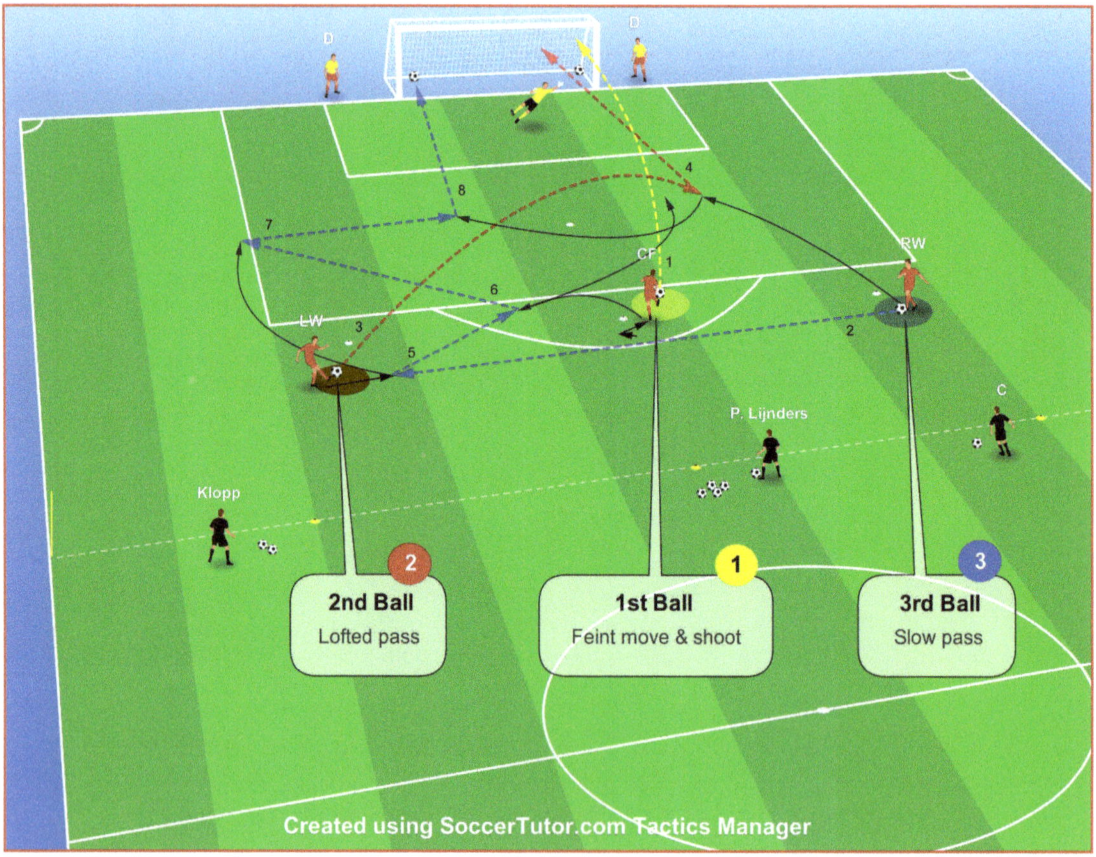

Practice Description

1st Ball (1). The centre forward (**CF**) has a ball, performs a feint, and shoots.

2nd Ball (3-4). The left winger (**LW**) plays a lofted pass into the box for the opposite right winger (**RW**) to score.

3rd Ball (2). The <u>slow pass</u> from the **RW** is played before the **LW's** lofted pass.

5-8. After the lofted pass, the **LW** steps across and plays a give & go with the **CF**, who moves across. The **LW** delivers a ground cross into the box for either the **RW** or **CF** to score (RW at near post in diagram example).

The 4th ball diagram and description follows on the next page...

Source: Jürgen Klopp's Liverpool training session at AXA Training Centre, Liverpool - 26th November 2020

Jürgen Klopp Practices: Multi-Ball Attacking Combinations and Finishing

4th Ball (3 v 2)

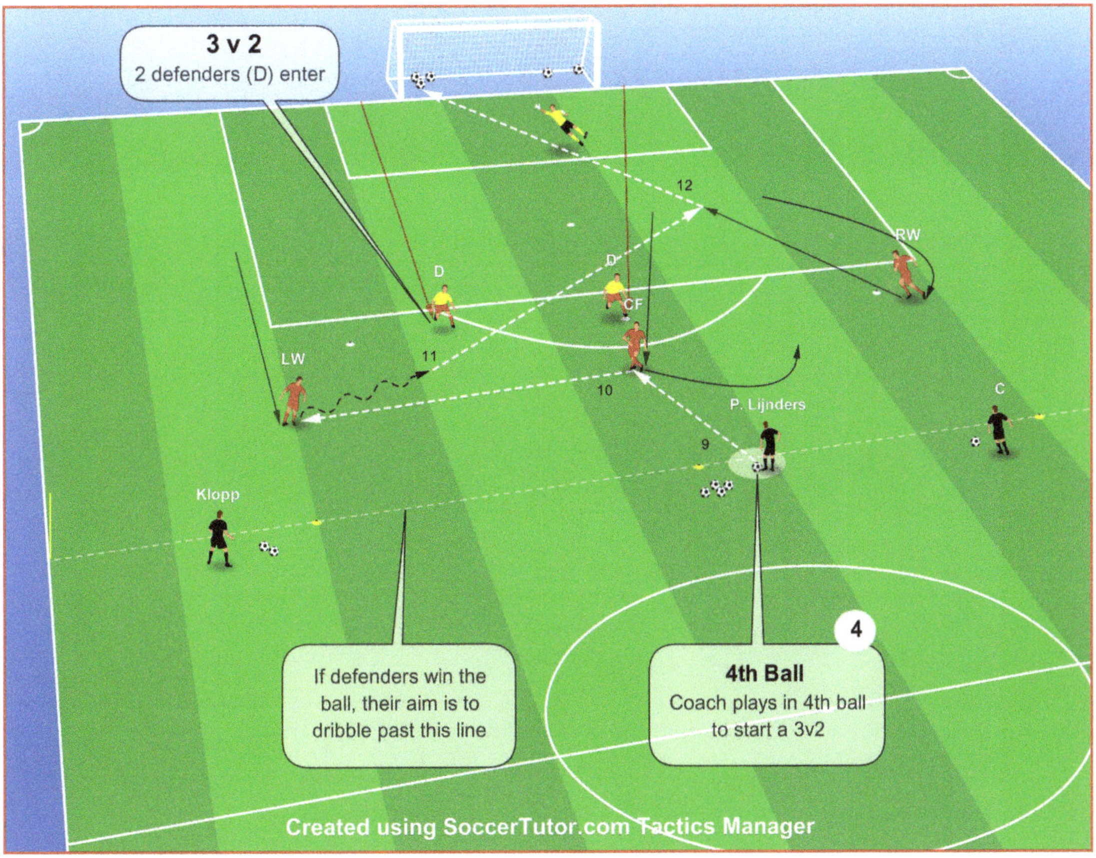

4th Ball (9-12). After the 3rd ball phase is complete and all the red players drop back into position, the Coach passes a new 4th ball in.

The 3 reds (**LW**, **RW** & **CF**) play 3v2 against the 2 yellow players (**D**), who move forward off the by-line to become the defenders.

In this example, the **CF** passes to the **LW**, who moves inside with the ball. He is then able to play a through pass in the gap between the 2 defenders. The **RW** has timed his run into the box well and scores.

If the yellow defenders win the ball, they aim to dribble past the marked out line shown.

Source: Jürgen Klopp's Liverpool training session at AXA Training Centre, Liverpool - 26th November 2020

Jürgen Klopp Practices: Multi-Ball Attacking Combinations and Finishing

14. Turn & Shoot, Lofted Pass, and Give & Go Finishing + 3v2 Attack

Balls 1-3 (Finishing)

Practice Description

The players are in 3 pairs (white, yellow, and blue). They start in the positions shown, with 1 player (B2) not involved.

1st Ball (1-3). W1 and Y1 play a one-two, then W1 turns and shoots.

2nd Ball (5-6). The same one-two, then W2 opens up and plays a lofted pass for R.

3rd Ball (4). The slow pass from R is played before W2's lofted pass.

7-10. After the lofted pass, W2 meets R's pass and plays a give & go with W1, who moves across. W2 delivers a ground cross into the box for either R or W1 to score.

The 4th ball diagram and description follows on the next page...

Source: Jürgen Klopp's Liverpool training session at Melwood Training Ground, Liverpool - 6th December 2018

Jürgen Klopp Practices: Multi-Ball Attacking Combinations and Finishing

4th Ball (3v2)

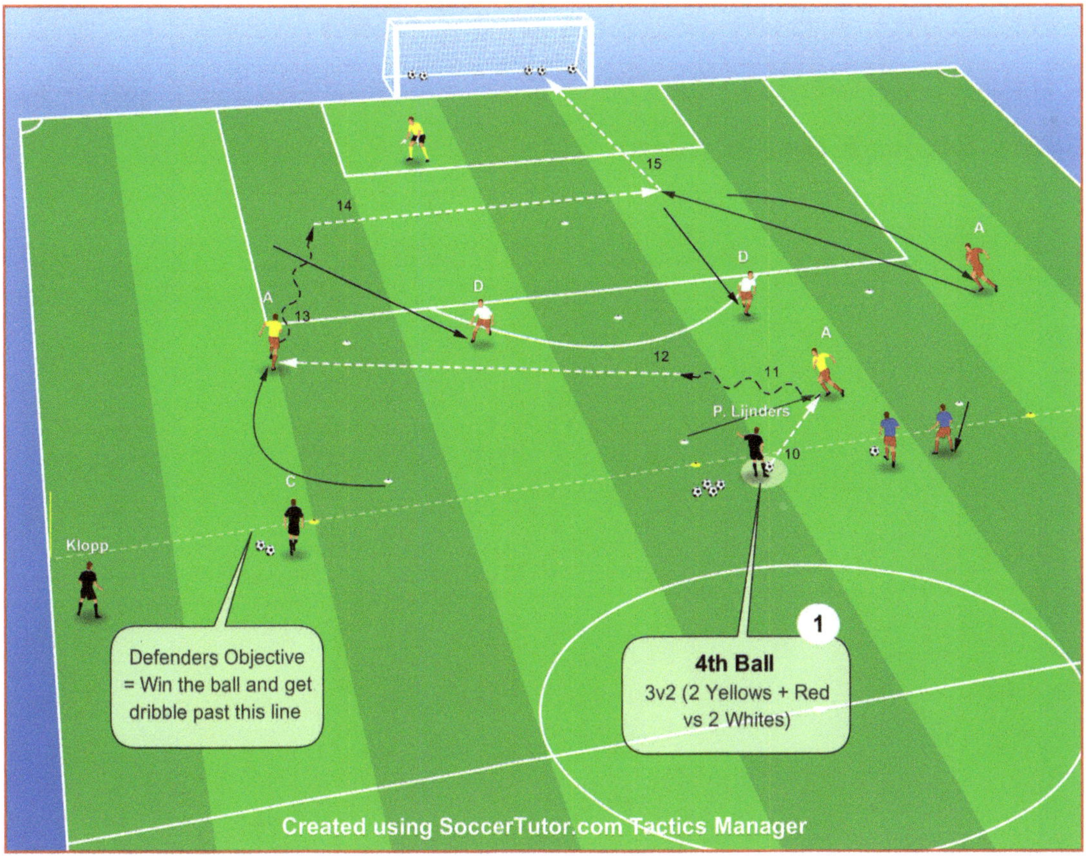

4th Ball (10-15). After the 3rd ball phase is complete, the white, yellow, and red players drop back ready to start a 3v2. The blue B1 drops out of the practice.

The Coach passes a new 4th ball in and the **2 yellow players + 1 red player (now labelled A) attack** and try to score.

The **2 white players (D) become defenders**. They must defend their goal and if they win the ball, their new objective is to dribble the ball past the marked out line.

In this example, the ball is played wide, and then dribbled into the box. The ball is passed across the box for the red player to score from close range.

Source: Jürgen Klopp's Liverpool training session at Melwood Training Ground, Liverpool - 6th December 2018

Jürgen Klopp Practices: Multi-Ball Attacking Combinations and Finishing

15. Pass, Receive, Shoot, Give & Go Finishing + 6v4 Attack in a 5-Ball Finishing Drill

Balls 1-4 (Give & Go Finishing)

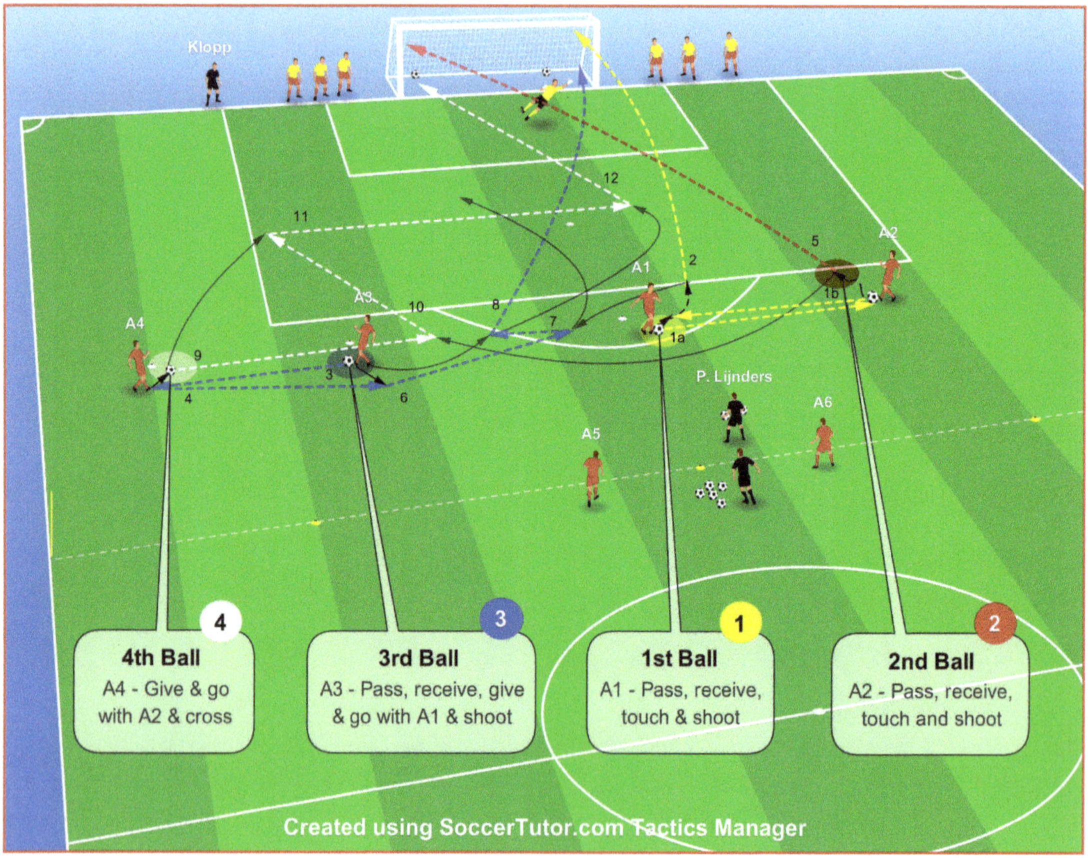

4th Ball — A4 - Give & go with A2 & cross
3rd Ball — A3 - Pass, receive, give & go with A1 & shoot
1st Ball — A1 - Pass, receive, touch & shoot
2nd Ball — A2 - Pass, receive, touch and shoot

Practice Description

1st Ball (1-2). **A1** and **A2** pass to each other. **A1** turns, and shoots.

2nd Ball (5). **A2** shoots from a wide angle.

3rd Ball (3). The one-two between **A3** and **A4** is before **A2's** shot.

6-8. **A3** passes to **A1**, who moves across. **A1** sets the ball for **A4** to shoot.

4th Ball (9-12). **A4** passes the 4th ball to **A2**, who moves all the way across from the other side of the pitch. He returns the pass for **A4's** run into the box (to complete a give & go).

A4 delivers a ground cross for either the **A1** or **A3** to score. In the diagram example, **A3** scores from the centre of the box.

Source: Jürgen Klopp's Liverpool pre-season training session in Evian, France - 1st August 2019

Jürgen Klopp Practices: Multi-Ball Attacking Combinations and Finishing

5th Ball (6 v 4)

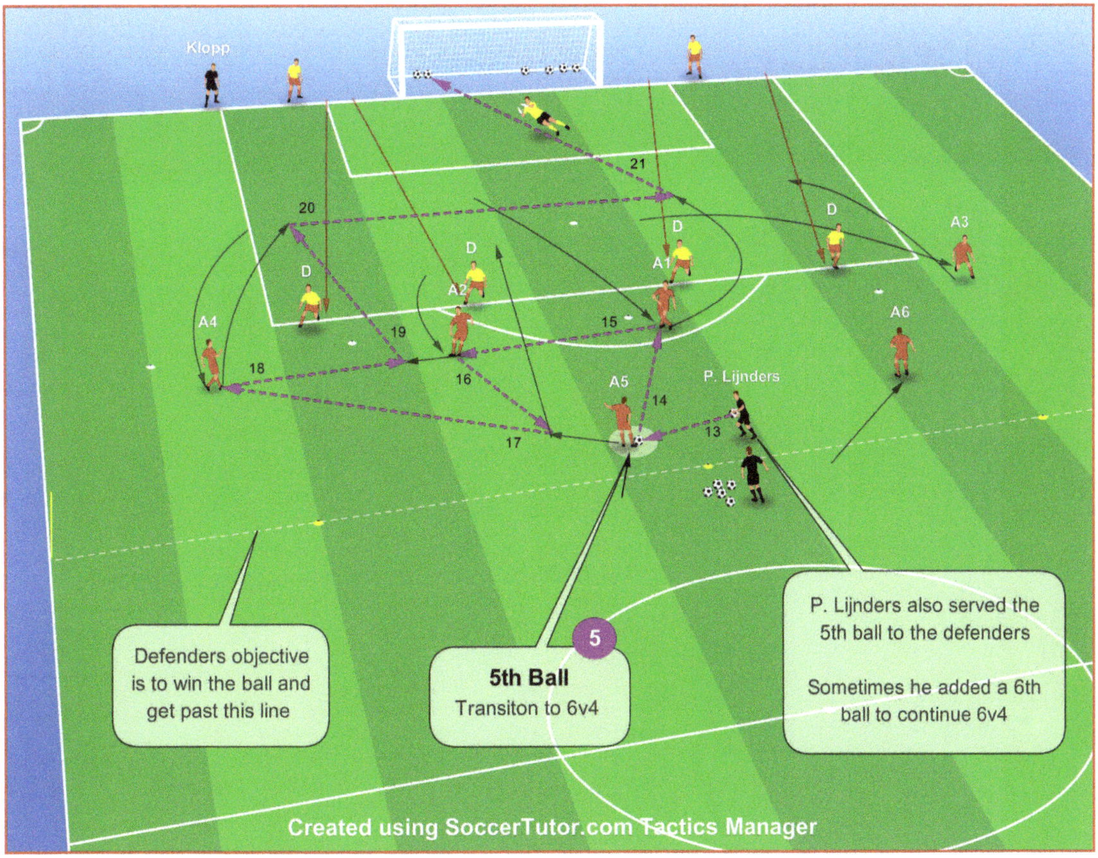

5th Ball (13). A5 and **A6** enter, and the Coach feeds **A5** the 5th ball. The red players use combination play to get in behind their opponents, and score.

4 yellow defenders run into play from the by-line to create a 6v4 situation. They must defend their goal and if they win the ball, their new objective is to dribble the ball past the marked out line.

14-17. In this specific example (diagram) observed during the Liverpool training session, **A5** passes to **A1**, who passes across to **A2**. **A2** passes back for **A5**, who passes out wide to **A4**.

18-19. A4 plays a give & go with **A2** to receive in behind the opposing defender and inside the box.

20-21. A1, **A3**, and **A5** make runs into the box to finish the attack. **A4** delivers a ground cross for **A1** to score.

NOTE: The Coach *(Pep Ljinders)* also sometimes served the 5th ball to the yellow defenders during this practice, and sometimes added a 6th ball to continue the 6v4.

Source: Jürgen Klopp's Liverpool pre-season training session in Evian, France - 1st August 2019

Jürgen Klopp Practices: Multi-Ball Attacking Combinations and Finishing

16. 4-Ball Finishing + Quick Transition to 7v4 Attack

Balls 1-3 (Finishing)

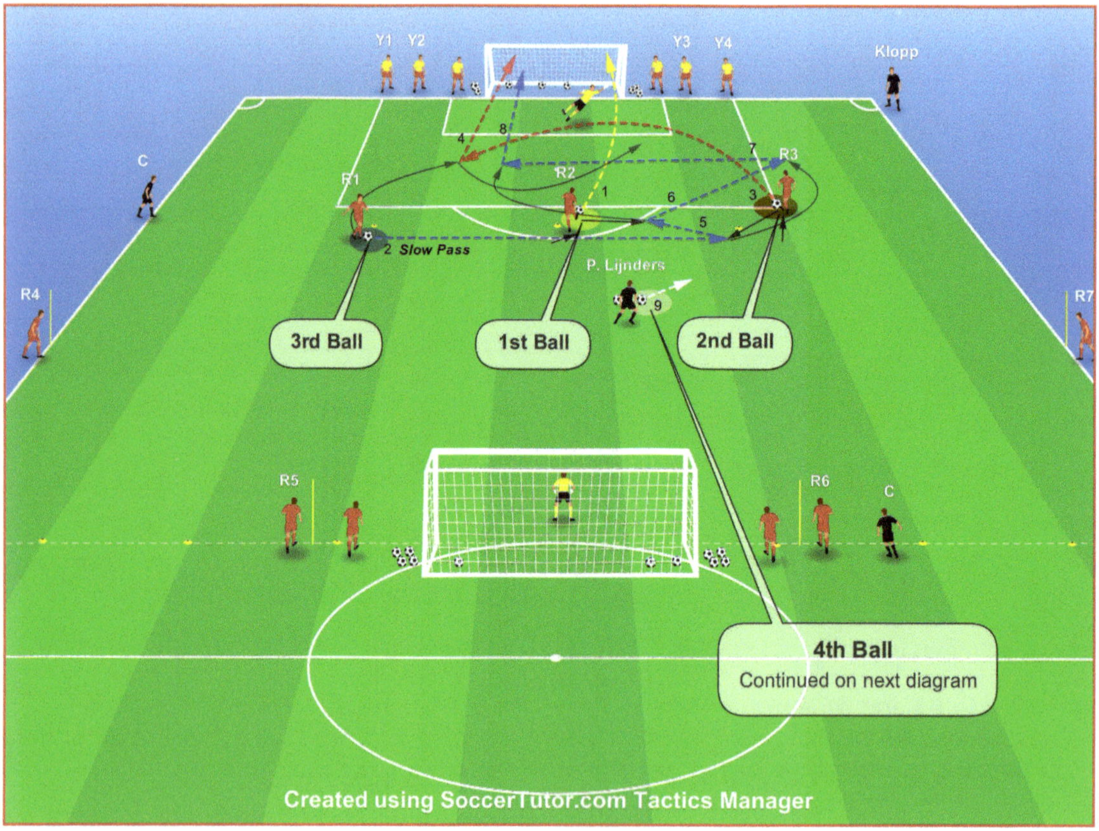

[Diagram showing 3rd Ball, 1st Ball, 2nd Ball positions and 4th Ball — Continued on next diagram]

Practice Description

1st Ball (1). R2 shoots from edge of box.

2nd Ball (3-4). R3 plays a lofted pass into the box for the run of R1 to score.

3rd Ball (2). The <u>slow pass</u> from R1 is played before R3's lofted pass.

5-8. After the lofted pass, R3 plays a give & go with R2 and passes across the box for either R1 or R2 to score.

The 4th ball diagram and description follows on the next page...

Source: Jürgen Klopp's Liverpool pre-season training session in Tyrol, Austria - 25th July 2021

Jürgen Klopp Practices: Multi-Ball Attacking Combinations and Finishing

4th Ball (7v4 Attack)

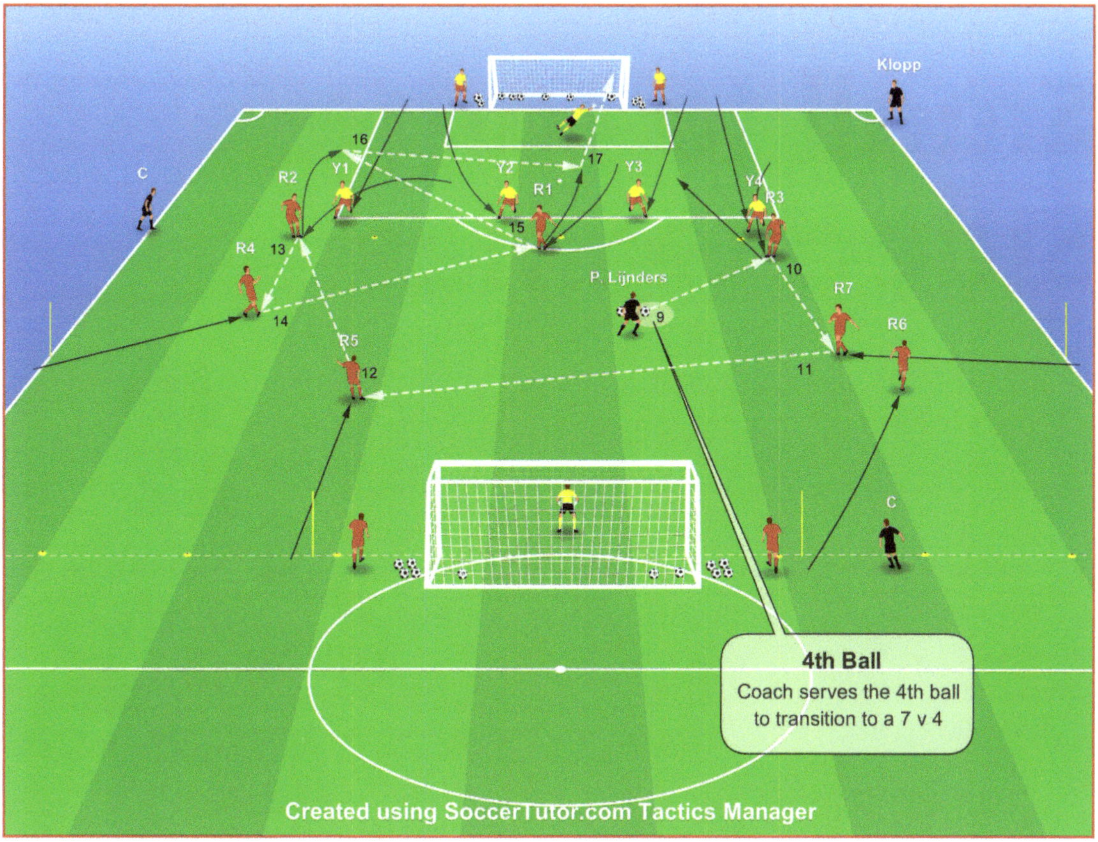

4th Ball (9). The Coach (*Pep Lijnders*) feeds a new 4th ball to a red player (**R3**). 3 new red players (**R4**, **R5** & **R6**) enter the pitch from different positions.

4 yellow defenders (**Y1-4**) run into play from the by-line to create a **7v4 situation**. Their aim is to defend their goal as a back 4.

10-11. In this specific example (diagram) observed during the Liverpool training session, **R3** passes back to **R7**, who has moved in from the sideline. **R7** passes across to **R5**, who has moved forward to receive.

12-14. **R5** passes forward to **R2** and he passes back to **R4**, who has moved in from the sideline. **R4** passes to **R1** in the centre at the edge of the box, as **R2** spins in behind his direct opponent (**Y1**)

15-17. **R1** plays a diagonal pass to **R2** in behind and he delivers a ground cross into the box for **R1** to score.

Source: Jürgen Klopp's Liverpool pre-season training session in Tyrol, Austria - 25th July 2021

Small to Large Sided Games

Direct from
Jürgen Klopp's
Training Sessions

"I prioritise what's more important to train and to let our ideas evolve - fundamental principles but in a less complex way. Then I create and contextualise specific exercises, where we want our players to learn, acquire and develop. I focus on what we can control, practice fundamentals of our game."

Pep Ljinders
Liverpool Assistant Manager

Jürgen Klopp Practices: Small to Large Sided Games

1. Receiving from a Throw-in and Breaking Out of Pressure in a 3v2 Game

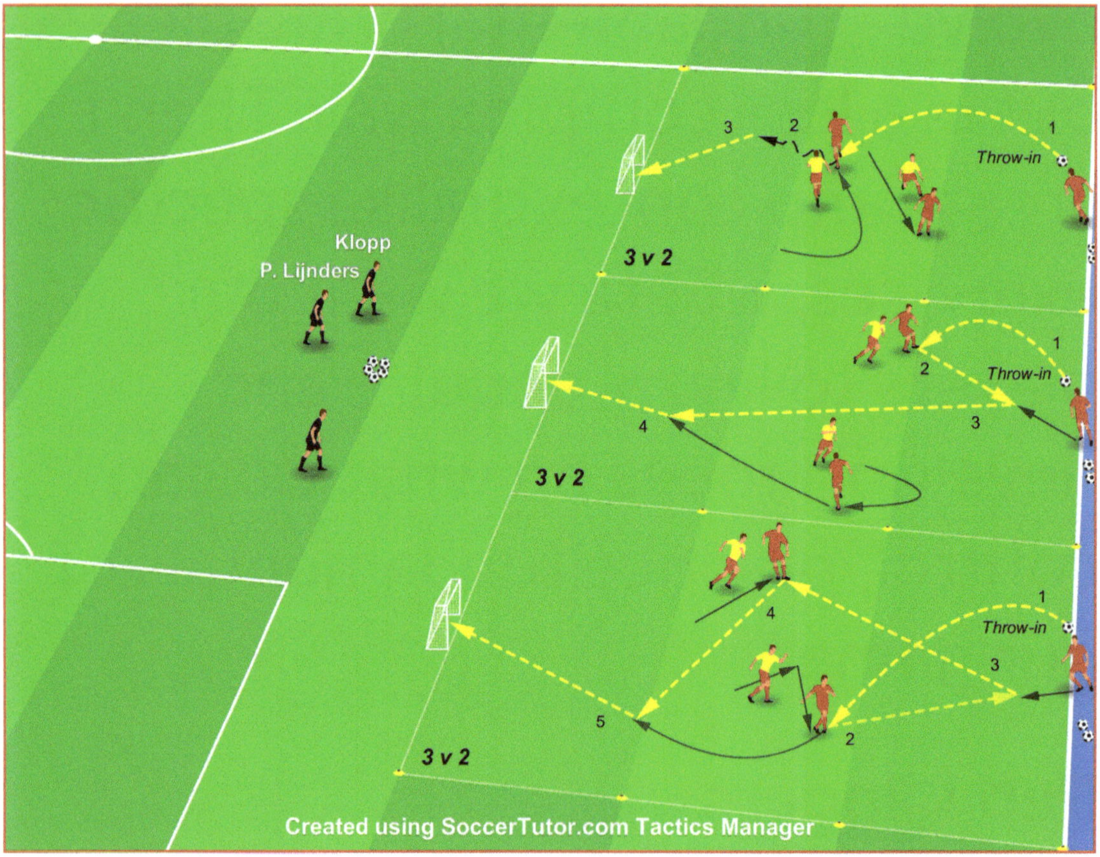

Practice Description

- The players are in groups of 5 playing 3v2 in marked out channels along the sideline with a mini goal at the other end.

- The **game starts with a red player taking a throw-in**. The reds aim to receive from the throw-in, play through the pressure of the 2 yellow defenders, and **score in the mini goal**.

- The 2 yellow defenders try to win the ball and then score themselves.

- If a goal is scored or the ball goes out of play, **always restart from with a new throw-in for the reds**.

Source: Jürgen Klopp's Liverpool pre-season training session in Salzburg, Austria - 23rd August 2020

Jürgen Klopp Practices: Small to Large Sided Games

2. Receiving from a Throw-in and Breaking Out of Pressure in a 5v4 Game

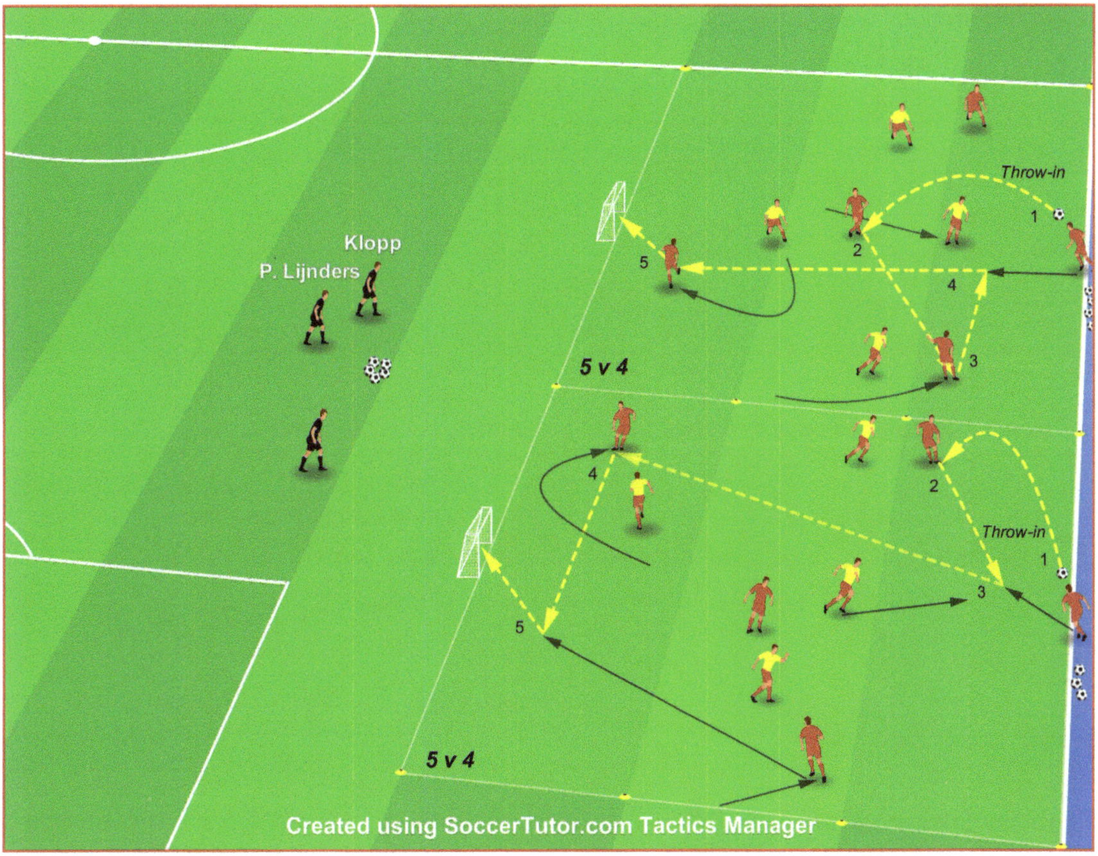

Practice Description

- The players are in groups of 9 playing 5v4 in marked out channels along the sideline with a mini goal at the other end.

- The **game starts with a red player taking a throw-in**. The reds aim to receive from the throw-in, play through the pressure of the 4 yellow defenders, and **score in the mini goal**.

- The 4 yellow defenders try to win the ball and then score themselves.

- If a goal is scored or the ball goes out of play, **always restart from with a new throw-in for the reds**.

Source: Jürgen Klopp's Liverpool pre-season training session in Salzburg, Austria - 23rd August 2020

Jürgen Klopp Practices: Small to Large Sided Games

3. High Tempo 4v4 (+GKs) "Shoot On Sight" Small Sided Game

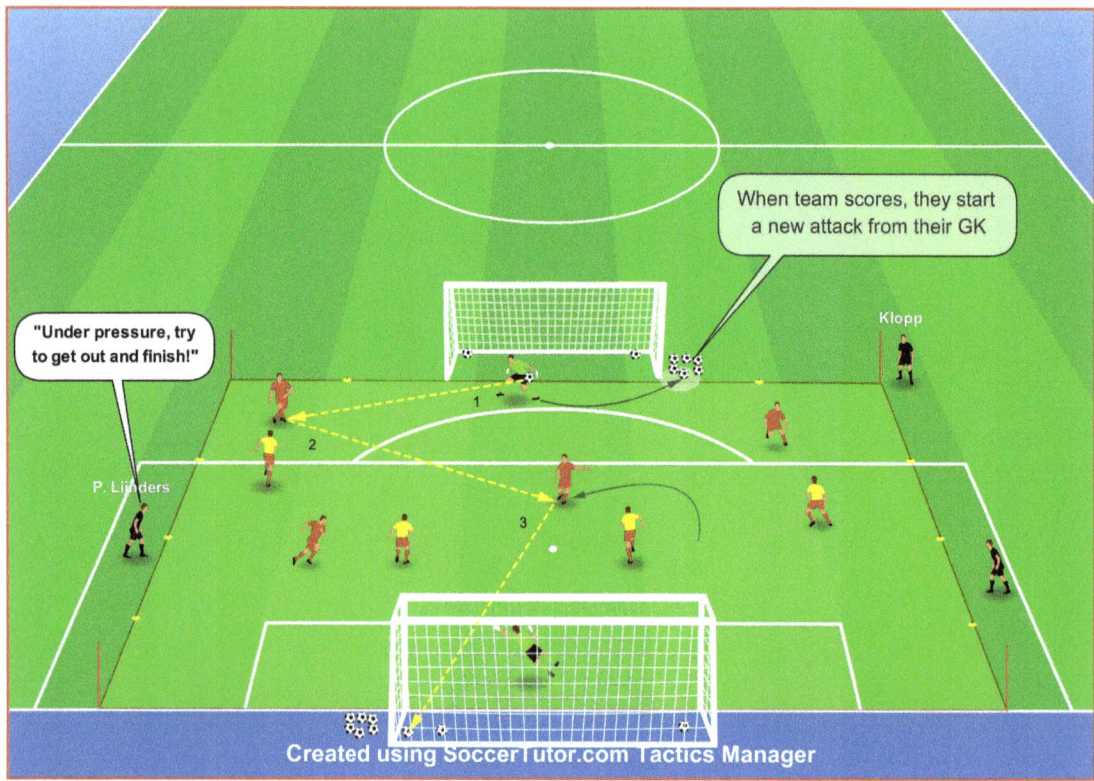

Practice Description

- In the area shown, the 2 teams play a normal 4v4 (+GKs) small sided game in **40 second bursts with rests** in between.

- The emphasis is to play at a **high tempo and shoot whenever there is space** and an opening to do so.

- The game starts with the GK and he distributes the ball by rolling it out to a teammate (short, medium or long).

- If a team scores, they always restart from their GK and try to score again.

- If a team wins the ball, they then quickly try to score themselves (early shots).

- If the ball goes out of play, the other team's GK starts with a new ball.

- The Coaches keep count of the score for the set period of time of the game.

Source: Jürgen Klopp's Liverpool pre-season training session in Tyrol, Austria - 27th July 2021

Jürgen Klopp Practices: Small to Large Sided Games

4. Shooting at Every Opportunity in a "Winner Stays On" 3v3 (+GKs) SSG

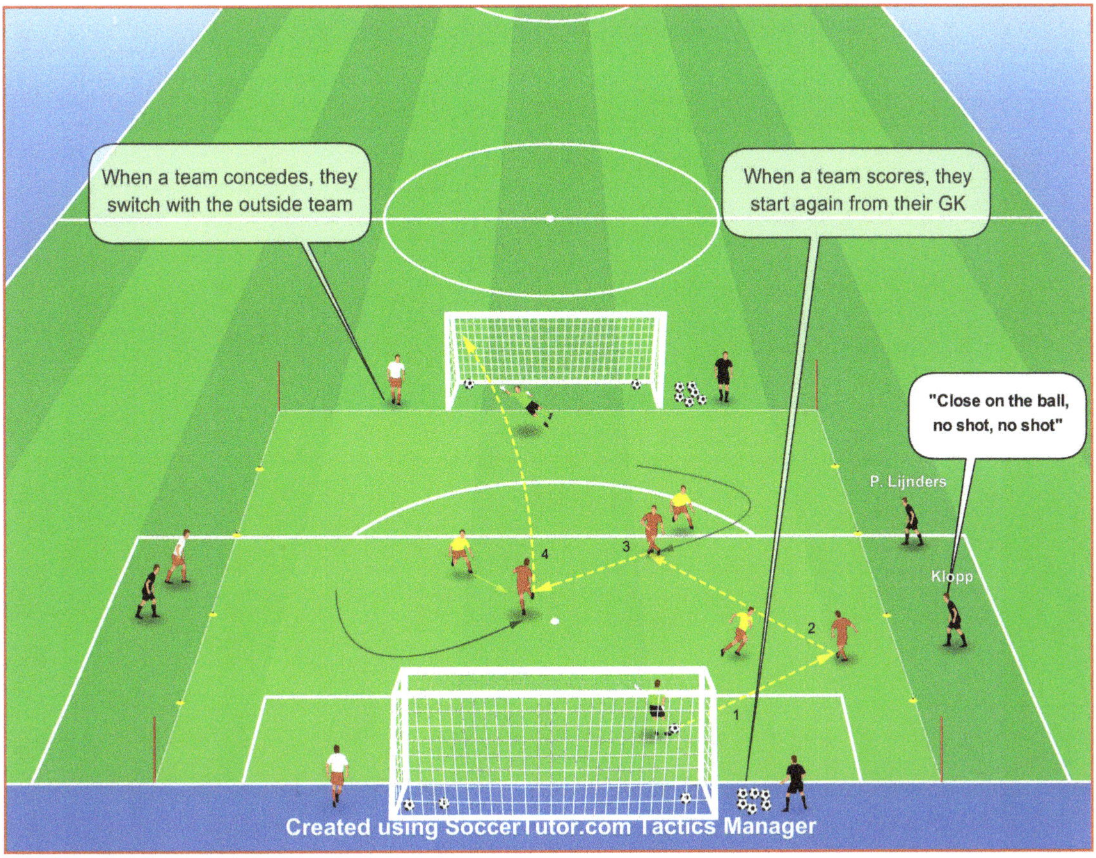

When a team concedes, they switch with the outside team

When a team scores, they start again from their GK

"Close on the ball, no shot, no shot"

P. Lijnders

Klopp

Practice Description

- In the area shown, the 2 teams play a normal 3v3 (+GKs) small sided game starting from the GK.

- The emphasis for the team in possession (reds) is to **shoot whenever there is sufficient space and opportunity**.

- The players can take **shots from deep positions**, and even the GKs try to score when not put under pressure.

- When a team scores, the play restarts with a new ball from their GK and another attack. The **team that concedes switches with the outside team** (whites).

- The defending team (yellows) try to win the ball, and then score themselves as quickly as possible.

- If a player kicks the ball out of play, the GK on the opposite team restarts the practice with a new ball.

Source: Jürgen Klopp's Liverpool training session at AXA Training Centre, Liverpool - 13th March 2021

Jürgen Klopp Practices: Small to Large Sided Games

5. Direct Play, Shooting Early and from Deep in a 4v4 (+GKs) SSG

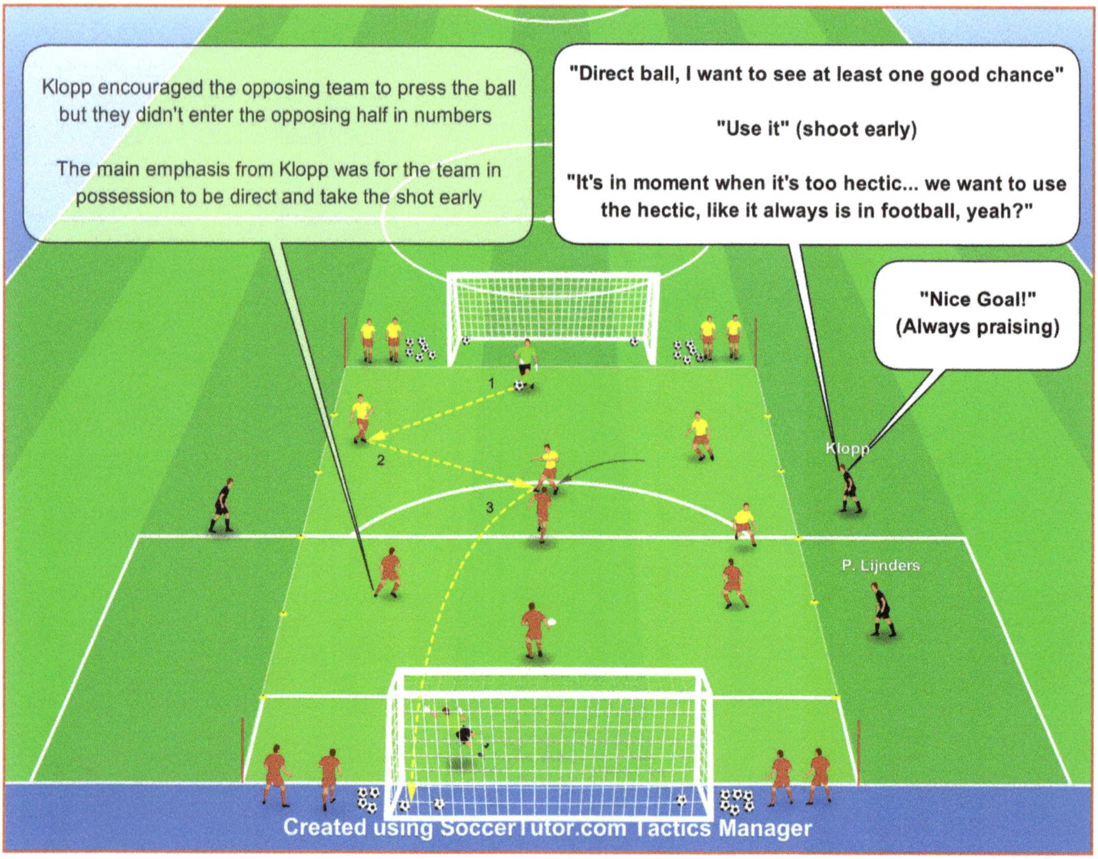

Practice Description

- In the area shown, the 2 teams play a normal 4v4 (+GKs) small sided game starting from the GK.

- The emphasis for the team in possession (yellows) is to shoot whenever there is sufficient space or opportunity, and there are **many shots from within teams' own defensive half**.

- When a team scores, the play restarts with a new ball from their GK and another attack.

- The defending team (reds) press the ball, try to block shots and win the ball, and then score themselves as quickly as possible.

- If a player kicks the ball out of play, the GK on the opposite team restarts the practice with a new ball.

Source: Jürgen Klopp's Liverpool pre-season training session in Evian, France - 31st July 2018

Jürgen Klopp Practices: Small to Large Sided Games

6. Support Play and Finishing in a 4v4 (+4) + GKs SSG with Outside End Players

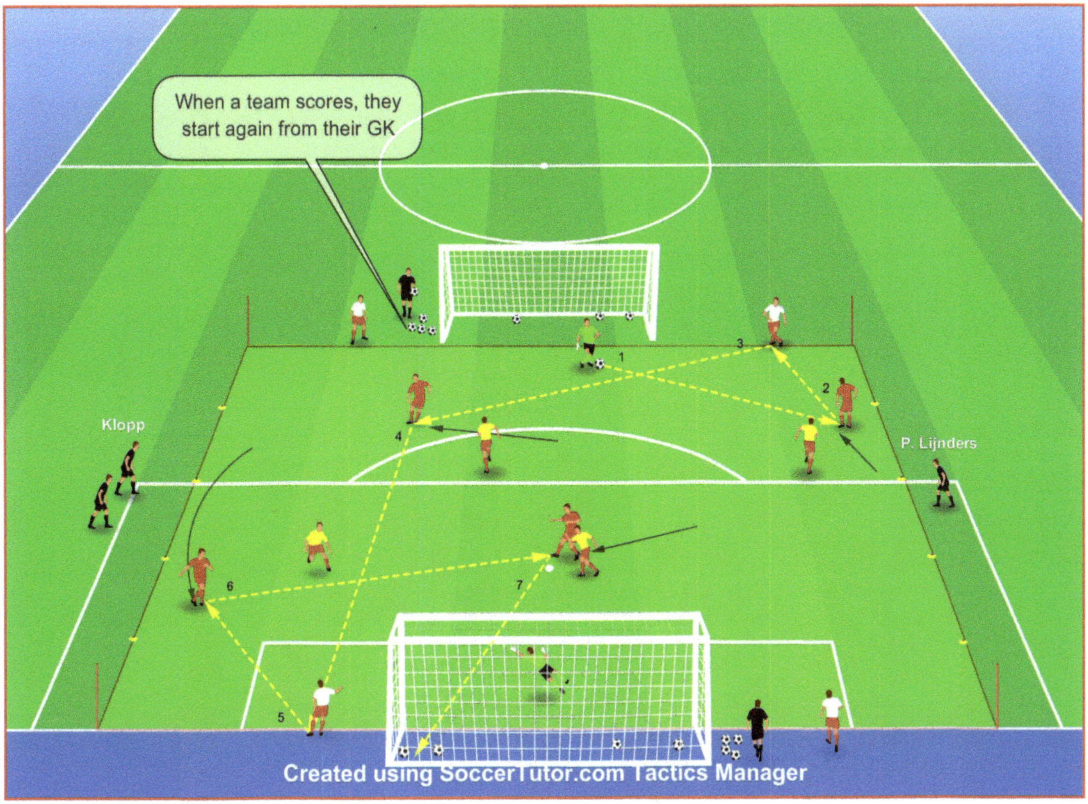

Practice Description

- In the area shown, 2 teams play a normal 4v4 +GKs small sided game with 4 additional outside players (1 positioned on each side of the goal).

- The aim is to utilise the outside players and the numerical advantage to maintain possession and create many goal scoring opportunities.

- The outside players use 1 touch, so the team in possession **bounce passes off them and quickly provide support**.

- When a team scores, the play restarts with a new ball from their GK and another attack.

- The defending team (yellows) press the ball and try to block potential passing lanes. If they win the ball, they make a quick transition from defence to attack and try to score (using the outside players).

- If a player kicks the ball out of play, the GK on the opposite team restarts the practice with a new ball.

Source: Jürgen Klopp's Liverpool training session at AXA Training Centre, Liverpool - 31st March 2022

Jürgen Klopp Practices: Small to Large Sided Games

7. Attacking Using the Full Width in a 5v5 (+GKs) SSG with Side Zones

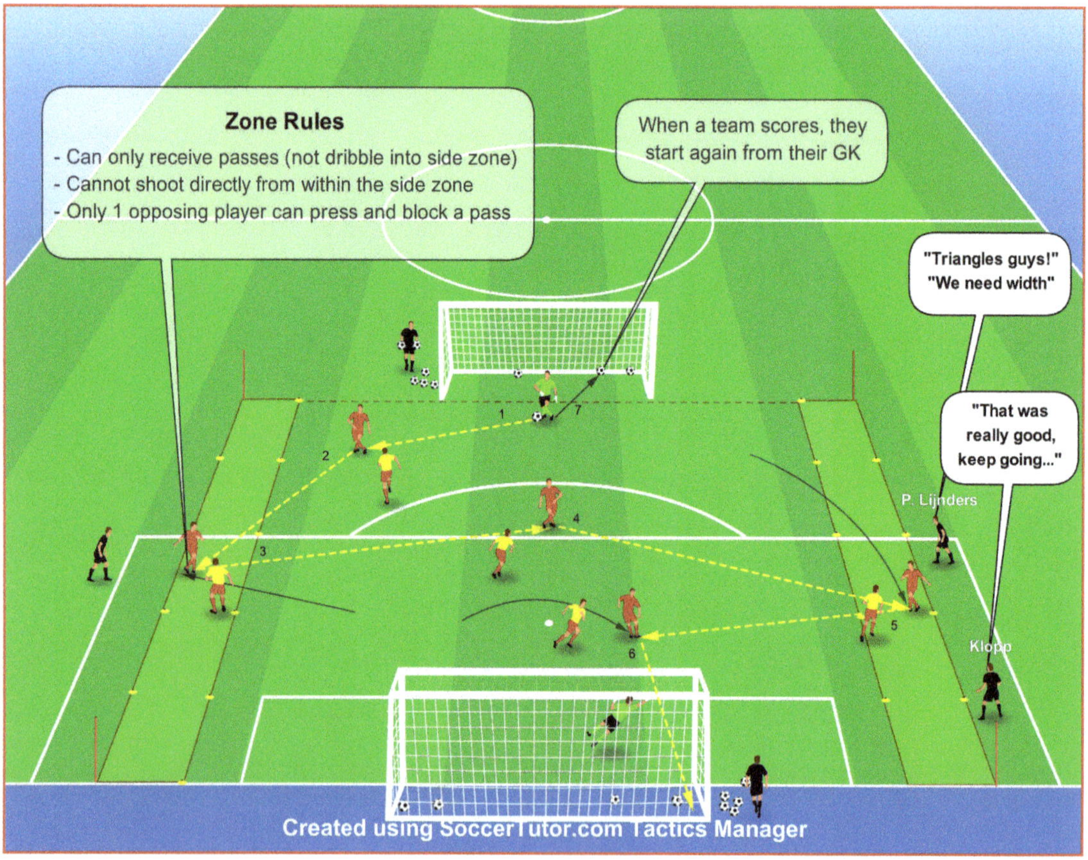

Zone Rules
- Can only receive passes (not dribble into side zone)
- Cannot shoot directly from within the side zone
- Only 1 opposing player can press and block a pass

When a team scores, they start again from their GK

"Triangles guys!" "We need width"

"That was really good, keep going..."

P. Lijnders

Klopp

Practice Description

- In the area shown, 2 teams play a normal 5v5 +GKs small sided game with 2 wide zones marked out, as shown.

- The game starts from the GK and the aim is to **utilise the full width of the pitch** to create openings and score.

- **ZONE RULES:** Players can only receive passes within the side zones, and cannot dribble the ball into them. Players are not allowed to shoot from within the side zones. Only 1 defending player (yellow) can move into the side zone at any time.

- When a team scores, the play restarts with a new ball from their GK and another attack.

- If the defending team (yellows) win the ball, they try to score with the same zone rules still applicable.

Source: Jürgen Klopp's Liverpool training session at AXA Training Centre, Liverpool - 23rd September 2021

Jürgen Klopp Practices: Small to Large Sided Games

8. Playing in Behind + Attacking Against a Low Block in a SSG with Changing Conditions

Game Conditions 1 - Playing in Behind

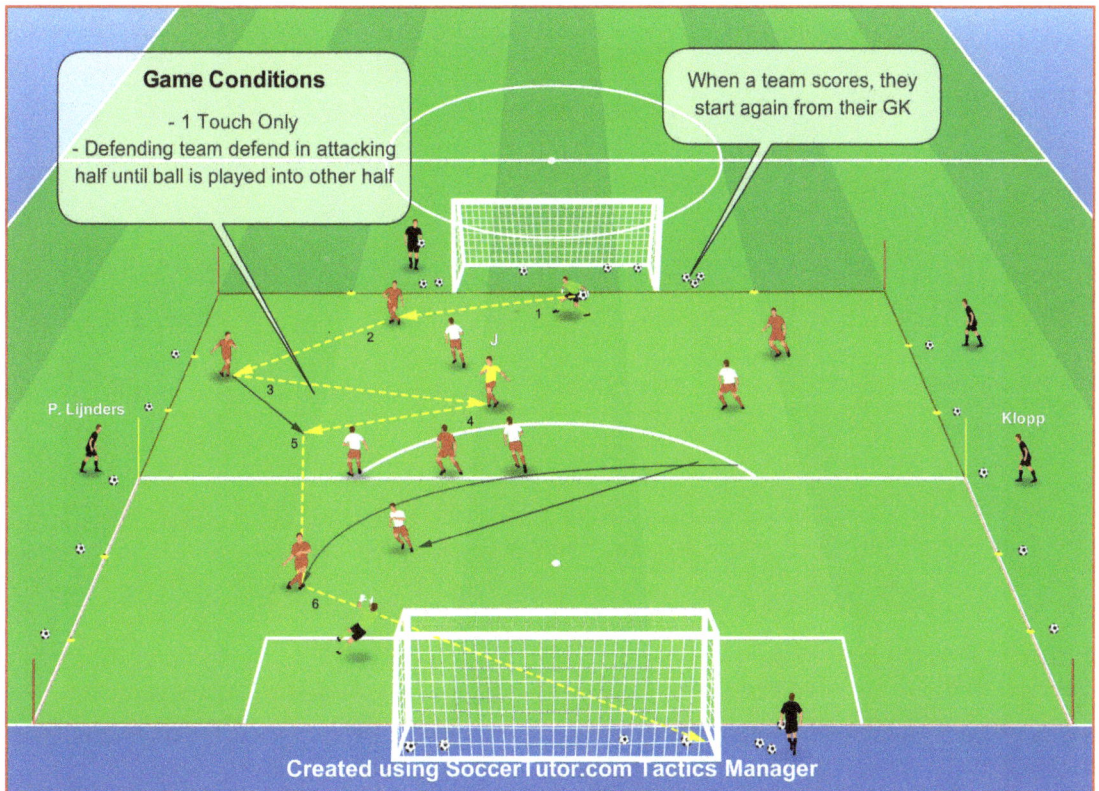

Practice Description

- In the area shown, 2 teams play a 5v5 (+1 Joker) +GKs small sided game with a clearly marked out halfway line.
- **GAME CONDITIONS:** The **defending team's players (whites) must all be in the red's half** trying to win the ball. They can move back after the ball has already been played in there.
- All players are limited to 1 touch.

- The game starts from the GK, and the reds aim to exploit their numerical advantage with the Joker and the high positioning of their opponents by **playing the ball in behind to score**.
- When a team scores, the play restarts with a new ball from their GK and another attack.
- If the defending team (whites) win the ball, they make a quick transition from defence to attack and try to score.

Source: Jürgen Klopp's Liverpool training session at AXA Training Centre, Liverpool - 18th February 2022

Jürgen Klopp Practices: Small to Large Sided Games

Game Conditions 2 - Attacking Against a Low Block

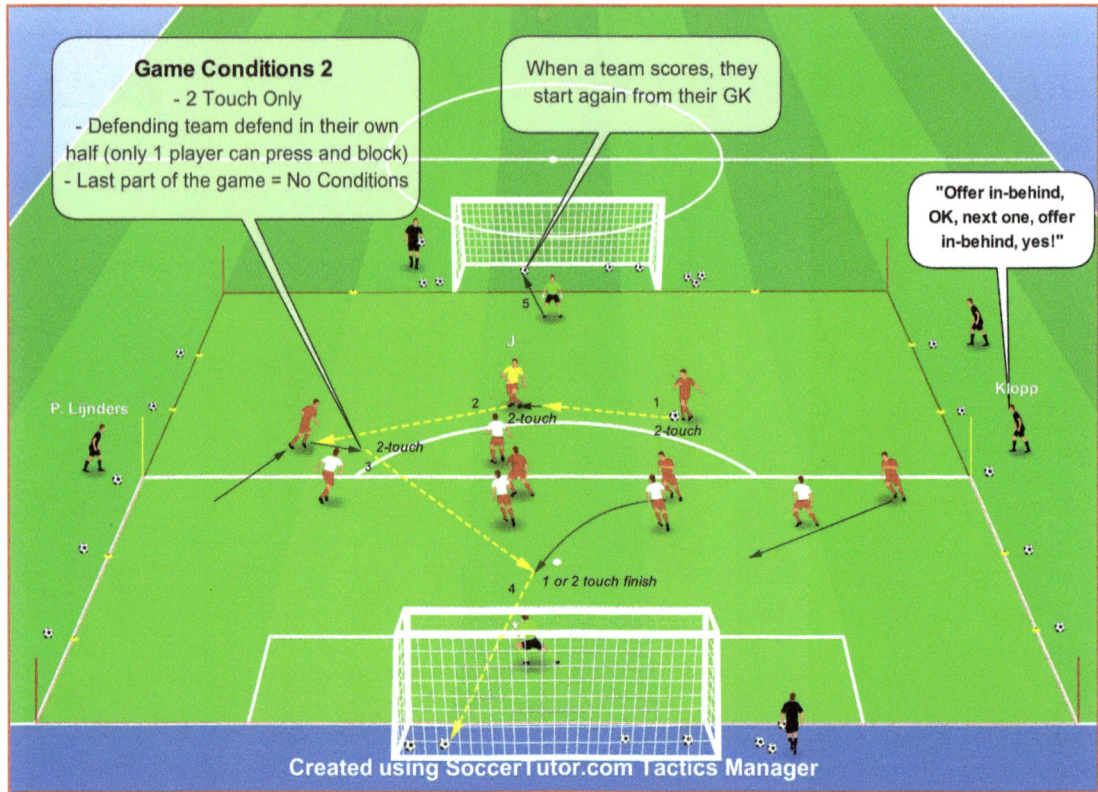

- **GAME CONDITIONS 2:** The defending team (whites) now **defend within their own half, with only 1 player allowed in the red's half** to press and block passes.

- All players are limited to 2 touches.

- The reds still try to exploit their numerical advantage with the Joker and play in behind their opponents, even though it is now made more difficult with their deeper defensive line.

- When a team scores, the play restarts with a new ball from their GK and another attack.

- If the defending team (whites) win the ball, they make a quick transition from defence to attack and try to score.

- **Game Conditions 3:** In the last part of the game, **all conditions are removed**, and the players play a normal 5v5 (+1) +GKs small sided game.

Source: Jürgen Klopp's Liverpool training session at AXA Training Centre, Liverpool - 18th February 2022

Jürgen Klopp Practices: Small to Large Sided Games

9. Play Out and Score Quickly in a 5v5v5 (+GKs) 3-Goal Game

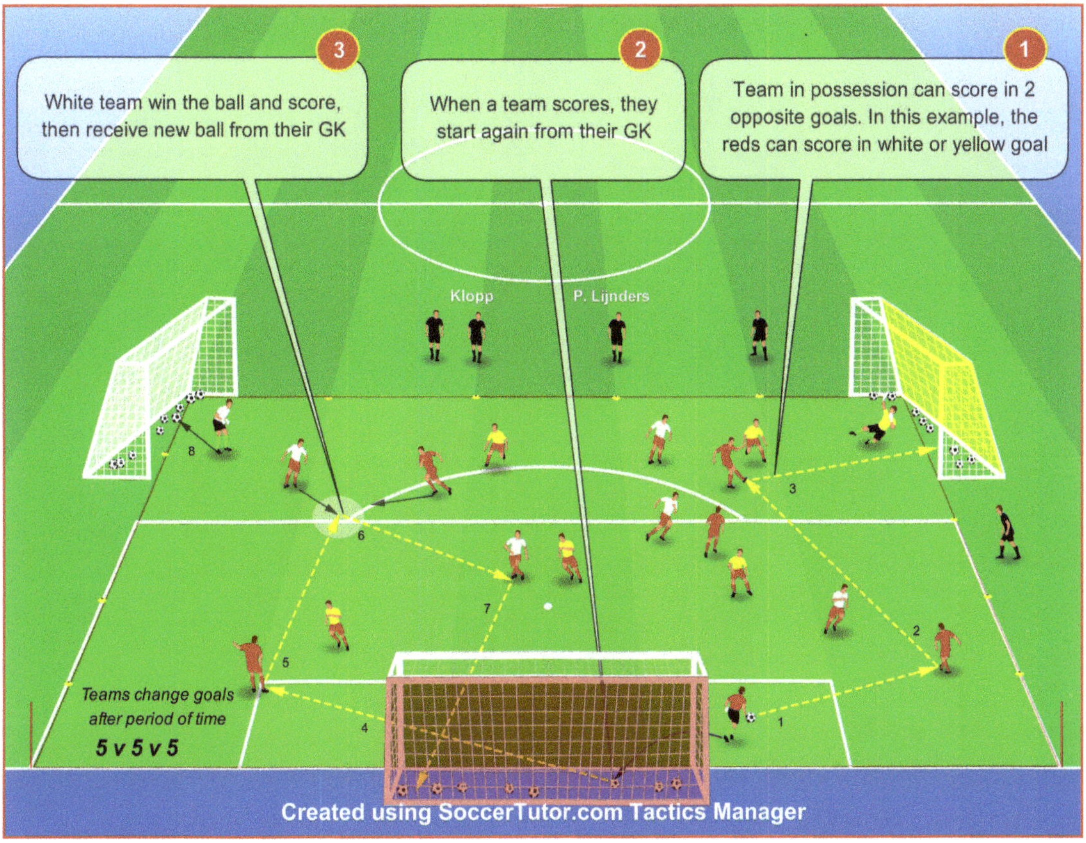

3 — White team win the ball and score, then receive new ball from their GK

2 — When a team scores, they start again from their GK

1 — Team in possession can score in 2 opposite goals. In this example, the reds can score in white or yellow goal

Teams change goals after period of time

5 v 5 v 5

Practice Description

In the area shown, 3 teams play a 5v5v5 game with 3 large goals + GKs as shown.

1. The game starts with a GK and the team in possession (reds) can score in either of the other 2 goals. In this example, the **reds can score in the white or yellow goals**.

2. When a team scores, the play restarts with a new ball from their GK and another attack.

3. Both of the other teams are trying to win the ball. If they do (whites in diagram), they then try to score in the red or yellow goal as quickly as possible. The play restarts with a new ball from their GK and another attack.

→ *The teams change goals after a set period of time.*

Source: Jürgen Klopp's Liverpool warm weather training camp in Tenerife, Spain - 22nd March 2017

Jürgen Klopp Practices: Small to Large Sided Games

10. Playing Through Pressure and Collective Defending in a 5v5 (+1) +GKs SSG

Practice Description

- In the area shown, 2 teams play a normal 5v5 (+1 Joker) +GKs small sided game starting from the GK.

- The emphasis for the team in possession (reds) is to **build up play through pressure**, use good combination play to create goal scoring opportunities, and score in the large goal.

- The **team in possession should utilise the Joker and the numerical advantage** to create chances and score goals.

- When a team scores, the play restarts with a new ball from their GK and another attack.

- The **defending team (yellows) press the ball**, try to block potential passing lanes, and win the ball.

- If the yellows win the ball, they make a quick transition from defence to attack and try to score.

- If a player kicks the ball out of play, the GK on the opposite team restarts the practice with a new ball.

Source: Jürgen Klopp's Liverpool training session at AXA Training Centre, Liverpool - 17th December 2020

Jürgen Klopp Practices: Small to Large Sided Games

11. 5v5 (+GKs) Small Sided Game with Possession Play Conditions

Practice Description

- In the area shown, 2 teams play a normal 5v5 (+GKs) small sided game starting from the GK.
- The **team in possession (reds) must complete 5 passes before they are allowed to shoot** and score. The Coach keeps count by calling out the numbers.
- When a team scores, the play restarts with a new ball from their GK and another attack.
- If the defending team (yellows) win the ball, they must also complete 5 passes before they are allowed to score.
- If a player kicks the ball out of play, the GK on the opposite team restarts the practice with a new ball.

Source: Jürgen Klopp's Liverpool training session at Melwood Training Ground, Liverpool - 25th September 2020

Jürgen Klopp Practices: Small to Large Sided Games

12. Attacking and Defending Corner Kicks + Counter Attacks in an 8v8 (+GKs) Game

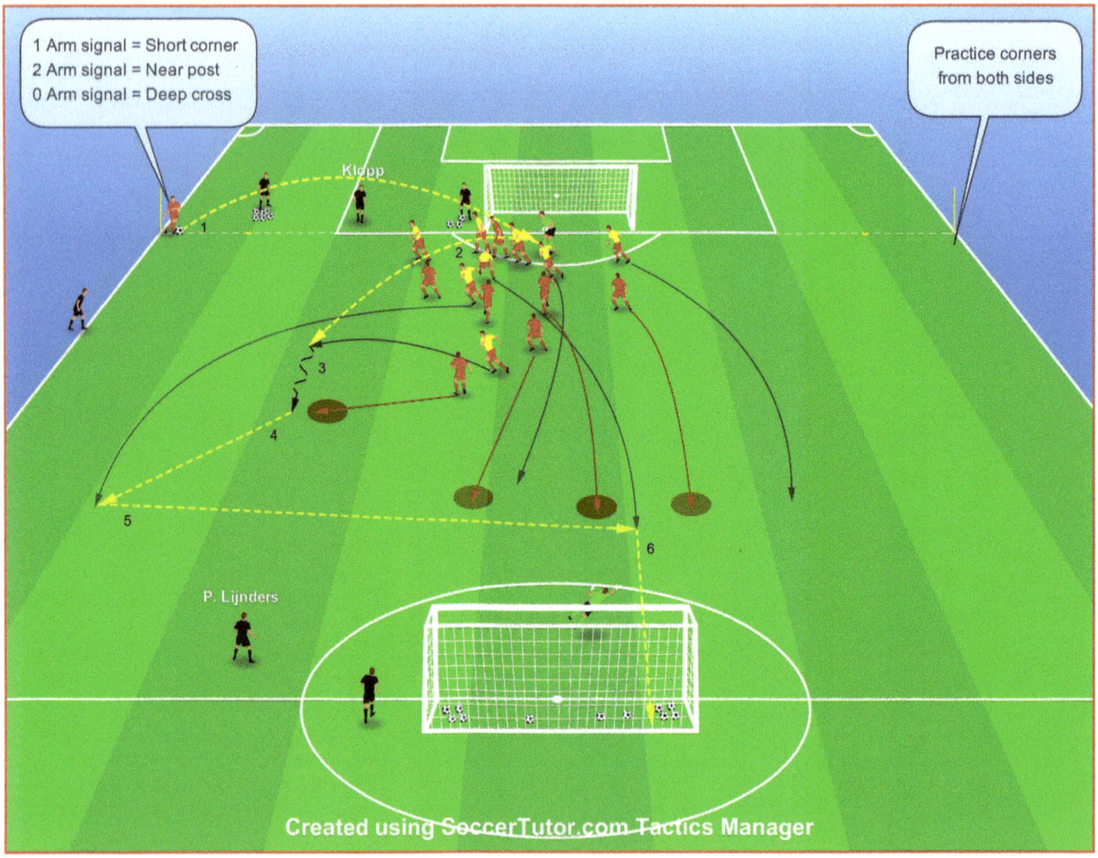

Practice Description

- This 8v8 (+GKs) game starts with a corner kick. If the player lifts up 1 arm up, it signals a short corner, 2 arms up signals a near post cross, and 0 arms up signals a deep cross.

- The reds try to score from the corner kick. If the ball is cleared, they try to win the second ball and continue their attack.

- The yellows aim to defend the corner kick, win the ball, and launch a fast counter attack to score in the opposite goal.

- If a goal is not scored in the first phase, the game continues as a normal game.

- If the ball goes out of play at any time, the **practice restarts with a new corner kick**. The Coach makes sure that corner kicks are practiced from both sides.

Source: Jürgen Klopp's Liverpool training session in Signal Iduna Park, Dortmund - 6th April 2016

Jürgen Klopp Practices: Small to Large Sided Games

13. Attacking and Defending Free Kicks + Counter Attacks in an 8v8 (+GKs) Game

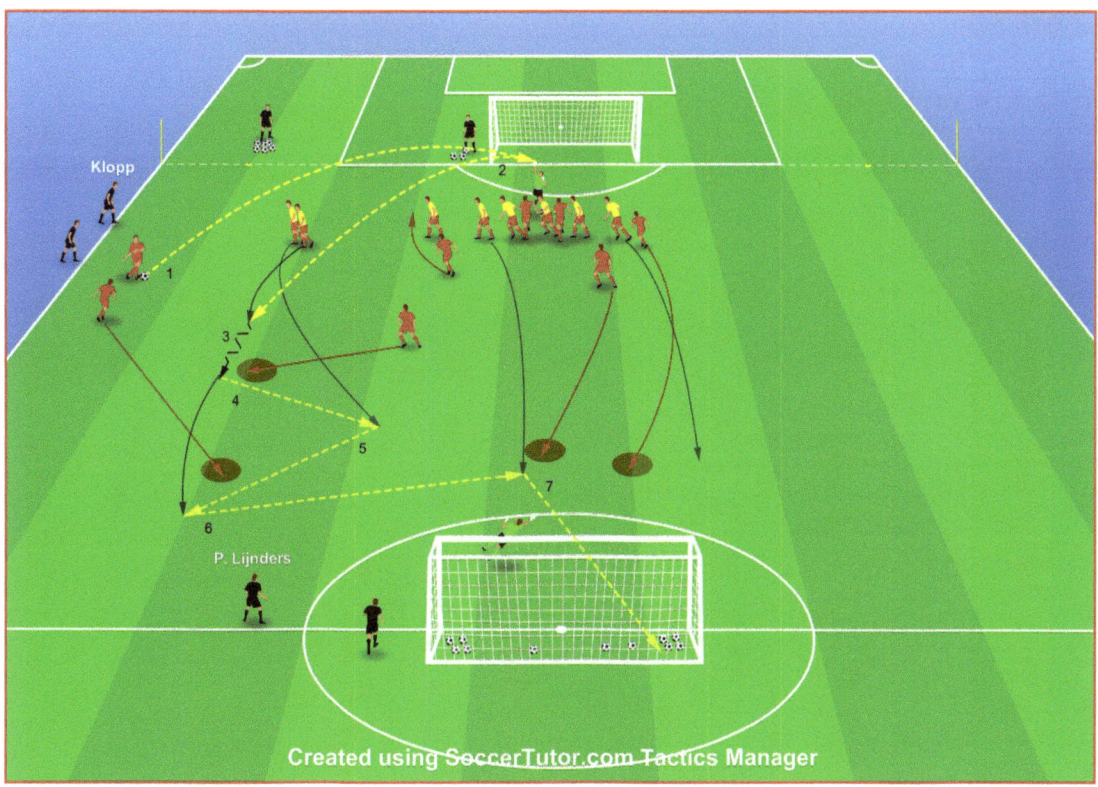

Practice Description

- This 8v8 (+GKs) game starts with a free kick. The free kick taker crosses the ball as shown, and 2 yellow players form a wall.

- The reds try to score from the free kick. If the ball is cleared, then try to win the second ball and continue their attack.

- The yellows aim to defend the free kick, win the ball, and then launch a fast counter attack to score in the opposite goal.

- If a goal is not scored in the first phase, the game continues as a normal game.

- If the ball goes out of play at any time, the **practice restarts with a new free kick**. The Coach makes sure that corner kicks are practiced from both sides.

Source: Jürgen Klopp's Liverpool training session in Signal Iduna Park, Dortmund - 6th April 2016

Jürgen Klopp Practices: Small to Large Sided Games

14. Possession Play in a Conditioned 10 v 10 (+GKs) 4-Sided / 4-Goal Game

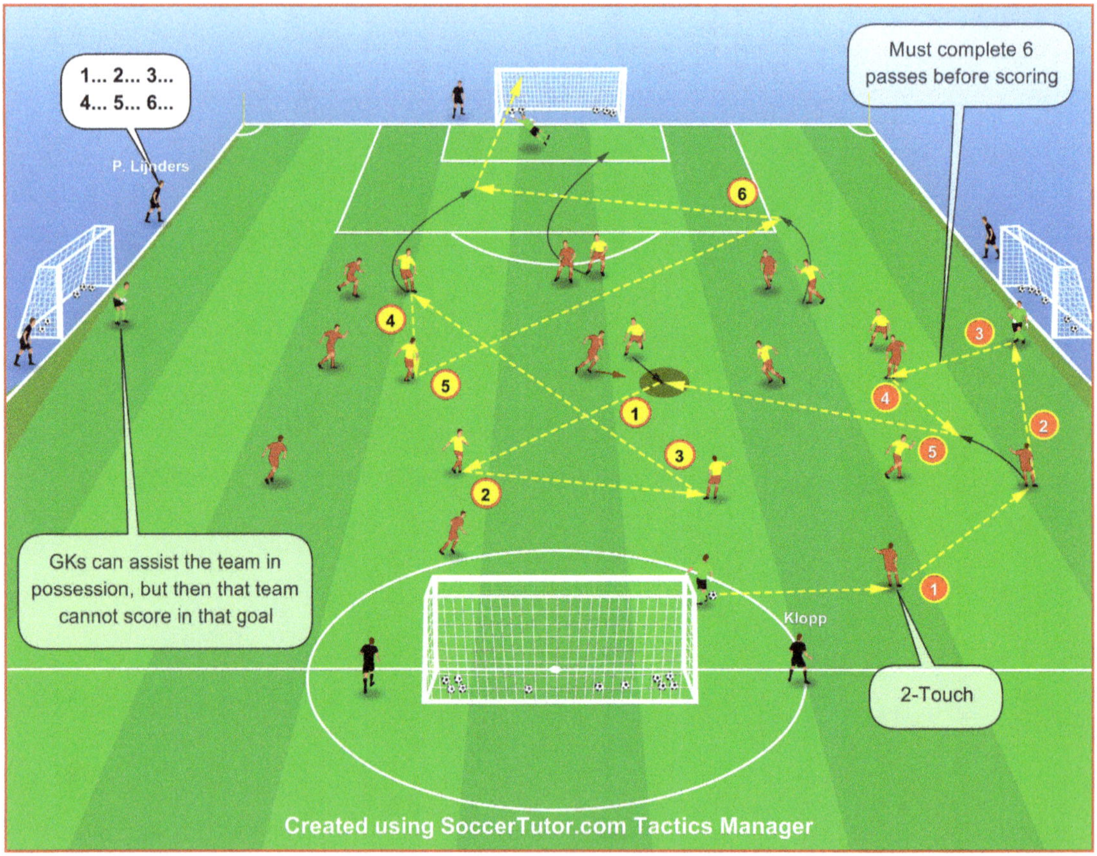

Practice Description

- In half a full pitch, 2 teams play a 10 v 10 (+4 GKs) game starting one of the GKs.

- The **team in possession (reds) must complete 6 passes before they are allowed to shoot** and score. The Coach keeps count by calling out the numbers.

- The teams are **allowed to score in any of the 4 goals** after they have completed their 6 passes.

- When a team scores, any of their players can then receive a new ball from any GK. They must again complete 6 passes before trying to score another goal.

- If the defending team (yellows) win the ball, they must also complete 6 passes before they are allowed to score.

- **NOTE:** *The GK can assist the team in possession, but then that team cannot score in that goal.*

Source: Jürgen Klopp's Liverpool training session at Melwood Training Ground, Liverpool - 25th January 2019

Transition Games

Direct from
Jürgen Klopp's
Training Sessions

"We want to attack the opponent non-stop when we have the ball, when we lose it and when the opposition have it."

Jürgen Klopp Practices: Transition Games

1. Supporting Runs to Score Quickly in a Dynamic 2v1 Attack / 3v2 Transition Game

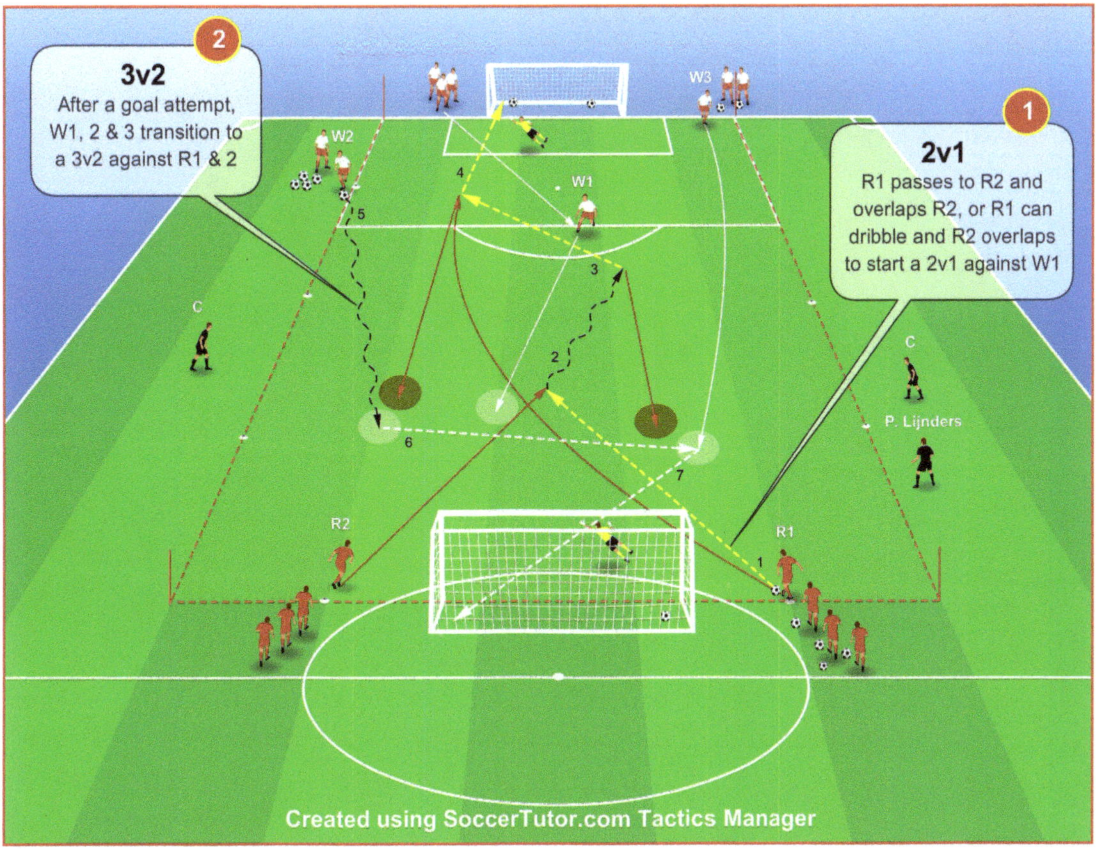

[Diagram showing the practice setup on a football pitch with annotations:
- **2v1**: R1 passes to R2 and overlaps R2, or R1 can dribble and R2 overlaps to start a 2v1 against W1
- **3v2**: After a goal attempt, W1, 2 & 3 transition to a 3v2 against R1 & 2]

Practice Description

1. The practice starts with **R1** passing into play for **R2** to run forward onto. **W1** runs in to become the defender for a 2v1 attack.

2. **R2** dribbles the ball forward and **R1** makes an overlapping run. The aim is to exploit the numerical advantage and score.

3. **R2** passes to **R1** on the overlap.

4. **R1** tries to score past the GK.

2nd ball (5). As soon as the first 2v1 attack is complete, **W2** dribbles a new ball into play from the side-line and **W3** also enters from the by-line.

6-7. We now have a 3v2 situation and the reds have to make a quick transition from attack to defence (sprint back to track runners and defend the goal). **W2** dribbles the ball forward at speed, and his 2 teammates make supporting runs. In this example, he passes for **W3** to score.

Source: Jürgen Klopp's Liverpool training session at AXA Training Centre, Liverpool - 14th December 2021

Jürgen Klopp Practices: Transition Games

2. Receive and Finish, 3v2 Transition + 4v6 Transition Game

Balls 1-3 (Receive & Finish + 3v2)

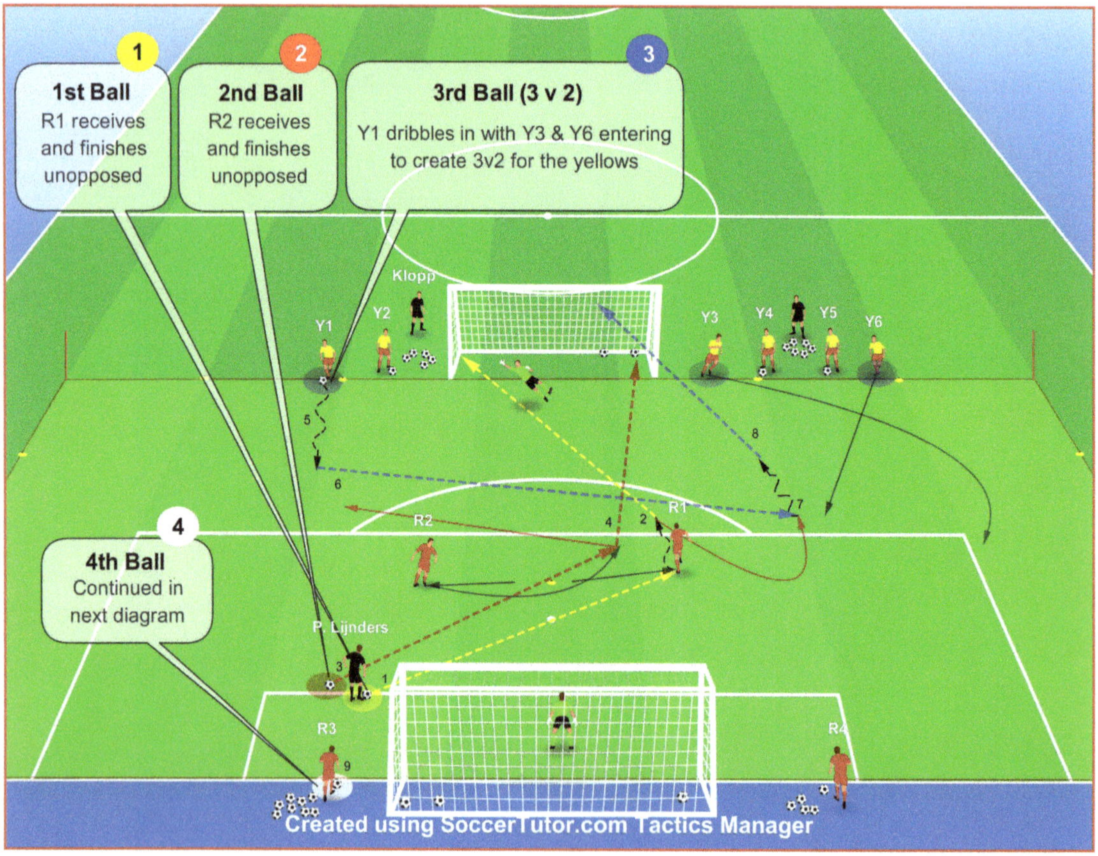

1 **1st Ball** — R1 receives and finishes unopposed

2 **2nd Ball** — R2 receives and finishes unopposed

3 **3rd Ball (3 v 2)** — Y1 dribbles in with Y3 & Y6 entering to create 3v2 for the yellows

4 **4th Ball** — Continued in next diagram

Practice Description

1st Ball (1-2). The Coach (Pep Ljinders) feeds the 1st ball in for **R1** to receive and finish on goal.

2nd Ball (3-4). The Coach feeds a 2nd ball in for **R2** to receive and finish on goal.

3rd Ball (2). **Y1** dribbles the 3rd ball into play. **Y3** and **Y6** also enter.

6-8. The yellows launch a **3v2 attack** and try to score. The reds must make a quick transition from attack to defence and try to win the ball. In the diagram example, **R1** is able to intercept **Y1's** pass and score.

The 4th ball diagram and description follows on the next page...

Source: Jürgen Klopp's Liverpool training session at AXA Training Centre, Liverpool - March 2019

Jürgen Klopp Practices: Transition Games

4th Ball (4v6 Transition)

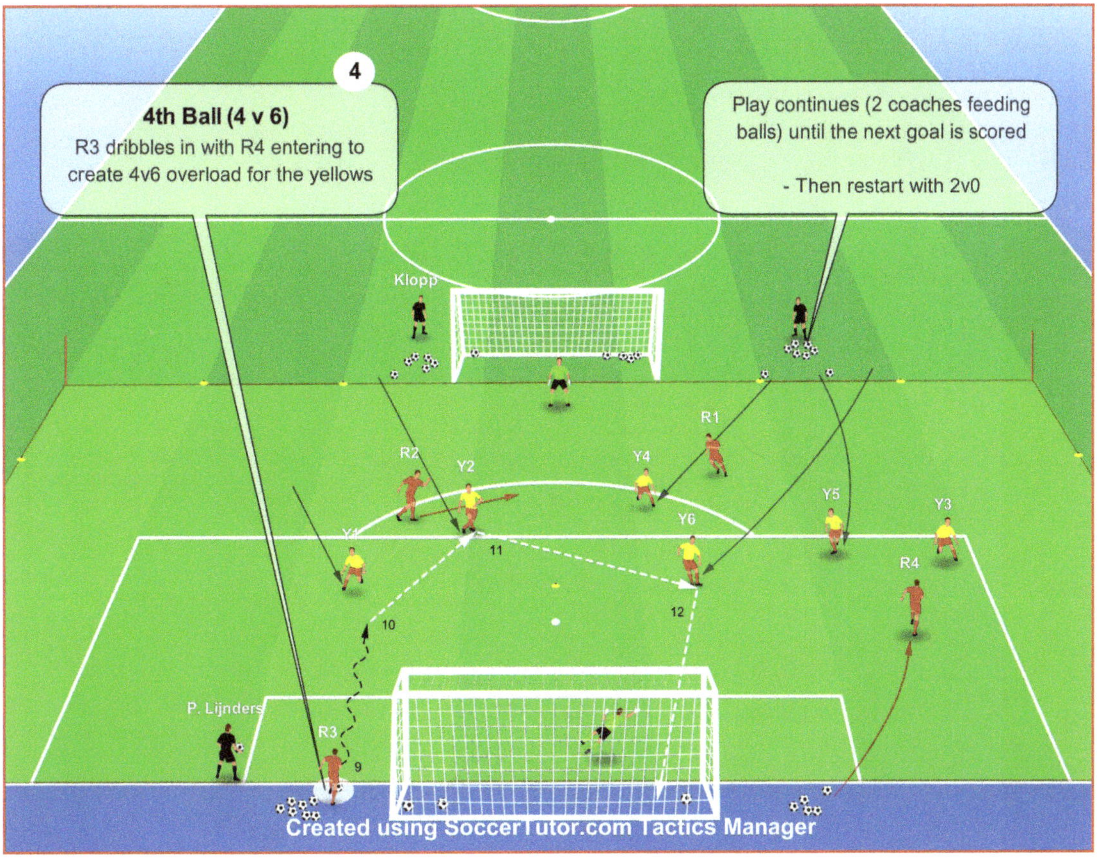

4th Ball (4 v 6)
R3 dribbles in with R4 entering to create 4v6 overload for the yellows

Play continues (2 coaches feeding balls) until the next goal is scored

- Then restart with 2v0

4th Ball (9). **R3** dribbles the 4th ball into play. **R4** also enters, as do 3 yellow players (**Y2**, **Y4** & **Y5**).

The reds launch a **4v6 attack** and try to score. The yellows try to utilise their 6v4 numerical advantage to win the ball and then score themselves (transition).

10-12. In this example, **Y2** intercepts **R3's** pass and quickly passes to **Y6** in space. **Y6** scores.

More Balls →. If (unlike the example above), a goal is not scored and the ball goes out of play, the Coaches keep feeding new balls in until a goal is scored...

Source: Jürgen Klopp's Liverpool training session at AXA Training Centre, Liverpool - March 2019

JÜRGEN KLOPP VOL.2: PRACTICES FROM KLOPP'S SESSIONS

Jürgen Klopp Practices: Transition Games

3. Receiving from Different Angles and Finishing + 3v3 Transition

Balls 1-3 (Different Types of Finishing)

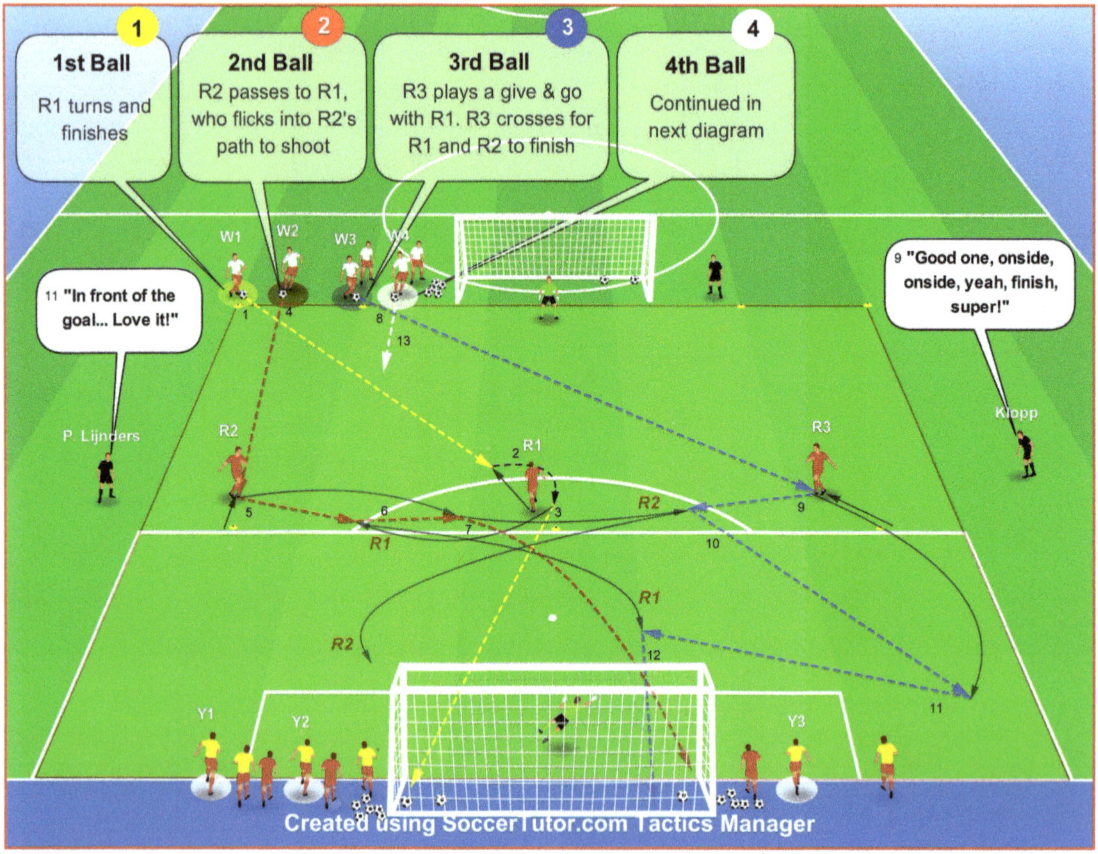

1st Ball - R1 turns and finishes

2nd Ball - R2 passes to R1, who flicks into R2's path to shoot

3rd Ball - R3 plays a give & go with R1. R3 crosses for R1 and R2 to finish

4th Ball - Continued in next diagram

"In front of the goal... Love it!" — P. Lijnders

"Good one, onside, onside, yeah, finish, super!" — Klopp

Practice Description

For this practice, we have 6 red players, 6 white players, and 6 yellow players + GKs.

1st Ball (1-3). **W1** passes into the centre for **R1**, who receives, turns, and shoots.

2nd Ball (4-7). **W2** passes to **R2** in a wider position and he passes inside to **R1**, who moves and sets the ball for **R2** to shoot.

3rd Ball (8-12). **W3** passes to **R3**, who drops to receive. **R3** plays a give & go with **R2**, who moves all the way across to provide support. **R2** cuts the ball back for one of his teammates to score in the box (**R1** in diagram example).

The 4th ball diagram and description follows on the next page...

Source: Jürgen Klopp's Liverpool pre-season training session in Tyrol, Austria - 25th July 2021

Jürgen Klopp Practices: Transition Games

4th Ball (3v3 Transition)

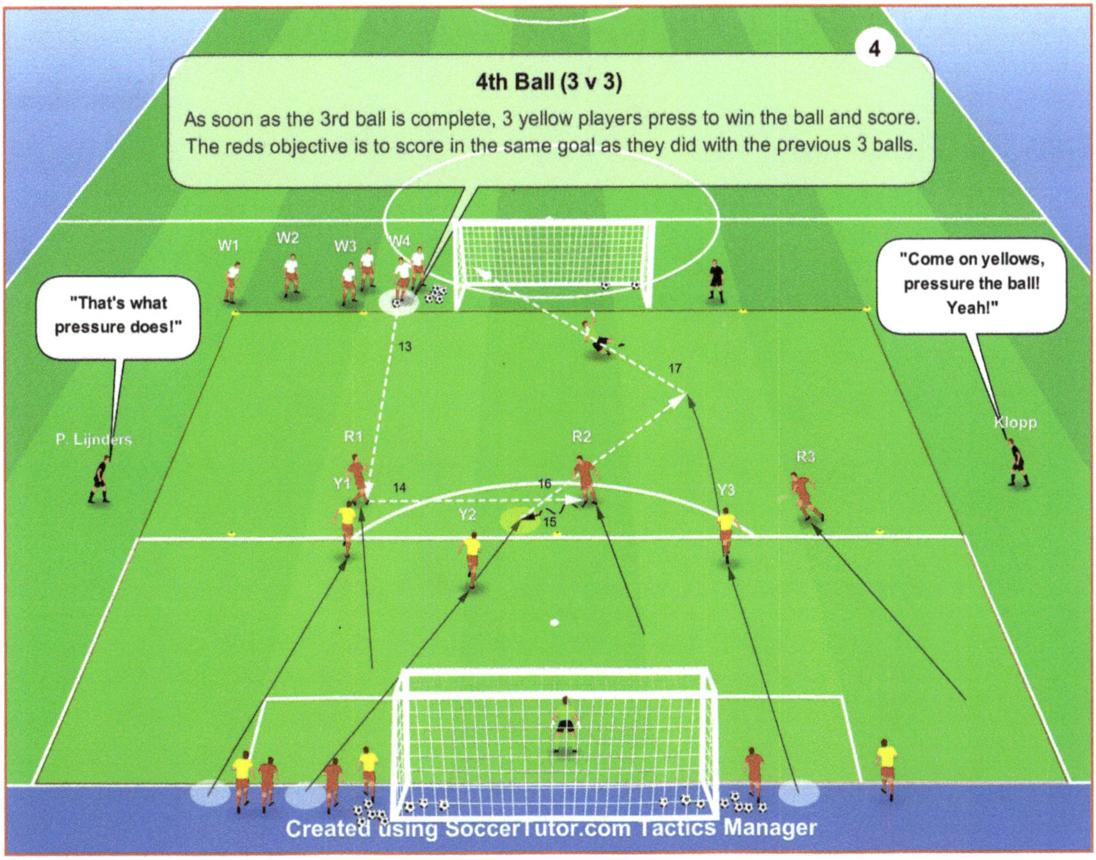

4th Ball (3 v 3)

As soon as the 3rd ball is complete, 3 yellow players press to win the ball and score. The reds objective is to score in the same goal as they did with the previous 3 balls.

"That's what pressure does!" — P. Lijnders

"Come on yellows, pressure the ball! Yeah!" — Klopp

4th Ball (13-17). As soon as the 3rd ball phase is complete, **W4** passes a new ball into play for the reds and their objective is to score in the same goal as they did with the previous 3 balls *(free play)*.

Y1, **Y2**, and **Y3** all sprint into the area to create a 3v3 situation.

The 3 yellow players press the reds and try to win the ball. If they succeed, they then make a quick transition from defence to attack (to score).

Source: Jürgen Klopp's Liverpool pre-season training session in Tyrol, Austria - 25th July 2021

Jürgen Klopp Practices: Transition Games

4. 5-Ball Finishing Drill with Give & Go + 4v4 (+4) Transition to Defend

Balls 1-4 (Finishing)

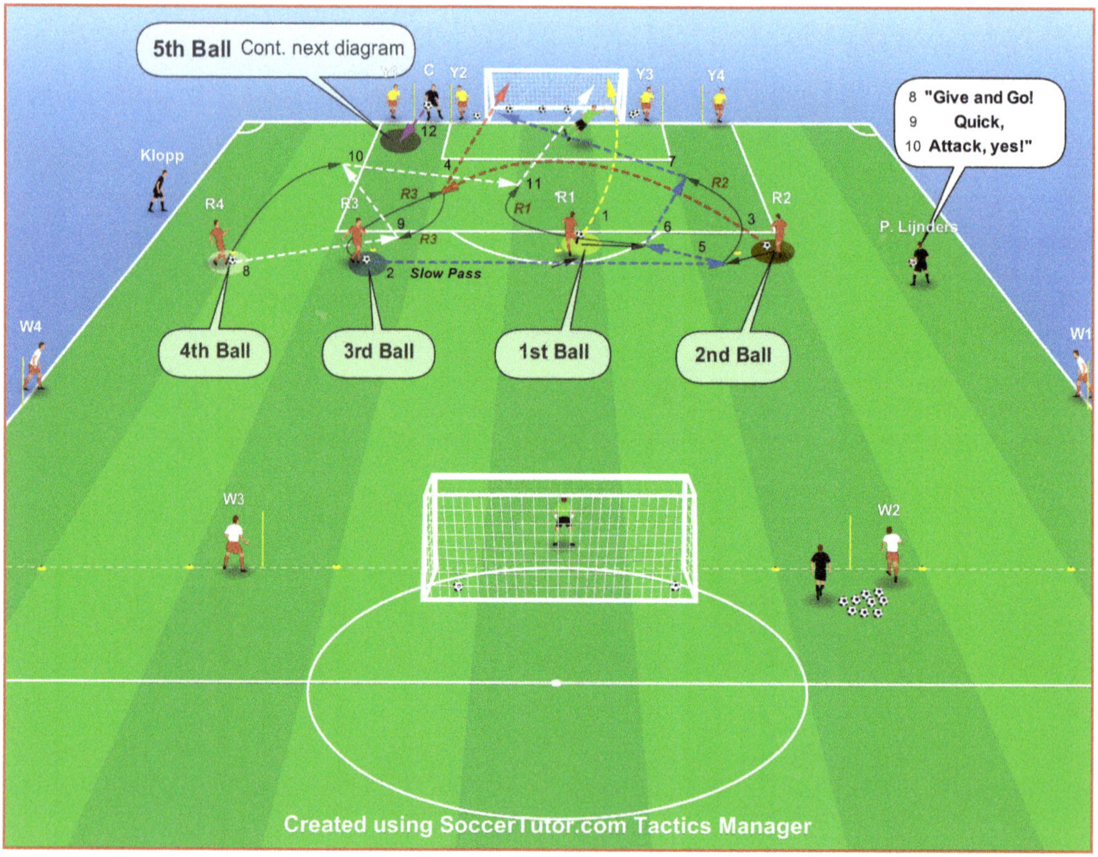

Practice Description

1st Ball (1). R1 shoots from the edge of the box.

2nd Ball (3-4). R2 plays a lofted pass into the box for the run of R3 to score.

3rd Ball (2). The <u>slow pass</u> from R3 is played before R2's lofted pass.

5-7. After the lofted pass, R2 plays a give & go with R1, and finishes inside the box.

4th Ball (8-11). R4 plays a give & go with R3, who drops back. R4 then cuts the ball back for R1 to score.

The 5th ball diagram and description follows on the next page...

Source: Jürgen Klopp's Liverpool training session at AXA Training Centre, Liverpool - 3rd March 2023

Jürgen Klopp Practices: Transition Games

5th Ball (4v4 +4 Transition)

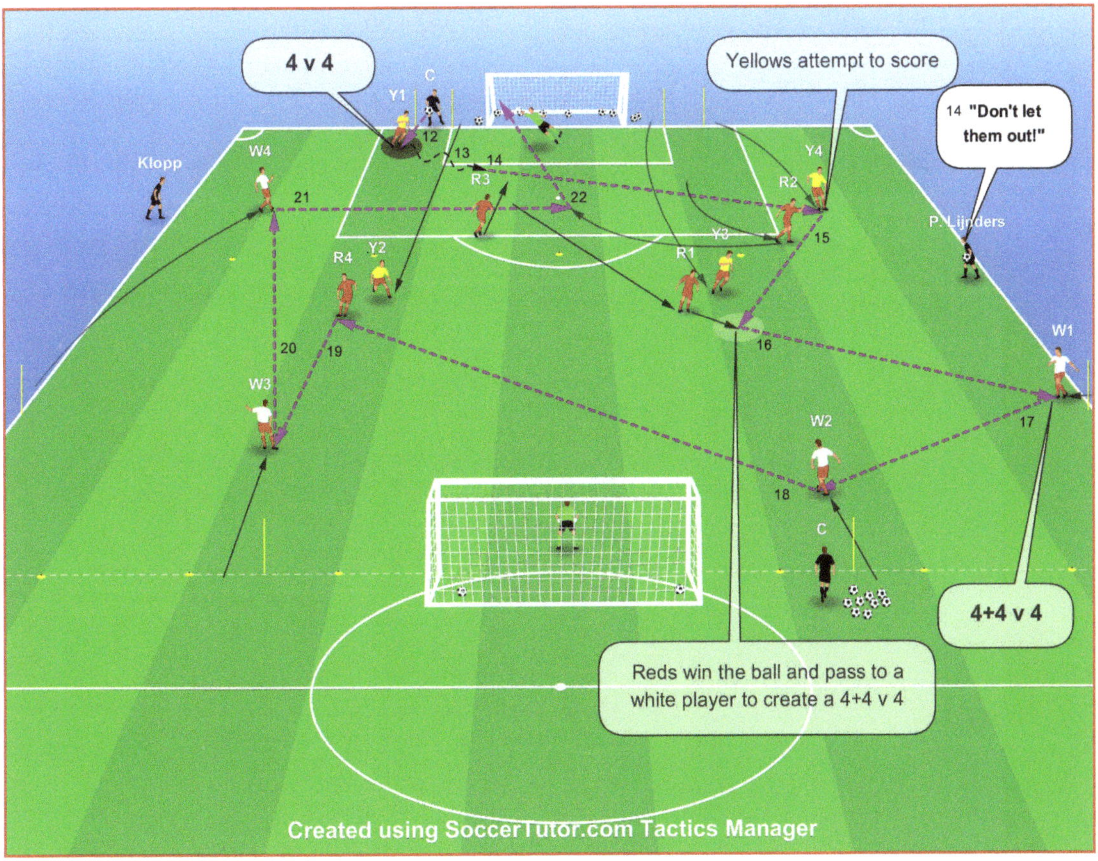

[Diagram: 4 v 4 in attacking third with Yellows attempting to score; Klopp and P. Lijnders coaching ("Don't let them out!"); Reds win the ball and pass to a white player to create a 4+4 v 4]

5th Ball (12-14). All 4 outside yellow players (**Y1-4**) enter the pitch and the Coach feeds one of them the ball. They launch a **4v4 attack** against the reds, who must make a **fast transition from attack to defence** by pressing the ball carrier and tracking the runners.

Y1 receives from the Coach, dribbles into the area, and passes across to his teammate **Y4**.

15-16. Y4 tries to play forward towards **Y3** and create an opening for the yellows to score. However, the pass is intercepted by **R1** who has tracked back well.

The 4 outside white players (**W1-4**) now enter to create a new **4v4 (+4) situation for a transition attack** (4 whites + 4 reds vs. 4 yellows = 8v4). **R1** passes to **W1**.

17-22. The whites/reds attack, and the yellows defend the goal. In this example, the ball is moved from **W1** to **W2**, to **R4**, who plays the ball back to **W3**.

W3 passes out to the **W4** in an advanced position on the left flank. **W4** delivers a ground cross and **R2** scores in a central position in the box.

Source: Jürgen Klopp's Liverpool training session at AXA Training Centre, Liverpool - 3rd March 2023

Jürgen Klopp Practices: Transition Games

5. 3-Ball Finishing + 4v4 Transition + 5v4 Transition Game

Balls 1-3 (Finishing)

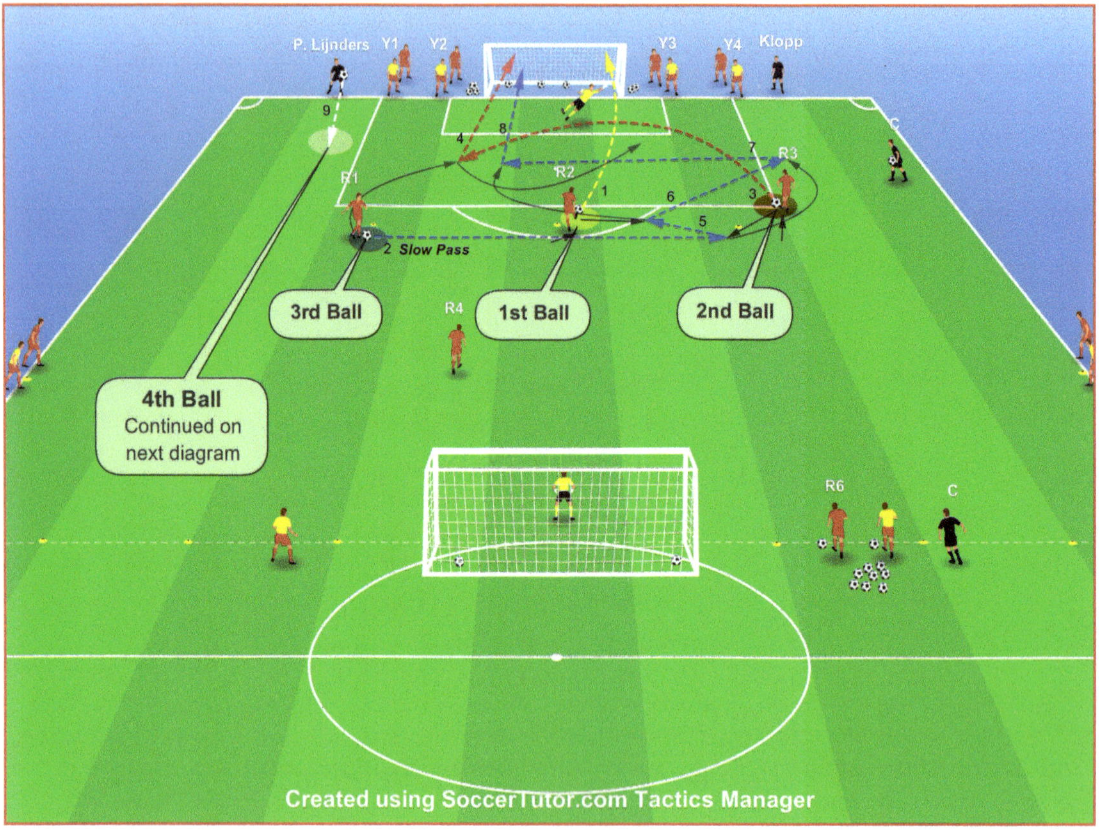

Practice Description

1st Ball (1). R2 shoots from edge of box.

2nd Ball (3-4). R3 plays a lofted pass into the box for the run of R1 to score.

3rd Ball (2). The **slow pass** from R1 is played before R3's lofted pass.

5-8. After the lofted pass, R3 plays a give & go with R2 and passes across the box for either R1 or R2 to score.

The 4th ball diagram and description follows on the next page...

Source: Jürgen Klopp's Liverpool training session at AXA Training Centre, Liverpool - 18th February 2022

Jürgen Klopp Practices: Transition Games

Balls 4-5 (4v4 + 5v4 Transition)

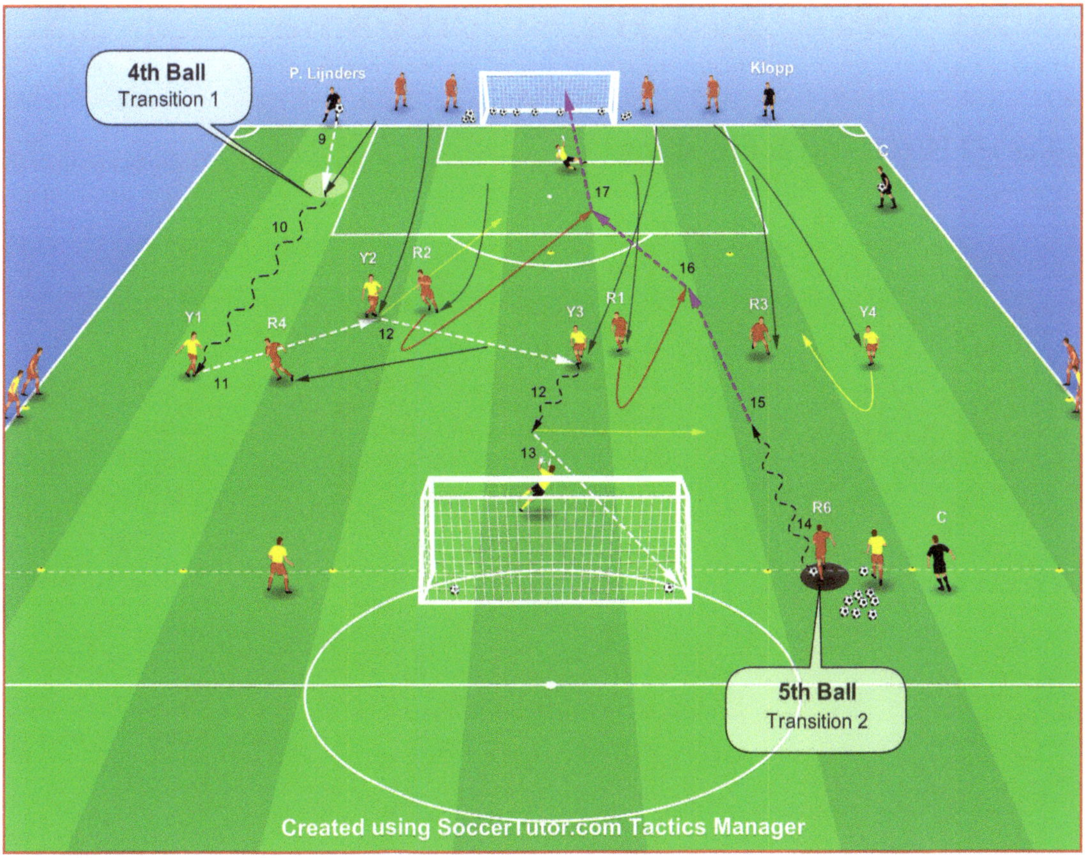

4th Ball (9-10). All 4 outside yellow players (**Y1-4**) enter the pitch and the Coach feeds one of them the ball. They launch a **4v4 attack** against the reds, who must make a **fast transition from attack to defence** by pressing the ball carrier and tracking the runners.

Y1 receives from the Coach and dribbles forward.

11-13. **Y1** passes inside to **Y2**, who passes inside again to **Y3**. In this example, **Y3** was able to dribble towards goal and score in a 1v1 versus the GK.

5th Ball (14-15). As soon as the 4th ball phase is finished, a new red player (**R6**) dribbles a 5th ball into play from the bottom of the pitch. The reds launch a new **5v4 attack** against the yellows, and make a **fast transition from defence to attack** by trying to score as quickly as possible.

In this example, **R6** dribbles forward and passes for the forward run of **R1**.

16-17. **R1** plays in behind and into the box for the run of **R2**, who scores past the GK.

Source: Jürgen Klopp's Liverpool training session at AXA Training Centre, Liverpool - 18th February 2022

Jürgen Klopp Practices: Transition Games

6. Crossing & Finishing with Side Zones + 5v4/5v8 Transition Game

Balls 1-2 (Crossing & Finishing)

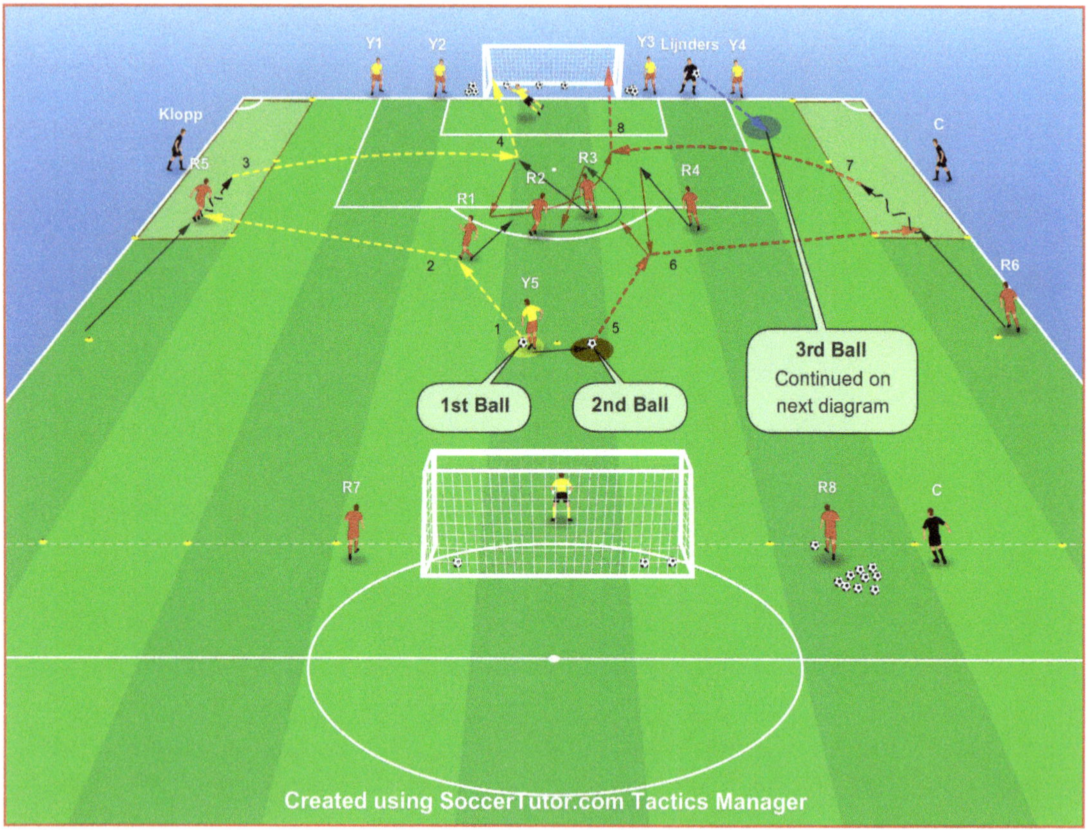

Practice Description

1st Ball (1-2). Y5 passes to **R1**, then **R1** passes out wide to **R5**, who moves forward to receive within the left side zone.

3-4. R2, **R3** & **R4** make runs into the box and **R1** moves into position for a possible cut back. In this example, **R1** delivers a cross into the front post area for **R3** to score.

2nd Ball (5-6). After the 1st ball phase is complete, all of the red players drop back into position. **Y5** passes the new ball to **R4**, and then **R4** passes out wide to **R6**, who moves forward to receive within the right side zone.

7-8. The same type of runs are made. In this example, **R6** moves forward with the ball and delivers a cross into the front post area for **R3** to score again.

Source: Jürgen Klopp's Liverpool training session at AXA Training Centre, Liverpool - 16th November 2021

Jürgen Klopp Practices: Transition Games

Balls 3-4 (Transition 1 + 2)

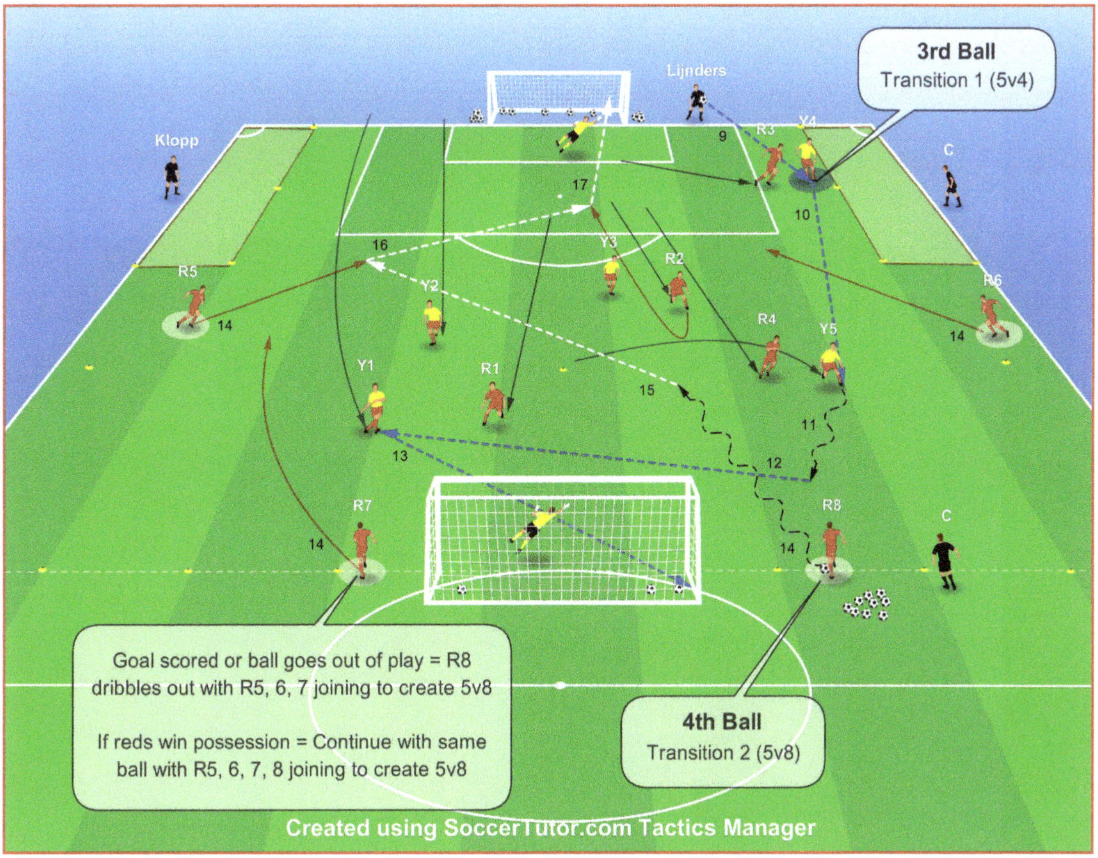

3rd Ball (9-10). All 4 outside yellow players (**Y1-4**) enter the pitch and the Coach feeds one of them the ball. They launch a **5v4 attack** against the reds, who must make a **fast transition from attack to defence** by pressing the ball carrier and tracking the runners.

Y4 receives from the Coach and passes forward to **Y5**.

11-13. Y5 dribbles forward and passes the ball across for **Y1** to shoot and score past the GK.

4th Ball (14). R8 dribbles the 4th ball into play and the other 3 outside red players (**R5**, **R6** & **R7**) enter too. The reds launch an **8v5 attack** and try to score. The yellows must make a quick transition from attack to defence.

15-17. In this example, **R8** plays a diagonal through pass to **R5**, who then delivers a final pass into the box for **R2** to score.

Source: Jürgen Klopp's Liverpool training session at AXA Training Centre, Liverpool - 16th November 2021

Jürgen Klopp Practices: Transition Games

7. Wingers/Centre Forward Finishing in and Around the Box + 9v7 (+GKs) Transition

Balls 1-3 (Return Passing & Finishing)

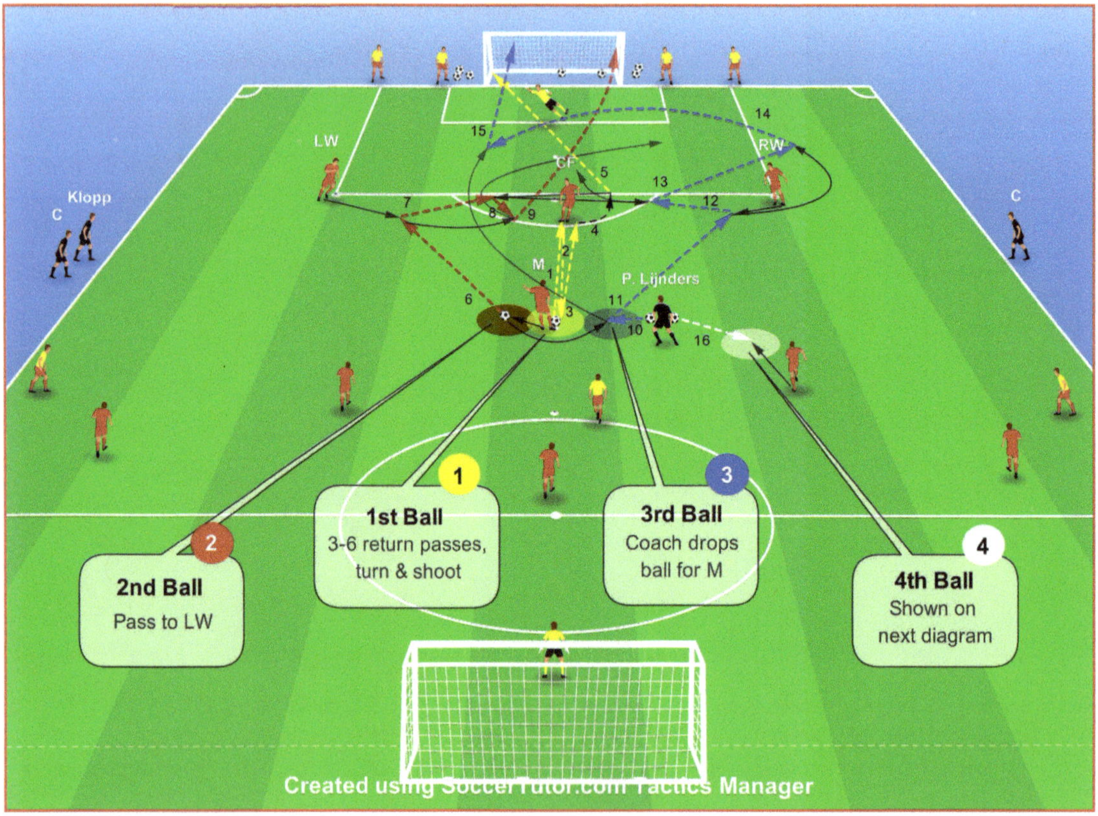

1st Ball — 3-6 return passes, turn & shoot

2nd Ball — Pass to LW

3rd Ball — Coach drops ball for M

4th Ball — Shown on next diagram

Practice Description

1st Ball (1-3). The midfielder (**M**) starts by exchanging 3-6 return passes with the centre forward (**CF**).

4-5. The **CF** receives, turns, and shoots.

2nd Ball (6-9). **M** passes the 2nd ball to the left winger (**LW**), who drops to receive. The **LW** passes to the **CF**, who moves towards the left side to set the ball for the **LW** to shoot.

3rd Ball (10-15). **M** passes the 3rd ball to the right winger (**RW**), who drops to receive. The **RW** plays a give & go with the **CF**, who has moved towards the right side.

The **RW** delivers a cross for either the **M**, **LW** or **CF** to score. In the diagram example, the midfielder (**M**) scores after a deep run into the box.

The 4th ball diagram and description follows on the next page...

Source: Jürgen Klopp's Liverpool training session at Melwood Training Ground, Liverpool - 3rd September 2020

Jürgen Klopp Practices: Transition Games

4th Ball (9v7 +GKs Transition Game)

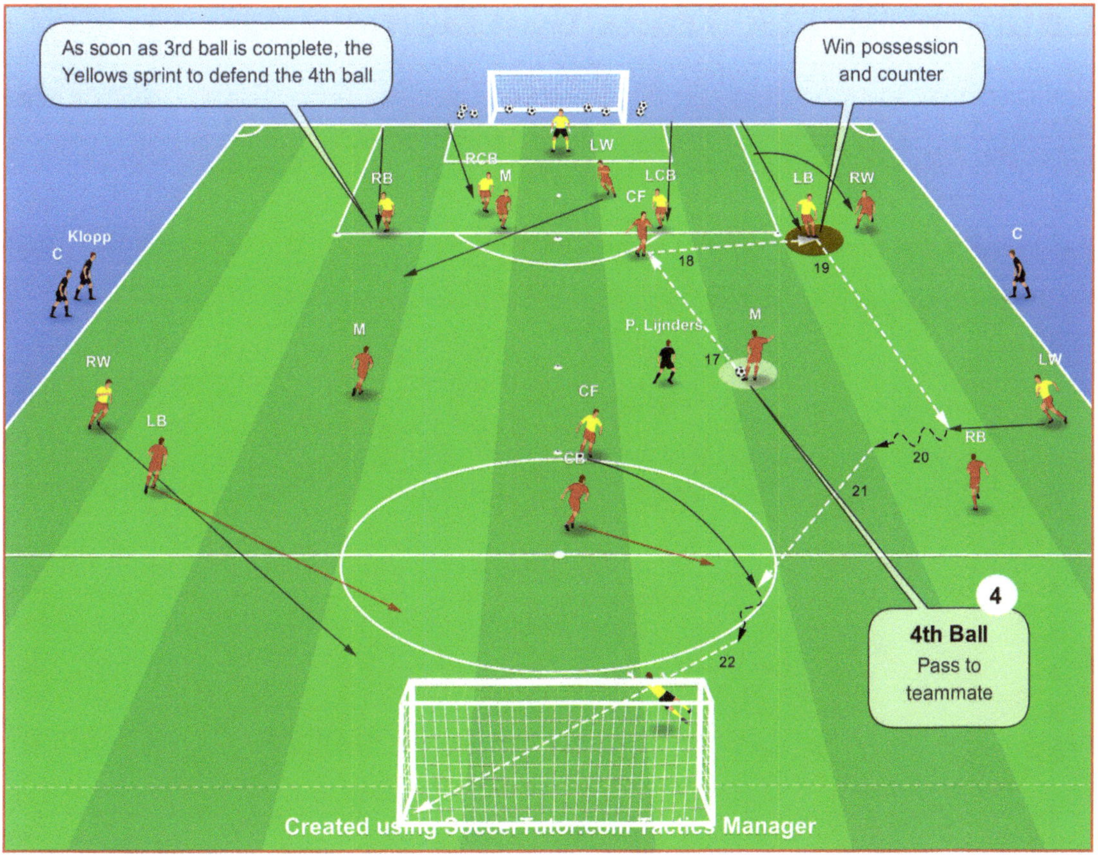

[Diagram: As soon as 3rd ball is complete, the Yellows sprint to defend the 4th ball. Win possession and counter. 4th Ball — Pass to teammate.]

4th Ball (17-22). As soon as the 3rd ball phase is complete, all of the **6 yellow players sprint to defend** the 4th ball.

The Coach drops a new 4th ball in, and the **9 red players try to score**.

If the yellow team win the ball, they launch a quick counter attack.

This happens in the diagram example when the yellow left back (**LB**) intercepts the ball. He plays to the left winger (**LW**), who cuts inside and plays a through pass to the centre forward (**CF**).

The **CF** scores in a 1v1 versus the GK.

Source: Jürgen Klopp's Liverpool training session at Melwood Training Ground, Liverpool - 3rd September 2020

Jürgen Klopp Practices: Transition Games

8. 3-Team 5v5v5 (+GKs) 2-Zone Counter Attack Transition Game

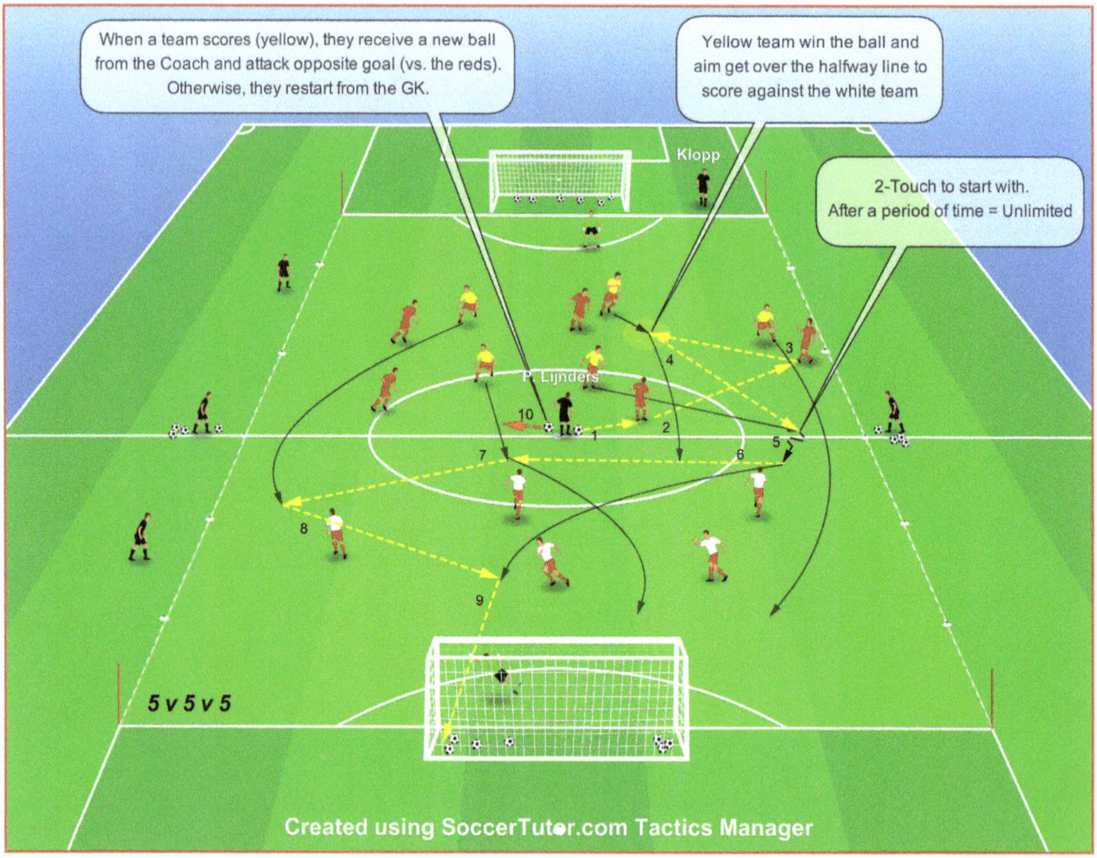

Practice Description

- In the marked out area shown, the game is split into 2 equal zones (halves).

- There are 3 teams of 5 players (red, yellow, and white). The red team start in possession within one half and try to score in a 5v5 against the yellows.

- The defending players (yellows) work together to press, block off passing lines and try to win the ball.

- If the yellows win the ball, they **aim to get over the halfway line** to attack the white team. The reds cannot leave the half.

- **When a team scores, they receive a new ball from the Coach and attack the opposite goal**. In the diagram example, the yellows score and then attack the reds. Otherwise, they restart from GK.

- *NOTE: The practice was 2-touch to start with and changed to unlimited touches after a period of time.*

Source: Jürgen Klopp's Liverpool training session at Melwood Training Ground, Liverpool - 13th July 2020

Jürgen Klopp Practices: Transition Games

9. 3-Team 6v6v6 (+GKs) 4-Zone Counter Attack Transition Game with Time Limit to Score

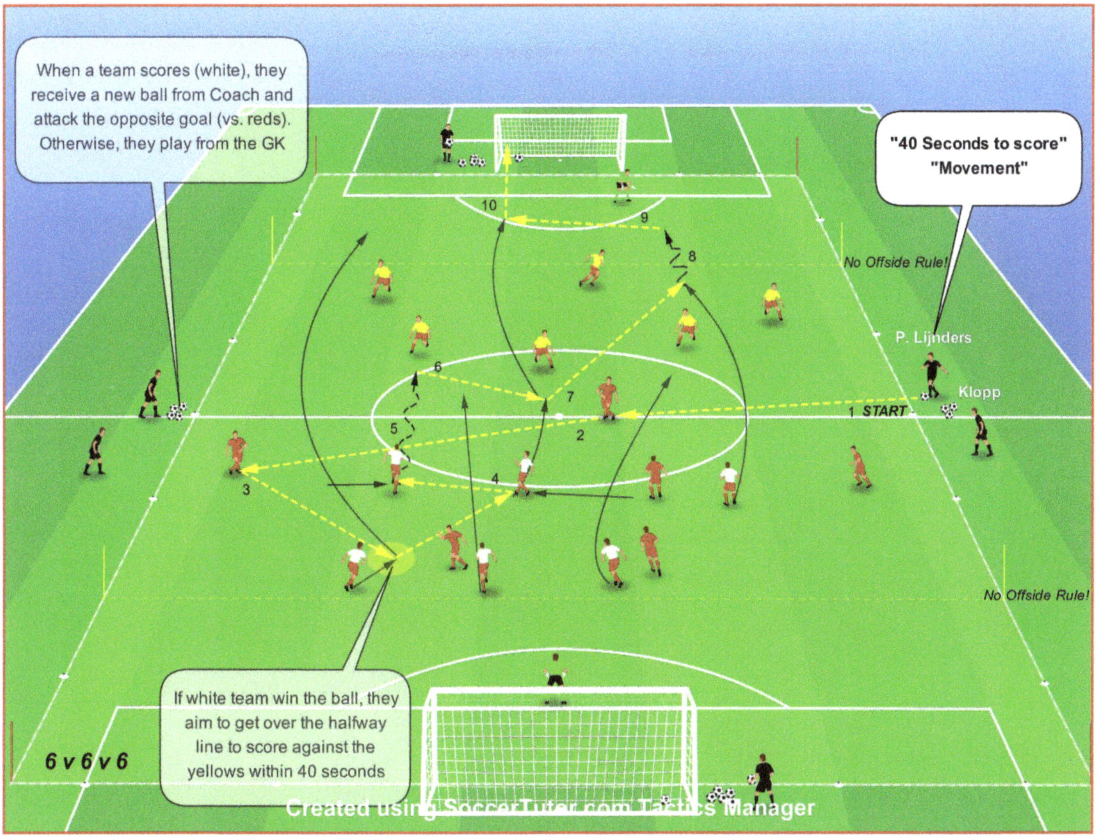

Practice Description

- In the marked out area shown, the game is split into 4 zones.

- There are 3 teams of 6 players (red, yellow, and white). The red team start in possession within one half and try to score in a 6v6 against the whites.

- The defending players (whites) work together to press, block off passing lines and try to win the ball.

- If the whites win the ball, they **aim to get over the halfway line** to attack the yellow team, and **score within 40 seconds**.

- The yellows cannot move into the final zone to defend but there is no offside rule applied.

- **When a team scores, they receive a new ball from the Coach and attack the opposite goal.** In the diagram example, the whites score and then attack the reds. Otherwise, they restart from GK.

Source: Jürgen Klopp's Liverpool training session at Melwood Training Ground, Liverpool - 20th August 2019

Jürgen Klopp Practices: Transition Games

10. 3-Team 6v6v6 (+GKs) 4-Zone Counter Attack Transition Game with Offside Rule

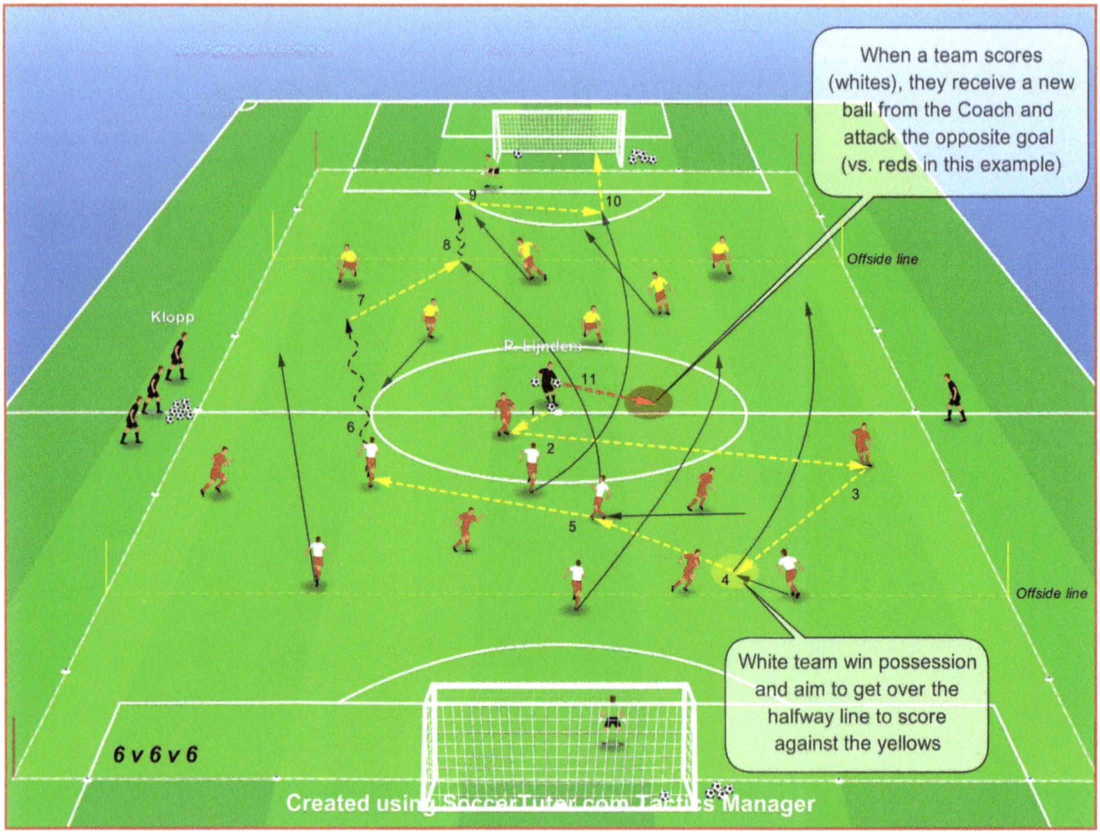

When a team scores (whites), they receive a new ball from the Coach and attack the opposite goal (vs. reds in this example)

White team win possession and aim to get over the halfway line to score against the yellows

Practice Description

- In the marked out area shown, the game is split into 4 zones.

- There are 3 teams of 6 players (red, yellow, and white). The red team start in possession within one half and try to score in a 6v6 against the whites.

- The defending players (white) work together to press, block off passing lines and try to win the ball.

- If the whites win the ball, they **aim to get over the halfway line** to attack the yellow team. The reds cannot leave the half.

- They yellows cannot move into the final zone to defend but the **offside rule is applied**.

- **When a team scores, they receive a new ball from the Coach and attack the opposite goal**. In the diagram example, the whites score and then attack the reds.

Source: Jürgen Klopp's Liverpool training session at Melwood Training Ground, Liverpool - 27th August 2019

Jürgen Klopp Practices: Transition Games

11. 3-Team 6v6v6 (+3) + GKs Counter Attack Transition Game with Side Zones

When a team that scores (white), they receive a new ball from the Coach and attack the opposite goal (vs. the reds). Otherwise, they play from their GK.

All players = 2-Touch

White team win the ball and aim to get over the halfway line to score against the yellow team

6 v 6 v 6 +3

Practice Description

- In the marked out area shown, the game is split into many zones including the side zones where only the wide Jokers operate. There is also 1 Joker who can play in either of the central halves.

- There are 3 teams of 6 players (red, yellow, and white). The red team start in possession with the Joker within one half (7v6 situation) and try to score against the white team.

- If the whites win the ball, they **aim to get over the halfway line** to attack the yellow team. They utilise the wide Jokers to score on the counter, as shown.

- **When a team scores, they receive a new ball from the Coach and attack the opposite goal**. In the diagram example, the whites score and then attack the reds. Otherwise, they restart from GK.

- *NOTE: All players limited to 2 touches.*

Source: Jürgen Klopp's Liverpool training session at AXA Training Centre, Liverpool - 23rd December 2020

Jürgen Klopp Practices: Transition Games

12. 8 v 8 (+3) + GKs "5-Second Rule" Fast Counter Attack Transition Game

Part 1/3 - Build-up Play + Score Unopposed within 5 Seconds

[Diagram: White team aim to get over the halfway line and score (unopposed) within 5 seconds. 8 v 8 +1]

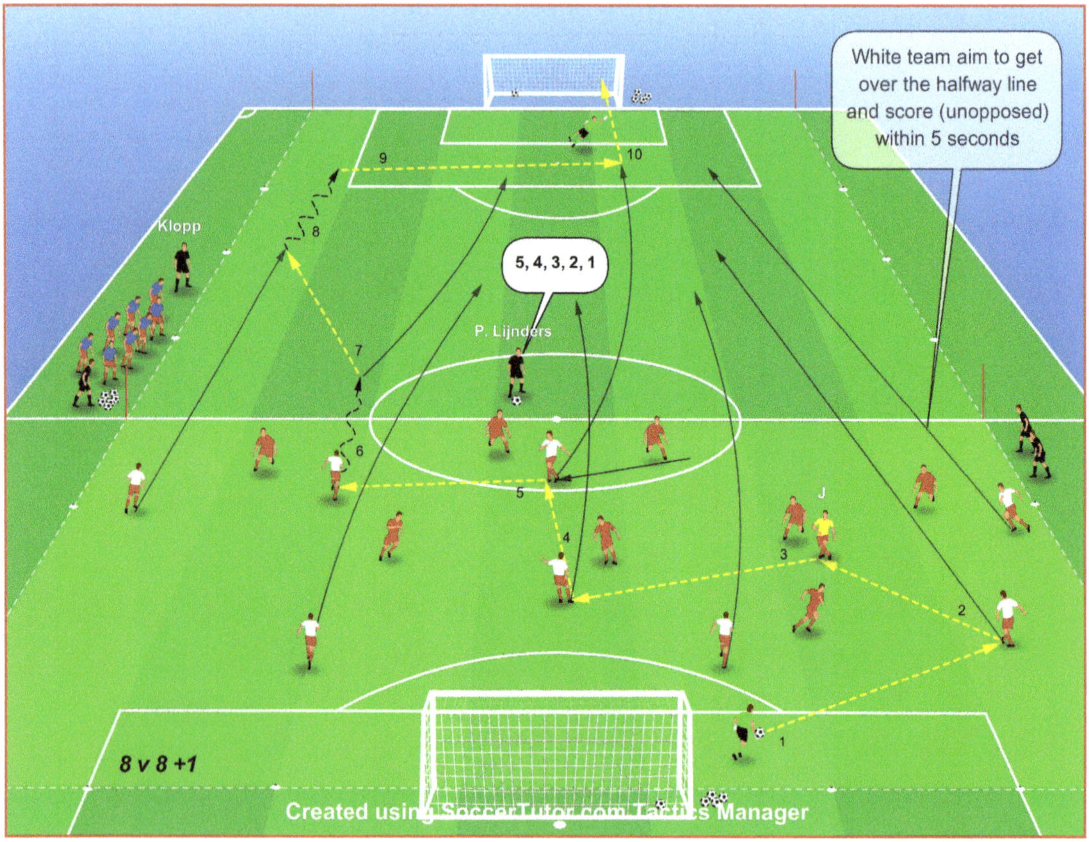

Practice Description

- The game starts with the GK and the white team in possession.

- The whites use the Joker and their **9 v 8 numerical advantage with the aim of building up play through pressure and dribbling into the attacking half**.

- When this is achieved, they then must finish their attack very quickly.

- Once crossing the halfway line, the white team **must finish their attack within 5 seconds** (counted out by the Coach).

- *The practice description continues on the next page...*

Source: Jürgen Klopp's Liverpool pre-season training session in Salzburg, Austria - 19th July 2021

Jürgen Klopp Practices: Transition Games

Part 2/3 - Win the Ball + Score

![diagram]

Reds win the ball and quickly transition to attack, trying to score

If the ball goes out of play, the Coach plays a new ball to a red player

8 v 8 +1

Practice Description

- If the white team fail to play into the attacking half and the white team win the ball, the reds then look to score themselves (as shown in the diagram example above).

- If the whites kick the ball out of play, the Coach gives a new ball to the reds.

- If the reds kick the ball out of play, the Coach gives a new ball to the whites for a free unopposed counter attack (score within 5 seconds).

Source: Jürgen Klopp's Liverpool pre-season training session in Salzburg, Austria - 19th July 2021

Jürgen Klopp Practices: Transition Games

Part 3/3 - Win Ball + Score Unopposed within 5 Seconds

White team aim to win the ball, dribble past the halfway line and counter to score (unopposed) within 5 seconds

8 v 8 +1

Practice Description

- If the reds start with a new ball and the white team are able to win it from them, then the whites launch a fast counter attack.

- Once crossing the halfway line, the white team **must finish their counter attack within 5 seconds** (counted out by the Coach).

Source: Jürgen Klopp's Liverpool pre-season training session in Salzburg, Austria - 19th July 2021

Football Coaching Specialists Since 2001

Jürgen Klopp

102 Passing, Counter-pressing Possession Games, Speed & Warm-ups Direct from Klopp's Training Sessions

Vol. 1

Coaching Books Available in Full Colour Print and eBook!
PC | Mac | iPhone | iPad | Android Phone / Tablet | Chromebook

FREE Coach Viewer **APP**

SoccerTutor.com

Football Coaching Specialists Since 2001

PEP GUARDIOLA
88 Attacking Combinations and Positional Patterns of Play Direct from Pep's Training Sessions
Vol. 1

PEP GUARDIOLA
85 Passing, Rondos, Possession Games & Technical Circuits Direct from Pep's Training Sessions
Vol. 2

Coaching Books Available in Full Colour Print and eBook!
PC | Mac | iPhone | iPad | Android Phone / Tablet | Chromebook

 **FREE** Coach Viewer **APP**

SoccerTutor.com

Free Trial

Football Coaching Specialists Since 2001

Tactics Manager
Create your own Practices, Tactics & Plan Sessions!

Tactics Manager App

   Soon! Soon!

SoccerTutor.com